economic transformation and human rights are some of his special areas of interest. He has also been on various academic and administrative committees and councils of various universities and committees and commissions of the government of Punjab.

**Jatinder Singh** is Assistant Professor at the Centre for Research in Rural and Industrial Development (CRRID), Chandigarh. He obtained his Ph.D. from Jawaharlal Nehru University (JNU), New Delhi and M.Phil from Centre for Development Studies (CDS), Trivandrum. His research areas include Foreign Direct Investment, Technology Development and Industrialisation in India. He has published extensively. He has completed six research projects funded by various national agencies and governments. He has worked in different capacities with various organisations including CDS, Trivandrum; Centre for World Trade Organization Studies, New Delhi; University of Delhi, New Delhi; and National University of Education Planning and Administration (NUEPA), New Delhi.

**Gurinder Kaur** is Assistant Professor at a reputed ICSSR research institute, Centre for Research in Rural and Industrial Development, Chandigarh, India. She has a Ph.D. in Anthropology from Panjab University, Chandigarh. Her academic training is in social anthropology and her research interest is in medical anthropology, particularly critical medical anthropology. Her research focuses on medical pluralism, cultural connotations of health and illness, social biography of drug addiction and structural and institutional factors influencing health and illness. She has published research articles in edited books and journals and has a book on Religion and Health: Narratives on Faith Healing.

# Dynamics of Drug Addiction and Abuse in India

This book analyses drug addiction and abuse from the perspectives of the state and community in India, with a special focus on the North-West regions of India. India lies in the transit route of two major global centres of heroin and cocaine processing: the Golden Triangle of Myanmar, Thailand and Laos towards the East and the Golden Crescent of Afghanistan, Iran and Pakistan to the West, making it vulnerable to drug trafficking. Curbing this has been a tough challenge for enforcement agencies.

This book looks at

- the nature and pattern of drug addiction across age, gender and occupational groups, both in rural and urban areas in India;
- the socio-economic causes of drug-use and addiction and the various socio-economic costs associated with it;
- the general perception of addicts and their family members, and civil society about the role of government machinery and political leaders on drug addiction as well as rehabilitation; and
- available mechanisms to address the issue at the level of family, society and government and the changes required in policy to curb drug addiction and use.

This interdisciplinary book will be of importance to students and researchers of economics, cultural and social anthropology, sociology, police administration, political science, and psychology. It will also be of interest to policy makers, government agencies, social scientists, departments of social and preventive medicine, social workers, civil society and drug-addicts and their families.

**Ranjit Singh Ghuman** is currently Professor of Eminence (Economics) at Guru Nanak Dev University, Amritsar. Prior to that, he was Nehru Chair Professor at CRRID, Chandigarh and Professor & Head of Economics Department at Punjabi University Patiala. He has published extensively on issues with socio-economic bearing. Development economics, rural and agricultural development, emerging water scarcity, international trade, drug menace and

# Dynamics of Drug Addiction and Abuse in India

Ranjit Singh Ghuman, Jatinder Singh and Gurinder Kaur

Routledge
Taylor & Francis Group
LONDON AND NEW YORK

First published 2024
by Routledge
4 Park Square, Milton Park, Abingdon, Oxon OX14 4RN

and by Routledge
605 Third Avenue, New York, NY 10158

*Routledge is an imprint of the Taylor & Francis Group, an informa business*



*British Library Cataloguing-in-Publication Data*
A catalogue record for this book is available from the British Library

ISBN: 978-1-032-25841-6 (hbk)
ISBN: 978-1-032-33063-1 (pbk)
ISBN: 978-1-003-31801-9 (ebk)

DOI: 10.4324/9781003318019

Typeset in Sabon
by Apex CoVantage, LLC

# Contents

# Preface

The book is the thoroughly revised version of our research programme on 'Dynamics of Drug Addiction and Abuse in India: Social, Economic and Political Implications' commissioned and funded by the Indian Council for Social Science Research (ICSSR), New Delhi. We thankfully acknowledge the ICSSR. We also owe our thanks to the members of the Advisory Committee of the Research Programme, Professors Sucha Singh Gill, N.K. Taneja, and M. R. Murthi, for giving their valuable advice from time to time which went a long way to improve the quality of our research work. The numerous taxpayers, out of whose pockets came the funding, also deserve our thanks.

We gratefully acknowledge the support and cooperation of the governing body members of the Centre for Research in Rural and Industrial Development (CRRID), where we completed the research programme. Late Mr. Rashpal Malhotra, the then-Executive Vice-Chairman of CRRID, deserves our special thanks as he always used to take a keen interest in the progress of our research programme. Our interactive sessions with Mr. Harpreet Sidhu IPS, Dr. Manmohan Singh IPS, Mrs. Gurpreet Deo IPS, Dr. Kaustubh Sharma, IPS, Dr. Swarajbir Singh IPS, (Retd.) and Editor, Punjabi Tribune, Mr. K.S. Sangha IAS, and Mr. Sandeep Rishi IAS helped us understand the administrative and legal nuances of the drug menace. Our occasional interactions with Dr. Jaspal Singh Sandhu, Vice-Chancellor, GNDU, Amritsar and Professors S. S. Jodhka, Ronki Ram, Surinder Kumar, Sukhpal Singh (IIM, Ahmedabad) and Ashok Pankaj added significant value to the study.

The fructification of this sensitive research programme could not have been possible without the support and cooperation of a galaxy of people and organisations, and we wish to put on record our sincere gratitude to all those people and organisations. We are especially grateful to numerous respondents (drug-addicts and members of their households, participants in FGDs and case studies), who, despite their pain and agony, came forward to share their views and experiences with the research team. Views of the participants in the workshop organised for sharing our preliminary findings are duly acknowledged.

Given the sensitive nature of the study, the collection of secondary and primary data/information would not have been possible without the formal approval from the concerned ministries and departments dealing with the issue of drug abuse and addiction. In this context, we are thankful to the concerned ministers and officials of the selected states (Punjab, Haryana, Himachal Pradesh, Rajasthan and Jammu and Kashmir) for granting us permission to collect secondary and primary data. We are especially thankful to the then-Deputy Commissioners and Senior Superintendents of Police of the sampled districts (Amritsar, Tarn Taran, Jalandhar, Ludhiana, Bathinda, Mansa, Moga, Sangrur from Punjab; Ambala and Sirsa from Haryana; Kullu and Kangra from Himachal Pradesh; Hanumangarh and Sri Ganganagar from Rajasthan; and Jammu and Kathua from Jammu and Kashmir) for their cooperation and support to the research work.

We are also grateful to the unknown referees whose valuable input has greatly helped us in improving the quality of the manuscript. Our thanks are also due to the entire team of Routledge India for evincing a keen interest at the various stages of the manuscript, which eventually led to publication.

Our sincere thanks and appreciation go to Shri Haqiqat Singh, Shri Gurbinder Singh and Shri Nirmal Singh, who have successfully completed the field work against numerous odds. Our thanks are also due to Dr. Rajeev Sharma and Dr. Sachna Arora for working with us in the initial stages of our work. We shall be failing in our duty if we do not appreciate the contributions of our Ph.D. scholars – Mankirat, Deepratan Singh Khara, Anuj Bhadhu and Ujjwala Singh – for helping us with computational work. Last, but not the least, we are grateful to our family members for their cooperation and support, even at the cost of facing neglect during our absorption in completing our study.

Ranjit Singh Ghuman
Jatinder Singh
Gurinder Kaur

# 1 Introduction

Though drug use and abuse have been part of all human societies since time immemorial, it has currently become more severe and widespread than ever before. People all over the world have been using and abusing drugs for centuries. A drug is a substance that alters the functions of the body, and addiction is the uncontrolled impulse to use a drug despite its multiple adverse effects. According to international agencies and a good amount of related literature, drug addiction and abuse is a multifaceted human phenomenon and dates back millennia but due to technological advances in communication and connectivity, the drug manufacturing and distribution of drugs has become a significant social problem since the latter half of the 20th century, on the rise over time. Recent global slogans such as the 'war on drugs' and the threat of 'narco-terrorism' are enough to believe that the contemporary world is facing a serious challenge of drug addiction and abuse. Drug abuse and addiction are not the same but tend to occur together. Drug abuse refers to the chronic and excessive use of a drug to a point when personal harm is likely to take place (Wilson and Kolander, 2011). According to the World Health Organization (WHO), drug or alcohol addiction is the repeated use of a psychoactive substance or substances to the extent the user (referred to as an addict) is periodically or chronically intoxicated, shows a compulsion to take the preferred substance (or substances), has great difficulty in voluntarily ceasing or modifying substance use, and exhibits determination to obtain psychoactive substances by almost any means.

Drug use and abuse has its roots across the globe and has spread its tentacles across societies and cultures. The problem of drug addiction and abuse is often embedded in the social, cultural, economic and political ground realities. In this context, drug addiction and abuse is socially constructed, socially transmitted and is socially located. It is like a cyclical process where certain social structures produce this kind of social behaviour, which in turn produces multiple sufferings, not just at the individual but also at the social level. Thus, the phenomenon is a complex one and needs to be understood and examined in the very structure of the society, economy and polity. The increased communication and connectivity have also become very handy to the drug producers and suppliers across borders. The issue has attracted

DOI: 10.4324/9781003318019-1

considerable attention from both national and international agencies since it is one of the largest threats to the safety of human beings world-over, after nuclear weapons and terrorism.

The prevalence of drug abuse and addiction is a global phenomenon, though there is a significant variation in the incidence of drug use and abuse and the types of drugs being used across regions and countries. In 2017, an estimated 271 million people (5.5 percent of the global population aged 15 to 64) had used drugs in the previous year, 30 percent higher than it was in 2009. In 2020, the figure went up to 376 million (best estimates) and 491 million (upper estimates) (UNODC, 2022). Clearly, the incidence has increased by 105 million to 220 million in just three years. In terms of percentages, the prevalence of drug use was highest in Oceania followed by the Americas, Africa, Europe and Asia. Cannabis, opioids, opiates, cocaine, amphetamines, prescription stimulants and ecstasy are the main drugs being used. Globally, 35 million people are suffering from drug use disorders that need treatment (UNODC, 2019). The number of drug related crimes is also rising over time. Thousands of persons have been killed in inter-gang violence and by drug lords across the globe (Thomas, 2005). When, as result of the American 'war on drugs,' the Columbian government and their US supporters increased pressure on the cocaine corporations, 500 police officials and 40 judges were killed during the late 1980s and early 1990s to undermine the legal attack launched against them. Numerous car bomb incidences caused the death of another 500 people, mostly civilians (Singer, 2008). The 2021 annual report of the International Narcotics Control Board (INCB) revealed that illicit financial flows related to drug trafficking serve as the lifeblood for organised criminal groups engaged in drug trafficking. This, in turn, is a threat to development and security, and curbing these illicit financial flows is therefore essential to addressing drug trafficking around the world.

Social analysis of drug addiction and drug abuse mainly concentrates upon the role of globalisation, which moved the definition of drug use towards drug abuse, customary use of drugs and structural factors that accentuate use of drugs, the impact thereof not only on the individual and the family but also on the society. With the increasing impact of globalisation, two narratives have emerged. One is associated with increased flow of drugs as commodities across international borders with multiple 'deleterious' effects on populations and, hence, became an issue of national security. Balze-Temple and Lo (1992), Beck (1998), Singh (2012), Page (2022) and Fox, Oliver, and Ellis (2013) have highlighted how the problem of drug abuse is adversely effecting the health and safety of people everywhere by adversely influencing the full-fledged development and functioning of society. There has been a consistent increase of drug trade in the economy over the years, implying an increase in demand and supply of the commodities involved. According to the UN (2005) the global drug trade has shown tremendous increases over the years amounting to billions of dollars (Nadeem et al., 2009).

# Dynamics of Drug Addiction and Abuse in India

Ranjit Singh Ghuman, Jatinder Singh
and Gurinder Kaur

Routledge
Taylor & Francis Group
LONDON AND NEW YORK

First published 2024
by Routledge
4 Park Square, Milton Park, Abingdon, Oxon OX14 4RN

and by Routledge
605 Third Avenue, New York, NY 10158

*Routledge is an imprint of the Taylor & Francis Group, an informa business*



*British Library Cataloguing-in-Publication Data*
A catalogue record for this book is available from the British Library

ISBN: 978-1-032-25841-6 (hbk)
ISBN: 978-1-032-33063-1 (pbk)
ISBN: 978-1-003-31801-9 (ebk)

DOI: 10.4324/9781003318019

Typeset in Sabon
by Apex CoVantage, LLC

The second narrative that evolved is the effort to counter this flow of drugs as a commodity in terms of laws and legality of the issue (Charles and Britto, 2001). Under the rubric of Single Convention on Narcotics Drugs, 1961, a system was established to control and "cover the cultivation of plants, which were the raw material of narcotic drugs" (Charles and Britto, 2001), which was ratified and implemented in the form of laws and acts by various nations. Charles and Britto (2001) and Charles, Bewley-Tylor, and Neidpath (2005) have presented the influence of globalisation on the issue of legality with respect to India's NDPS Act. These acts and laws were implemented to counter the growing impact of narcotic drugs. This, however, was also counter-productive to the traditional notions of functional, social and religious use of drugs.

Westermeyer (1976) cautioned about this counter-productive impact of implementation of anti-drug laws and conflict with customary usage of traditional drugs and increased use and addiction to derivatives like opium and other pharmaceutical drugs. Based on his study in the three East-Asian countries of Hong Kong, Thailand and Laos, he observed that

> after only months following the new law, a transition from opium addiction to heroin addiction began in these areas . . . Many former opium addicts switched to heroin use and all new addicts began to use heroin . . . not only did it occur in three different locations, but also at three different times.
>
> (p. 1137)

This observation projects that more than the temporal and spatial context of drug use, it is the blind implementation of laws without taking into the historical, social and cultural context of substance consumption which has led to this unintended consequence of a shift towards more harmful drug consumption practices.

In understanding the customary usage of drugs, use ranged from ecstatic, mind-altering states for religious rituals to medication or recreational purposes ever since ancient times. It was often a controlled usage where social institutions and structures maintained norms and sanctions associated with usage of drugs based on various markers like age and gender. Initially, it was a matter of "customary usage of drugs" which was highly sanctioned especially based on gender and age (Charles, Bewley-Tylor, and Neidpath, 2005). With changing technologies and circumstances, increasing flow of drugs as commodities across boundaries of nations, the use of drugs has in some cases been converted into abuse of drugs often reflected through the numbers of arrests, convictions and seizures of narcotics.

These two major narratives of globalisation and its role and impact on drugs production, manufacture, flow and consumption is synthesised by the arguments of Page and Singer (2010), who locate the topic in the historical context of colonial and post-colonial practices. According to them, globalisation in narcotics requires understanding that

> historic analysis suggests that drugs have played a far greater role in the construction of local, national, and international social relations and, as a result, in creation of broad social network . . . The starting points of this process in the modern era were the globalising changes introduced by Europe. The colonial administration . . . made significant contributions to the international spread of drug production and use throughout Asia and other parts of the world.
>
> (p. 91)

In this manner, the customary use of traditional drugs transformed into drug abuse of synthesised forms of drugs. An interesting aspect worth noticing is that the places of production remain(ed) those at the periphery (e.g., Afghanistan and Mexico where cultivation of drug producing crops like poppy is a source of livelihood and basic survival for many) and places of consumption at the core (countries in Europe and the West). This created a need for a system of checks and control over production and consumption of drugs, once again permeating from the core towards the periphery.

In the context of sociological and anthropological analysis, drug abuse is understood to be socially constructed and transmitted and a socially located issue (Singer, 1994; Parsons, 2022). Besides social factors, it has much to do with economic and political scenarios. Thus, it is imperative to understand the social structures and institutions as well as the politico-economic scenario. Initiation into use of drugs has been popularly attributed to factors like isolation, peer pressure, stress, familial history of drug abuse, religious ecstasy and the like, which all tend to locate the issue in the individual rather than the social.

One of the most significant studies that aptly represent the intersectionality between structural and institutional forces of social, economic and political nature with the issue of drug addiction is by Bourgois and Schonberg (2009). They present the issue of drug addiction interconnected with the problem of homelessness in the contemporary United States. Their focus was on heroin addicts of San Francisco. The authors demonstrated how these people indulged in criminal activities like burglary, theft and small economic activities like day labour to generate income for their drug dosage. The authors weaved their narrative around "themes of violence, race relations, sexuality, family trauma, and suffering, inequality and power relations" that result in a broader understanding of the life of drug addicts as embedded in the social factors and social structures rather than only in individuals.

In another extension of this argument, Bourgois (2012) highlighted how the neo-liberal forces of the Reagan era in the US led to cutbacks on welfare policies of the state for the marginalised sections of society, like the drug addicts, and still continue to impact the lives of people. Since the focus was on homeless drug addicts, he pointed out that rather than focusing on the public health and social welfare of these people, the statist measures focused upon criminality of the issue, thus incarcerating the addicts for long duration in prisons. As a result, devoid of any rehabilitation programme and with low skill development levels, these people, once released from prisons, again fall back into the same cycle of unemployment, homelessness and crime. The repercussions of this are evident from the fact that, as reported by International Narcotics Control Board (INCB, 2013), the majority of convicted individuals in the US committed crime under the influence of some drug.

Similar observations were made by Mcllwaine and Moser (2004) in their study on community tolerance on drug and alcohol consumption. In poorer sections of Colombia and Guatemala, the tolerance of the community to drug consumption was greater where it has been practised over a long period of time and where the mafias involved in the drug trade have filled up the empty spaces expected to be filled by state efforts, creating development activities in their localities. Thus, the spaces of structural and institutional vacuum were filled by those involved in the drug trade, leading to their acceptance by the community.

Drug users, especially drug addicts, face a high probability of stigmatisation that further accentuates their marginalisation. Not only do people who grapple with the issue of drug addiction face stigma and questioning of their morality, their family members, especially the immediate family members, are equally vulnerable to stigma associated with this (Room, 2005). It creates an identity of addicts for them, based on which they are often segregated and stigmatised as risk populations. Rather than having a preventive or curative effect, these aspects cause further suffering for the individual and those associated with him/her (Reith, 2004). This is tantamount to an atmosphere of victim blaming and added responsibilisation (Rose, 2000; Rabinow and Rose, 2006; Atici, 2022), with more focus on risk behaviour and categorizing certain sections as risk groups rather than looking into the detailed aspects of the cause and effect of such behaviour, both on the individual and society.

According to Singer (2012), consumption of substances to achieve an altered state of mind has been part of human civilisation, but with the changing political economy of the world, especially since the modernist era and the beginning of the 1900s, the identity of an addict and defining addiction started concretising. Earlier, those who consumed intoxicating substances were not labelled as addicts but as specific sub-sets of consumers, but by the 1900s the definition of addiction got associated with "the emergence of global capitalism and its desire for labour control," especially in the historical significance of the colonial context, with "addiction being used commonly to label possible unruly and resistant sectors within the dominant colonial societies."

In a similar context, Lin and Zhang (2014), in their study among synthetic drug users in urban areas of Shanghai, China, observed that, based on the colonial identity of an addict as someone who consumed opium, there is an extension in post-colonial times where drug addiction to any kind of drug is imprecated upon the past colonial experiences of drugs and is seen as a "symbol of imperialist aggression against China and loss of national sovereignty." This exemplifies the relationship between colonialism, the identity of an addict, stigma, and labelling against deviance from the expected role of a colonial subject.

In a study of women methamphetamine (popularly known as meth) users in Colorado, US, McKenna (2013) focused upon self-perception of stigma amongst these women. The way the women navigated stigma associated with meth use revolved around two narratives of "I'm not like them" and "I don't think they would hang out with me if they knew." While the first narrative implicated the other meth users over their uncontrolled use and dependency leading to acts such as crime, in the second scenario the stigma is directed at self, based on the popular perception of meth users in society because "the desire or perceived need to hide their meth use resulted from fears of negative treatment and judgment by non-users" (p. 375).

Another aspect that emerges through social analysis of the issue concerns the functional use of drugs. McKenna (2013), focusing on the functional aspect of drug use, argued that labourers used drugs as stimulants to enhance their work capacities and to work for longer durations. She associated this practice with capitalist economies, where rapid economic growth and increasing wealth disparities promote "functional use" of drugs. The perceived benefit of high alertness by meth use was located in the background of structural vulnerabilities "directly tied to homelessness or housing insecurity" (p. 176). It becomes a means for survival. Thus, rising inequalities in wealth and wellbeing, capitalist consumerism and insufficient wages tend to create an acceptable socio-cultural environment for enhancing the capacity of a labouring body (Das, 2015). Lin and Zhang (2014) also took a similar line of argument in their study among young people labelled as drug addicts in China's urban de-addiction centre in Shanghai. For their informants, "drug taking was a means to achieve socially acceptable goals" (p. 30) including those in business and service. Lasco (2014) also made similar observations among young meth users in the Philippines. He identified meth use as an enhancer of performance, especially among the marginalised youth involved in and surviving through the informal economy. He stated that "young people weigh the risks and benefits of drug use and evaluate the functions of various drugs in their everyday lives" (p. 784). Similar thoughts were presented by Hardon and Hyman (2014), Cohen (2014) and Lin and Zhang (2014) regarding the risk taking and enabling environment in which young meth users make decisions to consume the drug. These authors opine that the benefits of drug consumption far outweigh the risks and impact of drugs on their overall wellbeing. The youths in these studies emerge as pragmatic users of meth aware of the difference between the drug-addict and drug-user because they consume the drug to work rather than work to consume.

Also, social institutions like family, religion and kinship act as initiators of drug abuse and also act as institutionalised control mechanisms of drug abuse. Not only do they impact the issue of drug consumption, they also influence the intake of certain types of drugs and prohibit others. Hence, one kind of drug may get community or societal sanction and would be difficult to deal with at legal level (Mcllwaine and Moser, 2004). According to Gorsuch and Butler (1976), parental use of licit and illicit drugs, the influence of drug using peers and previous experience of drug use all contribute to the extent of drug abuse and, hence, drug addiction. Similar observations were made by Embleton et al. (2013) in their study among Kenyan street children, where the dual role by family and peers influences or impedes drug cessation. Thus, this section presents how the social, economic and political influence each other and complicate the matter of drug addiction. Not only do these forces produce this issue but they are also influenced by them in return.

This also reflects the linkages between consumption of drugs and the larger acceptance of it in the society. Mcllwaine and Moser (2004), based on their study in poorer sections of Colombia and Guatemala, argue that tolerance for consumption of any substance including drugs in a society is an important parameter for policy making on controlling addiction in any form. This toleration for consumption, however, does not reflect a unilinear relation with the community because associated issues and problems like violence, crime, debilitating conditions of the households, etc., act counterproductively to the threshold of toleration of consumption. They emphasised, "the need to acknowledge community tolerance as an important dimension in understanding the nature of drug and alcohol consumption" (p. 50). Factors like intra-family violence and conflict, gender-based violence, peer-pressure, structural factors like poverty and unemployment emerged as leading causes of drug addiction.

The nature of drug abuse and addiction varies considerably across countries. For instance, countries like Mexico, Brazil, Afghanistan, Russia, Slovakia, Iran, US, etc., have all been ranked on top in terms of drug usage, production and trafficking (World Drug Report, 2012). However, as depicted before, the problem of drug addiction and usage of mind-altering harmful substances (cocaine, methamphetamines and heroin, etc.) cannot be associated or confined to a particular culture, religion, demographic group, country or particular area. It is a common problem across all cultures, religions, regions and nations, though with a fair degree of variation.

Available evidence suggests that drug addiction of an individual may cause a heavy financial burden because maintaining a habit of such substances is a costly affair (Jiloha, 2009; INCB, 2013). The study by INCB (2013) for the US found that around 4.5 million people in the world in 2010 have taken treatment for drug abuse, costing about $35 billion annually. Further, the study also mentioned that if all drug users in 2010 could have received treatment, the estimated cost of treatment would have varied between $200 billion to

$250 billion. The study further estimated that out of 14 million drug users, 1.6 million suffered from HIV and 7.2 million and 1.4 million have been living with hepatitis C and hepatitis B, respectively.

Reflecting further on the costs of drug abuse, the World Drug Report (2016) pointed out that around 2 million people in the world lose their life due to drug use every year. Drug related deaths due to overdoses, adverse reaction, infection, etc., accounted for between 0.5 and 1.3 percent of all-cause mortality for people aged between 15 and 64 years.[1] The average age of death of drug users in Europe was mid-30s in 2010. In the same line, Global Burden of Disease Study (2015) identified that almost 12 million years of life loss (premature death and disability) was together accounted for by opioids, cocaine, amphetamines and cannabis in 2013.

Other than the previously noted costs, there are other forms of economic costs of drug abuse which can be viewed in terms of loss of productivity of drug user as well as non-participation in the labour market. Workers under the influence of drugs tend to be less productive because of a lack of commitment and under performance which increases their dependency on the economy (Nyameh et al., 2013). A study in Nigeria found that participation of Nigerian youths in drug abuse and trafficking reduced their involvement in economic activity, which led to a vacant labour market. Further, the productivity losses due to non-participation in the labour market amounted to as high as $120 billion in 2011 in the United States; 62 percent of it was drug-related costs. In case of Australia and Canada, drug abuse accounted for 0.3 percent and 0.4 percent, respectively, of loss in Gross Domestic Product (GDP) (INCB, 2013). Africa loses approximately 3.7 percent of its GDP to such flows every year (INCB, 2021). Drug related abuse also causes other types of abuse in the form of violence, theft, crime and other such activities, further adding to various types of social, economic and political burden (Mcllwaine and Moser, 2004).

Often people who are intravenous drug users (IDU) are highly vulnerable to HIV/AIDS. Their vulnerability is further increased due to stigmatisation. As a result, they may not report their HIV status and seek treatment for it, leading to loss in health and familial and social stability and may also become part of a risk population that might be the cause of further spread of this disease (Charles and Britto, 2001). According to United Nations Office on Drugs and Crime (UNODC) and United Nations Programme on HIV/AIDS (UNAIDS) (2001),

> drug injection, because of the health and social problems associated with it, remains the biggest cause of morbidity and mortality resulting

1 Annual figures of estimated drug related deaths are around 211,000 annually. Among the people aged between 15 and 49, drug use was named as the sixth most common reason for death.

> from the abuse of drugs . . . it is a major mode of transmission of HIV in many countries of Asia, Europe, Latin America and North America.

These evidences suggest that drug abuse causes serious costs for an abuser's family and society as well as for the economy as a whole. Variables of power, resistance and dominance in various forms and ways emerge as significant in interactions among culture, politics and economy (Carlson, 1996). Hence, it may be concluded that the issue of drug addiction, away from popular perceptions or limited understandings, must be understood as a complex issue which is deeply interlinked and embedded in social, economic and political structures, sharing a multi-pronged and multi-dimensional relationship with these forces.

### India's experience

Though the non-medical use of drugs in India started somewhere during the late 1960s, the visible change in drug use patterns commenced in the Indian context during the 1980s when India inadvertently became a part of a drug trafficking route between the Golden Crescent (West-Asian production centres) and the Golden Triangle (East-Asian demand centres). Border areas on both the western and eastern fronts of these countries became vulnerable to this trade route (UNODC, 2004). The changing pattern went from natural drugs to derivative drugs to synthetic drugs. The change in drug use pattern is also observable in the context of age category, where people as young as 16 years become victims of drug abuse (Charles, Bewley-Tylor, and Neidpath, 2005) and the previously sanctified norms and sanctions on use of drugs stood breached or broken.

United Nations Office of Drugs and Crimes (UNODC, 2011) identified the main pharmaceutical drugs abused in India as pain killers: codeine-based cough syrups, injectable opiates, antihistamines, benzodiazepines, sedatives, ketamine and anabolic steroids. Most of these medicines are medicines prescribed for treatment. In India, the maximum use of illicit drugs was observed among youth and early adolescents belonging to poor families (UNODC, 2011). The United Nations Convention Report (1988) found that around 50 percent of boys have tried at least one of the gateway drugs before they reached class nine. This number is 60 percent in the case of West Bengal and Andhra Pradesh and 35 percent in the case of Uttar Pradesh and Haryana. Basu et al. (2012) analysed the case of drug addicts in a sample of 6,608 individuals who were treated in the de-addiction centres. All the drug addicts were below the age of 35 and mainly used alcohol, opiates and cannabis. As most of the drug abusers are in the formative years, the loss of human capital for the nation is immeasurable. Drug abuse adversely affects their intellectual, moral, physical and psychological growth. Instead of becoming a part of the productive labour force, they become a burden for the family and society as well as for the nation. To tackle and control the rising phenomenon of drug abuse, use of drugs was brought under legal sanctions.[2] With this, the customary usage of drugs came under the ambit of legal control globally, mainly when many countries became signatory to the UN Convention on Narcotic Drugs in 1961. India passed its Narcotics Drugs and Psychotropic Substance Act[3] (NDPS) in 1985 and amended in 2001 and 2022. However, the desired results of the globalised legislation are still to be achieved, as is evident from the growing incidences of drug abuse and drug trafficking globally as well as nationally.

Ganguly (2008) observed that an increase in injection drug use began during the 1980s and 1990s for mainly two major factors: firstly, due to a diversion of legally cultivated opium towards making of opioid derivates like heroin, and secondly, due to the implementation of the NDPS Act of 1985 there was a shift in the consumption pattern from traditional drugs like opium and cannabis to more harmful derivatives like heroin. Ganguly, Sharma, and Krishnamachari (1995) had earlier raised a very pertinent question vis-à-vis the use of opium and cannabis in their traditional form and the possible unintended consequence of the implementation of the NDPS Act. They raised the issue of "whether these traditional users would continue to follow the age-old custom of raw opium consumption, or whether there would be a pro-heroin effect as has occurred in other South Asian countries after their governments adopted stringent legal measures" (p. 9). Their anticipated query holds certain stringent truth for present times as this gradual shift has been observed in many studies reviewed and mentioned here. The same observation has also been noted by Charles, Bewley-Tylor, and Neidpath (2005) in the pan-Indian context where "the implementation of law-enforcement dominated policies has generated a tense relationship between contemporary legislation and culturally ingrained drug use patterns . . . This situation is compounded by changing patterns of drug use within India" (p. 1–2).

Another aspect associated with drug use is the cultivation of drug yielding crops. In many states of India, particularly in the hilly terrains where ecological and cultural developmental activities have not reached, the cultivation of drug producing crops is a source of livelihood for many locals. This is not just an historical activity but has gained the significance of survival in present times. Vino (2014) studied the dynamics of ganja cultivation in a village in

2 According to the World Drug Report (2015), a quarter of a billion people used illicit drugs in 2013, falling in the age range of 15 to 64 years, making the prevalence rate 5.2 percent.

3 "An Act to consolidate and amend the law relating to narcotic drugs, to make stringent provisions for the control and regulation of operations relating to narcotic drugs and psychotropic substances, to provide for the forfeiture of property derived from, or used in, illicit traffic in narcotic drugs and psychotropic substances, to implement the provisions of the International Convention on Narcotic Drugs and Psychotropic Substances and for matters connected therewith" (NDPS, 1985) http://narcoticsindia.nic.in/upload/download/document_id08b2dbdc9ca941d237893bd425af8bfa.pdf on 3.7.2106 at 4.30 pm.

Ukhrul district of Manipur. The author noted that apart from cultivating vegetables and other items for subsistence, people also cultivated ganja due to non-availability of other sources of livelihood. The author observed that "40 per cent of the respondents engaged in the cultivation of ganja to purchase food items, particularly paddy, which is their staple food" because most people did not have enough resources and/or land to cultivate paddy for subsistence, and, hence, needed to buy it from the market. Another cause was the "desire for a descent standard of living" which "could improve only through investment in their children's and siblings education." Lack of development, especially in terms of education and health care, and a lack of state efforts and initiatives is directly related to the cultivation of drug producing crops by marginalised people in marginalised, remote areas of the country.

Punjab has been the focus of academicians and researchers for studying the nature and extent of intoxicants use (Modi and Modi, 1997), but those studies were mainly micro studies. Until recently, the problem of drug abuse in India was believed to be confined to the Northeastern states and some large cities, but available evidence on the issue suggests that in recent years a number of states in Northwest India have also been facing serious drug problems (Singh and Lal, 1979; Parshant, 1993; Nagla, 1995; Sidduqi, 1992; Ambekar and Tripathi, 2008; Basu et al., 2012). Punjab, located in North India on the Indo-Pakistan international border, and other neighbouring states have attracted widespread attention on the issue of drug abuse from independent researchers and other non-governmental organisations in recent years (Sandhu, 2009; Mahi et al., 2011; Singh, 2012; Indian Express, 2014; Sawhney, 2014; DNA, 2014, 2015). However, all the previous studies have a very limited scope and were mainly focused on some region of Punjab, Haryana and Delhi. Besides, the previous studies also included alcohol and tobacco in their analysis. Our study pertains to five states of North India, namely, Punjab, Haryana, Himachal Pradesh, Jammu and Kashmir (J&K) and Rajasthan. Moreover, we have studied only those drugs which are in the purview of the NDPS Act, 1985 so we have not studied alcohol and tobacco.

The extent of drug abuse in Punjab is evident from the fact that the state has accounted for maximum volume of drugs seized in the country in the recent past. It accounted for 52.26 percent of total drugs seized in the country in 2011 (Live Mint, 2016a). Similarly, the Election Commission seized 185,000 kg of drugs in India during 2014, Lok Sabha polls and Punjab alone accounted for 75 percent of seized drugs (Live Mint, 2016b). These numbers suggest that drug smuggling in Punjab has witnessed a phenomenal increase in the recent years.

Advani (2013) opines that the issue of drug supply in Punjab could not solely be attributed to international trafficking. He is of the opinion that synthetic drugs produced by pharmaceutical companies within the country are also an important source of drug abuse with the easy availability of over the counter drugs at pharmacies. These synthetic drugs have been the cause of increasing intravenous drug usage (IDU) in the state. A somewhat similar observation was made by Quraishi (The Tribune, June 29, 2016), former Chief Election Commissioner, during the 2012 Punjab assembly elections. He observed that,

> Punjab has emerged as a hub of drug trafficking due to its proximity to the golden crescent and 40 per cent of the highly potent drugs are transiting through the state . . . The districts of Bathinda, Mansa, Sangrur, Muktsar and Ferozepur, on the borders of Rajasthan and Haryana, are the worst affected. What is more disconcerting is that the menace is ruining the health, well-being and the future of the youth in Punjab, who fall prey to free supply of these substances as inducement during the polls.

One of the earliest studies on drug abuse was conducted by Lal and Singh (1979) in three districts of Punjab, namely, Sangrur, Bathinda and Ferozepur with a sample of 497 individuals. The authors observed:

> Opium is very extensively used by the rural population of Punjab . . . This is all the more remarkable since alcohol can be purchased openly while the entire amount of opium sold is smuggled from neighbouring states despite risks of detection and prosecution. The use of Cannabis in rural Punjab is on the other hand very limited.
>
> (p. 418)

This observation holds a truth for our present day scenario as well, where internal supply of opium within Punjab has been associated with Rajasthan, where its cultivation is licit under the law. Another significant observation made by authors was that "drug use in a community is a dynamic, changing process – the type and extent of drug use and abuse of any particular drug varying from time to time, depending on various social, psychological and economic factors" (p. 419). This is also in consonance with the present-day scenario observable in the state where decelerating growth, rising unemployment, geo-political scenarios and easy availability of money for some sections owing to land acquisition by the government and real estate companies has brought a change in the trend and type of drugs being consumed. Even if traditional drugs like opium have not vanished from the scene, the use of pharmaceuticals as drugs and synthetic and semi-synthetic derivates of traditional drugs has increased over time.

Similar observations in changing patterns of drug use have been made by Sachadev, Yakhmi, and Sharma (2002) in a study conducted among patients of a de-addiction centre in Faridkot, Punjab. They observed that with the implementation of the NDPS Act of 1985 there has been a decrease in consumption of opium but there has been an increase in the use of pharmaceutical drugs and synthetic and semi-synthetic drugs.

The growing volume of drug smuggling in Punjab has also made it notorious for being one of the states with the highest number of drug addicts in

India. It is evident, as 67 percent of the households in Punjab had at least one drug addict during the first half of the last decade (Mint, 2016b). Another study (Sandhu, 2009) has revealed that 73 percent are youth among the drug addicts. Interestingly, based on this study, the government of Punjab submitted an affidavit in the Punjab and Haryana High Court that 70 percent of the youth in Punjab are drug addicts. This was an erroneous interpretation of the study, as Sandhu's entire sample was of drug addicts and, amongst them, 73 percent were youth.

While analysing the case of Maqboolpura village in Amritsar district, Phillip (2007) met a number of women in the village who narrated the same tragedy of her husband's or son's death because of drug addiction. Maqboolpura is known as "widow village" today. Mahi et al. (2011) examined the degree of drug abuse by analysing the case of Chhajli village in the Sangrur district of Punjab. The study reveals the prevalence of substance abuse among the village population was 39.3 percent and the average age of substance users varied between 15 and 24 years. Another study by Yardley (2012) reported the case of Kazikot village (District Tarn Taran) near the India-Pakistan border. Opium, heroin and other synthetic drugs are the main drugs being used in the village and a majority of the drug addicts are in the age group of 15 to 35 years. Shockingly, some schoolboys also take a small black ball of opium paste with tea before their classes. The study noted that the widespread problem is impossible to measure as it has reached an alarming stage. Yardley interviewed Dr. Manjit Singh Randhawa (a civil surgeon in Amritsar) who said, "I'm getting calls from people saying they have lost their children, they have lost their breadwinners. In every village, people are falling prey to this drug abuse."

A study by Gupta et al. (2014) in ten de-addiction centres in Punjab observed that the most commonly used drugs included propoxyphene, *bhukki*, opium, cannabis and Buprenorphine. Oral consumption was the most common method of consuming drugs. However, the authors observed an increasing trend towards IDUs. The authors opined that even with increasing reportage of drug addiction across Punjab over the years, many private de-addiction centres have come up in the state, especially in rural areas, but the major pitfall remains in the domain of rehabilitation, a lack of which remains the major cause of relapse in a majority of the cases.

A survey by the New York Times reports that 75 percent of the population of border districts of Punjab are exposed to drugs in one form or another (Kanwar, 2012). According to this survey, one out of three college students in border districts is an addict. The use of heroin is quite prevalent among the rich whereas the poor are depending on synthetic drugs supplied by the local pharmacy. The study by Society for Promotion of Youth and Masses, & NDDTC, AIIMS (2016) reported that in 2012, Punjab had 836 drug users per 100,000 people whereas the figure was 250 at the all of India level. Further, 76 percent of opioid dependents in Punjab belonged to the 18 to 35 years age group and 56 percent of opioid dependents were residents of rural areas. 53 percent of drug addicted individuals were using heroin and 33 percent of drug addicts reported using opium/*doda*/*bhukki*. One-third of opioid addicts were injecting drugs. Kalra and Bansal (2012) also made similar observations in their study of 200 patients at a de-addiction centre in a village in district Bathinda, Punjab, where the average age of an addict was 25 years and the most commonly consumed drugs were *bhukki,* pharmaceutical drugs like tramadol and cough syrups.

Ambekar (2012), in a study on HIV prevention among injecting drug users, made the alarming argument that the IDU phenomenon exists in many smaller towns and even villages of Punjab" (p. 9). The author opined that if the supply of heroin gets disrupted due to high vigilance, the shift towards injecting pharmaceutical drugs increases. Regarding the supply of drugs in Punjab, the author also stated that "besides pharmacies, which are the principal source of pharmaceutical drugs for IDUs, many peddlers also sell pharmaceutical drugs along with the injecting equipment to IDUs" (p. 10).

The usage of drugs is not only confined to illiterates, labourers, and educated unemployed, but it is prevalent among school students as well. In 2009, the Government of Punjab filed an affidavit wherein it stated that every third male and every tenth female student has taken drugs on some pretext (Preet, 2012). On average, 7 out of 10 college students were hooked on some kind of drug. Some of the young respondents were taking 10 pills a day and a cough syrup. It was also reported that at least half of the students in schools were taking drugs.

In a nation-wide study on the magnitude of substance use in India by the National Drug Dependence Centre, AIIMS, New Delhi (2019) observed that at the national level 2.8 percent of people between the age group of 10 to 75 years (3.1 crore) were recorded as current users of cannabis. In terms of harmful use or dependent use of cannabis, the national average was 0.66 percent. Punjab was among the states with a higher proportion than the national average, at 2.2 percent. In terms of opioid use, the report observed that "of the total estimated approximately 77 lakh problem opioid users . . . in the country, more than half are contributed by . . . Uttar Pradesh, Punjab, Haryana, Maharashtra, Rajasthan, Andhra Pradesh and Gujarat." (p. 4). In terms of the percentage of the population affected, Punjab was among the top states. In another study by PGI, Chandigarh (Avasthi et al., 2018, 2019) found that opium and opium-based drugs are the most commonly used drugs in Punjab with a higher incidence in rural than in urban areas.

Most of the previous studies focused on the type of drugs used, changes in patterns of drug addiction and demographic trends in terms of age, gender and the rural-urban divide of the populations under study. The gap, however, remains in terms of what Charles, Bewley-Tylor, and Neidpath (2005) refer to as the customary usage of traditional drugs in communities. Only a few of the studies reviewed, in passing, refer to this aspect. The use of traditional drugs like *bhang* has been part of the culture of the whole region of

Northwest India, particularly among the Sikhs and the Rajputana that has been recorded by various British commissions in Colonial India. The Report on the Indian Hemp Drugs Commission (1884) mentioned:

> The hemp plant grows spontaneously throughout the Himalayas. . . . Its prevalence seems to be most notorious in the districts of Hoshiarpur, Gurdaspur, and Jullundur. . . . The growth decreases in frequency very rapidly as the Himalaya is left behind. It appears, however, from the evidence to maintain its hold in the Amritsar, Lahore, Karnal and Shahpur districts.
>
> (pp. 24–25)

The same Commission report also mentions that consumption of ganja is least followed by *charas*. *Bhang*, however, was noticed to be consumed commonly, especially in the western half of the Punjab States.

Royal Commission on Opium (1894) also reflects upon the customary usage of opium amongst certain sections of Indian population. The Commission report mentioned:

> The consumption of opium by the people of India generally is infinitesimally small; it has been consumed for centuries by certain classes in Northern India. It is an indisputable fact . . . that these classes, especially the Rajputs and Sikhs, are precisely the finest races physically in all India.
>
> (p. 62)

The same report also mentions the consumption of *post* by the Sikh soldiers. An important point is that many places in the report refer to consumption of opium as better than consuming alcohol. Its consumption is definitely debated in the context of banning or regulating, but evidence from witnesses to the Commission report emphasizes that had the consumption of opium been abusive and harmful, the Sikhs and Rajputs would not have been the physically martial races that they have been over the centuries. In reply to the Commission's suggestion to ban or regulate opium in Punjab State, the Government of Punjab replied:

> The ratio of consumption of opium to population is not so high . . . among certain classes of population, it is of old standing, and does not seem to do much harm. . . . The people on the contrary assert that they find it a protection against fever.
>
> (p. 142)

The Commissioner of Excise in the same regard warns that "any attempt to prohibit the sale of opium, except for medicinal purposes, would in this province be most unpopular and consequently politically inexpedient" (p. 142).

The preceding discussion on India and Punjab raises a pertinent question about how a society that permitted the customary use of traditional drugs moved towards increased consumption of hard drugs like heroin from the 1980s onwards. The probable answer to this lies in observations by Westermeyer (1976) that the implementation of anti-drug laws and conflict with customary usage of traditional drugs increased the use and addiction to derivatives of opium and other pharmaceutical drugs. This begs an explanation in the context of India where the opening of a new route between the Golden Crescent and the Golden Triangle for the trade of drugs and simultaneously whether the implementation of a law like the Narcotic Drugs & Psychotropic Substances (NDPS) Act 1985 had any impact on the consumption pattern of drugs in the country and the region in particular. It is well known that there are three major global centres of heroin and cocaine processing. They are the Golden Triangle (Myanmar, Thailand and Laos) in the East; the Golden Crescent (Afghanistan, Iran and Pakistan) in the West; and South America. India is the transit route of the first two centres with the US and EU as targets. The third centre does not need India to push heroin and cocaine by virtue of its geographical location. India is, thus, vulnerable to narcotic drug trafficking because of its location between the two largest opium producers of the world. To curb this trafficking is the real challenge for the enforcement agencies. The World Drug Report 2014 reported that, out of the total heroin seized in India, most was of Southwest-Asian origin and the rest originated in India. This view gained credence after the seizure of 10 tonnes of acetic anhydride (used in processing opium into heroin) in Delhi (Dikshit, 2019).

In the case of Rajasthan, a study by Lakshminarayana and Singh (2009) in the western desert districts of Rajasthan based on a survey of 1,200 households in 45 villages of Barmer, Jaisalmer and Bikaner districts revealed that males of this region were highly addicted to opium, specifically those in their middle age. The addiction rate was 8.4 percent in Barmer, 7.9 percent in Jaisalmer and 6.9 percent in Bikaner districts of Rajasthan. The authors also observed that the state maintains a very strict vigil on the illegal spread of drugs, especially in rural areas; however, in spite of this vigil, the drugs reach these areas illegally. According to Singh (2016), there are 19,000 licensed vends in Rajasthan where opium and its derivatives like *doda* and *bhukki* are easily available. Opium is cultivated illicitly in Rajasthan under the license by Central Bureau of Narcotics.

A narrative most commonly acknowledged in the newspapers is that widespread drug addiction among the youth in Punjab is owing to the presence of licit shops/vends in the districts of Hanumangarh and Ganganagar in Rajasthan, which also border the state of Punjab. The sale of poppy husk and opium at these vends was stayed by the order of the Rajasthan High court on June 30, 2015 in a case filed by the Chandigarh-based NGO, Arrive Safe Society. However, the stay was lifted by the Supreme Court of India on September 4, 2015 due to the pleas of local shop owners (The Tribune, September 5, 2015).

In Haryana, according to a study by Ambekar and Tripathi (2008), the likely size of population which are IDUs ranges between 265 to 15,858 individuals. Another report in Chandigarh Tribune (July 27, 2016) mentioned that the peripheral area of the UT Chandigarh had easy availability of drugs at Panchkula, Mani Majra and Baltana. All these places fall under the administration of district Panchkula. Haryana government has also been organising various drives to tackle the issue of drug addiction ranging from large scale seizure and destruction of the narcotics to organising awareness camps, competitions for school and college youth, marathons, etc., specifically targeting the youth of the state. At the level of the political sphere, the current health minister of the state acknowledged the issue of drug addiction among the youth, blamed the state of Punjab as the cause of this and also proposed the idea of putting under CCTV surveillance several border areas between the two states (The Tribune, May 6, 2016).

According to Dr. Gupta from Indira Gandhi Medical College, Shimla the prevalence and pattern of substance abuse in Himachal Pradesh revealed that nearly 29 percent of youth in the state were cannabis users and 3.4 percent were addicted to opium (The Tribune, June 26, 2016). Even the government of Himachal Pradesh acknowledged the high prevalence of drug abuse among the youth and emphasised the need to tackle the issue in its state youth policy. Charles (2001), in a study on drug trade in Himachal Pradesh noted that cultivation and trade of traditional drugs, mainly cannabis, is highly acceptable by the local community and has been part of historical and cultural practice in many parts of the state. With changing legal, economic and geo-political scenarios, trade and cultivation of cannabis is still acceptable to locals. It is also seen as a lucrative business and the thriving of this business involves an active nexus of local, national and international dealers, local cultivators, national and international tourists and active support of "legal machinery and those holding political positions." (p. 2437). The author has cited the absence of adequate development of certain regions within the state, along with rising aspirations of the people, particularly the youth, and national and international exposure of the locals owing to increased tourism as major contributors to drug trade in the state. Also the state houses proliferate the pharmaceutical industry in a Baddi, district Solan. Exercises similar to those in Haryana have also been undertaken by the state government of Himachal Pradesh to make people aware about the implications of drug abuse and addiction. Most of these activities were aimed at the youth of the state. The role of chemists and pharmaceutical units in the states was highlighted in some of the reporting on the issue (The Tribune, May 7, 2015; June 17, 2015; Chauhan, 2015). The narrative on the state of Punjab also emerged in news reporting in Himachal Pradesh, whereby security at border points between the two states was occasionally beefed up, especially in the event of seizures of drugs from either state (The Tribune, June 19, 2015).

The previously mentioned studies and media reports are majorly exploratory in nature and highlight that amongst the addicts there is very high proportion of youth and most of them are male. There is transition from traditional drugs to derivative drugs and synthetic (pharmaceutical, over the counter) drugs and there has been a significant increase in number of

Injection Drug Use (IDU) over the years. There are co-morbidities like HIV/AIDS associated with drug abuse. Main causes of drug abuse among males are paradoxical: lack of job opportunities, ennui and consumerism associated with prosperity. Some studies have correlated lack of development and cultivation of drug producing crops. Some of the studies highlight the relationship between structural vulnerabilities like homelessness, unemployment and survival for basic daily livelihood and drug production and drug addiction.

Two main formats of research studies emerge on the issue of drug abuse in context of Northwest India. Some studies (Pathak, 2016; UNODC, 2004; Advani, 2013; Singh, 2010; Sawhney, 2014) have attempted to relate the two important facts of geographic location and the state of economy vis-à-vis the state of Punjab with the much talked about issue of drug abuse. These studies made use of various parameters from content analysis to primary field-based information. The other typology of research (Lal and Singh, 1979; Singh, 2010; Society for promotion of youth and masses[4]; Mahi et al., 2011; Kalra and Bansal, 2012[5]; Sachadev, Yakhmi, and Sharma, 2002; Ambekar, 2012[6]; Dube et al., 2014[7]) conducted on the issue of drug abuse refers mainly to the demographic trends and typology of drug used and is mainly epidemiological in nature. The demographic trends indicate that age of initiation ranges between 18 to 35 years. Thus, the youth tend to be the main prey of drug addiction and youth from both rural and urban areas are vulnerable to drug addiction.

It is clear from the foregoing studies that there are some micro and case studies on drug abuse in Northwest India. Hardly any study has done a comprehensive and holistic exposition of drug addiction and abuse. Besides, none of these studies has specifically covered the states of Punjab, Haryana, Himachal Pradesh, Jammu and Kashmir and Rajasthan as a whole. These studies and local media reports have highlighted the issue and there is an acknowledgement of its seriousness. In most of the narratives that circulate through the media coverage, the focus has been on blaming one state or the other as a cause of drug addiction. However, what remains missing, hence, vulnerable to misrepresentation, requires addressing the real, innate causes rooted in the structural and institutional factors that contribute towards

4 Study by Society for promotion of youth and masses was based on drug addicts undergoing treatment at government de-addiction centers in ten districts of Punjab. Of the total sample of 3,620, 76 percent were opioid users in the age group of 18 to 35 years, with 54 percent married, 53 percent each opioid dependent and IDU and 55 percent belonging to rural areas (Society for Promotion of Youth and Masses, & NDDTC, AIIMS, 2016).

5 Kalra and Bansal (2012) studied a sample of 200 drug addicts with 85 percent from a rural background, 76 percent married and with 14 years as minimum age of initiation.

6 Ambekar (2012) noted the increase in IDU in small towns and rural areas of Punjab, which otherwise was more of an urban phenomenon.

7 Dube et al. (2014) found an increasing prevalence in 15 to 44 year age group, with 71.9 percent ofdrug addicts married.

this practice. Also, a holistic perspective in terms of inter-state studies is absent in the existing literature. In order to fill this gap, the present study includes neighbouring states of Rajasthan, Haryana, Jammu and Kashmir and Himachal Pradesh for gaining a fulfilling insight into the issue of drug addiction. There is also an apparent lack of comprehensive studies dealing with multiple aspects such as socio-cultural and politico-economic causes, implications and solutions of drug addiction and abuse in Northwest India as a whole.

At times, the non-contextualised spread of information harms not only society at large but also further stigmatises the people who need help and treatment for this problem and also those who are closely associated with them, especially their family members, neighbours and friends. This is where the contribution of academia becomes significant in order to deconstruct the popular narratives and give them a contextual and nuanced understanding. Our study has tried to contextualise the entire phenomena of drug addiction and abuse embedded in socio-cultural and politico-economic

## Northwest India with special focus on Punjab

The wide coverage of the drug menace in Indian media, especially in Northwestern states, for the last ten years points out that drug use, drug abuse and drug addiction is no doubt a serious problem (Sharma, 2017). There were, however, some early warnings in the media (The Tribune, January 16, 2001; November 22, 2005; September 21, 2008). The news reports pertaining to the matters of drug use, drug abuse and drug addiction were reviewed starting from the period of the election campaign in the state of Punjab in 2012, and especially the 2017 assembly elections. The national daily, The Tribune, was specifically chosen for this purpose because of the spread of its coverage and readership in the Northwestern region, particularly Punjab. The national daily also has a history of non-partisanship and apolitical stance vis-à-vis a political party reflecting any particular ideology. Its reportage does not cater to political patronage of any particular political party and highlights critical issues impacting the region in general, and state in particular.

The open politics on drug addiction in Punjab dates back to 2013 with the arrest of dismissed Punjab Police DSP, Jagdish Singh Bhola, in the multimillion drug racket (Rs. 6000–7000 crore drug smuggling). Bhola's name figured in a probe by the Punjab Police Special Task Force (STF) and the ED (Enforcement Directorate of Government of India). Bhola, along with some others, was convicted by the Mohali CBI Court on February 13, 2019 (The Tribune, February 14, 2019). One of the wanted smugglers in this drug haul was Sarbjit Singh Sander (whose name also figured in the previous case and who was hiding in Canada along with 11 other smugglers), killed in Canada on February 10 (The Tribune, February 24, 2022).

This arrest opened a Pandora's Box for the political, police and NRI segment of the state. The role of NRIs in acting as active and passive couriers for smuggling of drugs gave this issue an international angle. It was also claimed in the news reports that apart from the NRIs, drugs manufactured in Baddi (Himachal Pradesh) worth crores were also being smuggled across the world. The alleged involvement of a senior minister in the then Badal government in Punjab was fodder that was made a major political issue in the state. The then-chief minister of the state, Shri Prakash Singh Badal, commented that "Shiromani Akali Dal (SAD) cannot be blamed for the misdeeds of any individual associated with the party" (The Tribune, November 17, 2013). In 2014, reports revealed that synthetic drugs were increasing in the state and these were easily available through local chemist shops in the villages. The drugs were also being ordered over phone and delivered at the destination of the addict. The naming of two powerful politicians from the then-ruling party of the state by Jagdish Bhola was dismissed by them as a "cheap plot cooked up by the Congress" (The Tribune, June 2, 2014). The incident resulted in stricter vigilance in terms of arrests and seizures in the state at the time.

By 2015, the drug problem became a political issue resulting in crackdowns on addicts and peddlers. The then BJP state president mentioned that the "drug menace in Punjab is more serious than terrorism and has to be dealt at that level only" (The Tribune, June 27, 2015). Apart from the media highlighting the issue of drugs in the state, the issue was also debated in the Rajya Sabha in mid-2016. By the end of the year, with preparation on full scale, the Election Commission (EC) of India also recognised the need for special cognisance on the matter of drugs in Punjab by announcing the constitution of special squads to check the flow of drugs in the state during elections. This projects a shift where additional focus was also on drugs rather than only on money or distribution of alcohol or other intoxicants during elections. The actual politicising with a focus on drugs began in the early months of 2016, wherein the Punjab and Haryana High Court questioned the government and police machinery for not handling the inflow of drugs into the jails in the state. The issue of locating drugs like opium and heroin in the jails of Amritsar was highlighted as early as the year 2013.

The Bollywood movie, *Udta Punjab* (released in 2016), gave a push to politicisation of this issue not only in Punjab but also at the national level. Despite the fact that the movie became highly controversial, it drew attention of all the stakeholders in and outside Punjab. The reportage of this controversy in the national media, particularly through television, brought light to the issue of drugs in the state with people across sections of society and politicians claiming the movie reflected Punjab in a negative role. The movie released with a disclaimer:

> For almost decade, Punjab has been waging a lone war against the latest form of terrorism – Narco Terror. Drugs are not produced in Punjab but being pushed through its porous border with Pakistan. The lure of easy money and changing social fabric has seen many youth of Punjab

> being addicted to drugs. . . . Punjab has been a highway of drugs and not the end consumer.

Similarly, Khosla's documentary on the same issue reveals that nearly 50 percent of jail inmates in Punjab are drug addicts and about 30 to 40 percent of addicts are HIV positive. Further, most of these drug addicts finance the expenses incurred from drugs by way of drug peddling (The Tribune, October 12, 2016). A former Additional Director General of prisons also highlighted the issue of drug addiction in Punjab's jails.

With the approaching state legislative elections in 2017, the stage was set for drugs to become an issue of imperative debate and discourse in political, academic and societal spheres. In the 2017 elections to the Punjab Legislative Assembly, the drug phenomenon got a prominent place in the manifestoes of all the contesting political parties. The manifestos of all political parties promised zero tolerance for those involved in the drug trade, a permanent cure and rehabilitation for the addicts and economic empowerment and education to the masses to wean the youth away from drugs. The manifesto of parties other than the SAD-BJP also highlighted the role of SAD-BJP government (2012–17) in the spread of drugs in the state and patronising the drug mafia. The Congress manifesto promised an end to the drug menace in the state within one month of the Congress coming to power in the state, if elected to power.

The then-Congress President Captain Amarinder Singh, in the run up to Punjab State Assembly elections in 2017, took a vow with *gutka sahib* (a small holy book of Sikh religion) in his hands to end the drug menace in one month after coming to power. The Congress came to power but the drug menace went on as usual. The Parliamentary election in 2019 witnessed the same promises by every political party. In view of the elections, the top leadership of the Punjab Congress held a meeting with the top national leaders implicating the "big fish" of drugs as one of the three major issues. The new DGP of the state, who took charge on February 9, 2019, also acknowledged the presence of narco-terrorism in the state. The 2022 elections to the Punjab State Assembly again got much wider attention for all the political parties, and every party made the drug menace a major election plank and promised to uproot the problem after forming government within a specified period. In fact, drugs and sacrilege were the two main poll planks in 2022 elections.

With the reported death of 23 drug addicts during the month of June 2018 in Punjab, a number of measures, such as a dope test for getting an arms licence, for new recruitment in the government service and screening for prisoners, were initiated. The issue of smuggling of drugs from across the border was also taken up with the central government as it was being alleged that the state is the victim of Pakistan sponsored narcotic terrorism. Punjab, being a border state, is not only the transit point, but also a big market for drugs. Heroin is routed through the porous India-Pakistan border, opium and poppy husk is smuggled from Rajasthan and Madhya Pradesh, where its cultivation is legal, and *charas* and hashish come from Himachal Pradesh. Officials say high-quality heroin from Delhi is suspected to be routed through Gujarat, Rajasthan's Ganganagar and Hanumangarh districts or Jammu and Kathua districts in J&K (The Tribune, July 5, 2019).

There have been big seizures of heroin and other illicit drugs in recent years (The Tribune, April 27, 2022). As per media reports, some of the caught 'consignments' were as big as 2,988 kg of heroin at the Mundra Port in September 2021, 206 kg from Gujarat on April 25, 2022, 200 kg on April 21, 2022, 102 kg heroin at Attari ICP, Amritsar in April 2022 and 62 kg heroin from IGI Airport, Delhi in May 2022. In June 2019, 532 kg heroin was caught from Amritsar. Ironically, the concerned agencies are yet to reach the logical conclusion to break the supply chain. Most of the drug seizures in Punjab, either by the Punjab police or by the Border Security Force (BSF), were located in the border districts of Punjab particularly Amritsar and Tarn Taran. Other districts that reported seizures of drugs were Ferozepur, Fazilka and Muktsar. The most common drugs seized included *charas*, heroin, opium, poppy husk, tramadol and capsules. Considering the seriousness of the issue, Punjab and Haryana High Court directed the enforcement directorate "to book within three months all drug trafficking convicts for money laundering in Punjab and Haryana" (The Tribune, April 13, 2019). It is envisaged that this step would deter the supply of drugs due to fear of attachment of property under the NDPS Act. However, what remains to be seen is how the verdict will translate into action. Also, the SSP of Ferozepur district of Punjab, at a public platform, accepted the connivance of certain police officials in propagating the supply of drugs in the state (The Tribune, June 16, 2019). Following this, the Congress party MLA from Kapurthala also endorsed the claim.

The Aam Admi Party (AAP) government in Punjab, after coming to power with a thumping majority in March 2022, is also aiming to have a drug-free Punjab with effective enforcement, de-addiction and prevention thorough community participation (The Tribune, March 22, 2022; May 8, 2022; July 8, 2022). It constituted a new Special Task Force (STF) on the issue but a report is awaited. Paradoxically, all the political parties have acknowledged that Punjab and a number of other states, especially bordering with Punjab, have been facing the problem of the drug menace for more than a decade but nothing much has been achieved, despite the number of measures taken by the governments. Over 40 percent of inmates in Punjab jails are hooked to narcotics (The Tribune, July 18, 2022). The acknowledgement of drug addiction in the state by the political parties reflects the acceptance of this as a problem.

The Haryana Chief Minister launched an action plan for a drug free state (The Tribune, June 27, 2022). Acknowledging the drug menace in the state, the Himachal Pradesh (H.P.) Chief Minister also agreed to constitute an ADGP-headed special task force (The Tribune, June 27, 2022). In view of the rising drug smuggling, the police and other security forces in J&K are tightening the vigil (The Tribune, July 18, 2022).

The number of addicts, peddlers and prisoners under the NDPS Act has been on the rise. To begin with, most of the Act's statements were more of rhetoric than a reality. However, with increasing pressure from various sections of polity, society and judiciary some prominent actions were taken over a period of time. The efficacy of these would, however, be revealed with the passage of time. The election time, whether state or central, appears to be the most prominent time for political statements over the issue of drug addiction. This issue has also been a major test for the present AAP-government in Punjab.

Probably, the first time a major decision was made by the special CBI Court, in mid-February 2019, that held Jagdish Bhola guilty and sentenced him to 12 years of incarceration and a fine of Rs. 0.22 million in a synthetic drugs scam worth Rs. 7,000 million. Apart from him, 22 other accused were also held guilty by the court. These included some prominent NRIs as well. It was during the investigations of this case that names of certain prominent politicians were revealed by Bhola as part of the drug scam. In late December 2021 (ahead of the 2022 Assembly elections) a former cabinet minister, Bikram Singh Majithia, in the SAD-BJP government in Punjab was arrested for alleged drug smuggling under the NDPS Act. The case has been registered on the basis of a 2018 report of the STF probe into the drug racket (The Tribune, December 22, 2021).

## Scope and methodology

The foregoing discussion brings home the fact that the issue of drug addiction cannot be understood in isolation from historical, systemic, structural, social, psychological, political and economic factors. In view of the collective influence and action of these aspects, the main focus of this study is to understand the issue of drug addiction and abuse from multiple perspectives and multiple locations in India, especially in the Northwestern states. It is in this context that we have tried to look into the dynamics of drug addiction and abuse both from theoretical and empirical standpoints. The empirical evidence has been generated from both the secondary and primary data, quantitative as well as qualitative. The primary data was collected through an intensive and extensive field work in five states of Northwest India, namely, Punjab, Haryana, Himachal Pradesh, Jammu and Kashmir and Rajasthan. The states, apart from Punjab, were chosen for a holistic insight into the issue of drug addiction and abuse in Punjab. Rajasthan was selected due to the legally allowed production and easy availability of poppy and its derivatives whereas Haryana was chosen owing to its cultural, economic and political proximity with Punjab. Himachal Pradesh was selected owing to high tourism spots in the districts of Kullu and Kangra and the presence of certain areas in these districts famous for locally made *charas* drugs. Jammu division of Jammu and Kashmir was selected owing to its strategic location vis-à-vis international and national significance.

Our study includes only those illicit drugs which are in the purview of Narcotic Drugs and Psychotropic Substances (NDPS) Act, 1985 and does not include liquor and tobacco. The main objective of our study was to understand the socio-cultural and politico-economic dynamics of drug addiction and abuse and not to estimate its extent. As such, we have studied only the addicts who were either taking treatment in drug de-addiction centres (DDCs) or were undergoing follow-up treatment, and through them we reached into their households. We also studied the hidden drug addicts (those who did not fall in the previous two categories but were addicted to drugs without the knowledge of their household members) by identifying them through the snowball sampling method.

Primary data has been collected from 950 addicts and their household members (950), 190 hidden addicts, 616 control group households (households with no addicts). It is pertinent to mention that, in compliance with the ethical requirements of the study, we got prior consent of all the respondents. However, in view of their privacy, we have not disclosed their names. Though the Research Programme was commissioned by the Indian Council of Social Science Research (ICSSR), Ministry of Education and the Government of India, we also got the permission from the concerned authorities of all five states.

The sampling of the control group respondents was done from the same locations to which belonged the addicts. The drug addicts were selected from 73 drug de-addiction and rehabilitation centres (run by the government, private sector and NGOs) located in the states under study. Among them, 23 are government, 33 were private and 17 NGOs. Amongst the government, 14 are from Punjab, 2 each from Haryana, H.P. and Rajasthan and 3 from J&K. Amongst private centres 21 are from Punjab, 3 from Haryana, 2 from H.P. and 7 from Rajasthan. Amongst the NGOs, 4 each are from Punjab and Haryana and 3 each from H.P., J&K and Rajasthan. The hidden drug addicts were reached by snowball sampling. The selection of addicts was made from these centres and it was through them that we approached their family members. The selection of districts from states other than Punjab, inter alia, is based on their proximity to Punjab, as the major focus of the study is Punjab and its neighbouring states. The statewide selection of districts and number of addicts and respondents from the control group is given in tables 1.1 and 1.2, respectively.

In addition, qualitative data was also collected through 77 focus group discussions (FGDs) with 640 participants (Table 1.1A in annexure) and 40 case studies across the states. Thus, the empirical part of the study dwells on the quantitative and qualitative data and information collected from 3,386 respondents. Given the size of the sample and spatial spread of the respondents, we can safely say that ours is a representative study and is the first of its kind. The participants in the focus group discussions included elected

*Table 1.1* Selected states and districts

| *S. No.* | *Punjab* | *Haryana* | *Himachal Pradesh* | *Rajasthan* | *J&K* |
|---|---|---|---|---|---|
| 1 | Amritsar (Amritsar + Tarn Taran) | Ambala | Kullu | Ganganagar | Jammu |
| 2 | Jalandhar | Sirsa | Kangra | Hanumangarh | Kathua |
| 3 | Ludhiana | | | | |
| 4 | Moga | | | | |
| 5 | Sangrur | | | | |
| 6 | Bathinda (Bathinda + Mansa) | | | | |
| Total | 8 | 2 | 2 | 2 | 2 |

*Note:* Tarn Taran and Mansa districts were earlier parts of Amritsar and Bathinda districts, respectively.

members of rural and urban local bodies (ULBs); academic institutions, teachers and students; religious and spiritual organisations; social pressure groups and youth/sports clubs; medical experts of civil hospitals, de-addiction centres and psychiatrists; police officials; members of civil; and other knowledgeable individuals, officials and volunteers serving in controlling and treating the drug-addicts. The state-wise composition of FGDs is shown in Table 1A in annexure.

The main focus of the study is Punjab for multiple reasons, the prominent ones being its projection in the media, the higher proportion of addiction reported in national and state level studies on drug addiction and the geopolitical location of the state. All these factors have projected Punjab, directly or indirectly, as the epicentre of drugs. The empirical work is mainly focused on social and economic parameters of the respondents and, hence, we tried to capture the nature and pattern of drug addiction and abuse across age, education, gender, occupation and location. We have also tried to examine institutional as well as structural issues and mechanisms to address drug addiction/abuse besides looking into the social and economic cost for an individual, family, society and the economy. Besides examining the causes behind drug addiction, the study also reveals the demand–supply pattern across the states.

The book has been organised into eight chapters. The following chapter presents the trends and patterns of drug addiction in India based on secondary data. Chapters 3–7 dwell on the primary data. Chapter 3 discusses the socio-economic profile of the addicts and their households. Chapter 4 analyses the process of drug addicts' initiation into addiction. Pattern of drug addiction is examined in Chapter 5 while Chapter 6 discusses the socio-economic cost of drug addiction. Chapter 7 dwells on the community perception about drug addiction and abuse. Summary, implications and recommendations are given in the last chapter.

*Table 1.2* Sample size across states

| *Determinants* | *Punjab (8 districts)* | | | | *Other states (8 districts)* | | | |
|---|---|---|---|---|---|---|---|---|
| | *Schedule A* | *Schedule B* | *Schedule C* | *Schedule D* | *Schedule A* | *Schedule B* | *Schedule C* | *Schedule D* |
| Inpatient DDC | 330 | 330 | | – | 240 | 240 | | – |
| Follow-up | 220 | 220 | | – | 160 | 160 | | – |
| Hidden | | 110 | | – | – | 80 | | – |
| Non-drug users* | | | | 408* | – | – | | 208** |
| Total (per state) | 550 | 660 | 45 | 408 | 400 | 480 | 28 | 208 |

*Note:* * 30 rural+20 urban, ** 15 rural+10 urban

*Schedule A pertains to socio-economic status of the 950 respondents from the households; Schedule B to 1140 drug addicts (670 in-patients, 380 follow-up and 190 hidden addicts); Schedule C to De-addiction and rehabilitation centres (73 Nos.); and Schedule 'D' to 616 respondents from control group households.*

# 2 Trends and patterns of drug addiction in India

## Revelations from Narcotic Drugs & Psychotropic Substances (NDPS) Act

The issue of drug abuse has attracted considerable attention of both the national and international agencies because, after nuclear weapons and terrorism, it is one of the biggest threats to the safety of human beings the world over. Rapidly increasing magnitude of the problem of drug abuse is causing immeasurable harm to the health of human beings and safety of the world society and is also adversely influencing the peace, development and functioning of society (Balze-Temple and Lo, 1992; Beck, 1998; Singh, 2012; Fox, Oliver, and Ellis, 2013).

India, too, is caught in this vicious circle of drug abuse, and the cases of drug addicts are increasing day by day. Some estimates reported that India is home to one million heroin addicts and, unofficially, there are as many as five million. The most frequently used drugs in India are cannabis products (*Charas, Bhang and Ganja*), heroin and Indian-manufactured pharmaceutical drugs containing narcotic drugs. Based on the information of people treated for drug abuse, it is observed that 73 percent of drug abusers in India use opioids, 19 percent use cannabis, 5 percent use sedatives and the rest use cocaine and inhalants (World Drug Report, 2009).

The broader objective of this chapter is to provide an overview about the drug related incidence reported at the national level and across major Indian states between 2001 and 2017. To analyse the trends and extent of drug related incidence, we have used secondary information available in the annual reports of the National Crime Record Bureau (NCRB) on various indicators and information collected from State Crime Record Bureau.

### Empirical analysis

In this section, we cover various issues related to the intensity of the drug problem across states. The first part of this section contains details about the persons arrested under the NDPS Act in India. The second part outlines the gender composition of arrested persons. The third part analyses the age-wise distribution of arrested persons under the NDPS Act and the last part of this section informs about the incidence of cases reported under NDPS Act.

DOI: 10.4324/9781003318019-2

## Persons arrested under NDPS Act

The details of the number of persons arrested under the Narcotic Drugs & Psychotropic Substances (NDPS) Act, 1985 during 2001–2017, in absolute terms for major states of India are given in Table 2.1. It is evident that the total number of persons arrested under the NDPS Act has increased from 26,825 in 2001 to 56,006 in 2017 in India. Out of all the major states of India, Maharashtra has shown the greatest increase in the number of arrested persons under the NDPS Act over the period of 15 years (2001–2015), which is followed by Punjab. The number of persons arrested in Maharashtra and Punjab increased from 2,058 and 5,308 in 2005 to 19,996 and 12,171 in 2015, respectively. However, it is surprising to note that a significant decrease was recorded in the case of Maharashtra in 2017.

For the present study, five states (Punjab, Haryana, Himachal Pradesh, Rajasthan and Jammu and Kashmir) in India were selected to understand the phenomenon of drug addiction in social, economic and political terms. The data reveals that the number of arrested persons under the NDPS Act has shown a consistent increase in four states, namely, Punjab, Himachal Pradesh, Rajasthan and Jammu and Kashmir. However, fluctuation is observed for Haryana.

*Table 2.1* Number of persons arrested under NDPS Act during 2001–2017

| *State/UT* | *2001* | *2005* | *2010* | *2015* | *2017* |
|---|---|---|---|---|---|
| Andhra Pradesh | 676 | 855 | 720 | 1555 | 2042 |
| Assam | 187 | 248 | 239 | 282 | 569 |
| Bihar | 597 | 631 | 861 | 605 | 309 |
| Gujarat | 182 | 139 | 131 | 77 | 123 |
| Haryana | 1438 | 1560 | 1082 | 2241 | 2397 |
| Himachal Pradesh | 273 | 279 | 732 | 775 | 1211 |
| Jammu & Kashmir | 154 | 189 | 566 | 899 | 1331 |
| Karnataka | 520 | 399 | 434 | 564 | 1841 |
| Kerala | 616 | 530 | 893 | 4629 | 8915 |
| Madhya Pradesh | 1305 | 1460 | 1516 | 1533 | 1773 |
| Maharashtra | 638 | 2058 | 1967 | 19996 | 995 |
| Odisha | 150 | 164 | 240 | 737 | 946 |
| Punjab | 2487 | 5308 | 6416 | 12171 | 13958 |
| Rajasthan | 955 | 1416 | 1589 | 1364 | 1774 |
| Tamil Nadu | 4307 | 4423 | 1742 | 1868 | 3682 |
| Uttar Pradesh | 10293 | 11047 | 13475 | 6984 | 6734 |
| West Bengal | 735 | 607 | 1018 | 1939 | 1501 |
| Total States | 26130 | 31898 | 34166 | 59047 | 55681 |
| All-India | 26825 | 33895 | 34544 | 59625 | **56006** |

*Source*: NCRB (Various Reports).

–Refers to non-availability of data.

The percentage share of each state to all of India's number of arrested persons under the NDPS Act is shown in Table 2.1A in annexure. It is clear that the number of arrested persons, in terms of percentages, has consistently increased in Punjab in the last one and a half decade (2001 to 2017). It has gone up from 9.27 percent in 2001 to 24.92 percent in 2017, whereas in Haryana it has declined from 5.36 percent (2001) to 3.13 percent (2010) and then marginally increased to 4.28 percent in the recent year (2017). Rajasthan has recorded an increase from 3.56 percent (2001) to 4.6 percent in 2010, which later declined to 3.17 percent in 2017. The rest of the two selected states, Jammu and Kashmir and Himachal Pradesh, did not shown a uniform trend in this regard (Table 2.1A in annexure).

It is interesting to note that Punjab ranked second after Maharashtra in terms of percent of total number of persons arrested under NDPS in 2015. Maharashtra accounted for 33.54 percent of total arrested persons in 2015, followed by Punjab (20.41 percent percent) and Uttar Pradesh (11.71 percent percent). In 2017, a sharp decline was noticed in the case of Maharashtra and a sudden jump was recorded in the case of Kerala. In 2017, Kerala accounted for 15.92 percent of the total arrested persons, then declined to 1.78 percent in the case of Maharashtra (Table, 2.1A in annexure). It is pertinent to note that the size of Punjab (both in terms of population and geographical area) is much smaller than Maharashtra and Kerala. In that sense, the intensity of drug abuse and addiction in Punjab is much higher when compared with Maharashtra and Kerala. In a comparison to Uttar Pradesh, again the drug abuse and addiction is much higher.

### *2.1.2 Gender-wise composition of arrested persons*

A gender-wise composition of arrested persons under the NDPS Act for major states of India from 2005 to 2015 is presented in Table 2.2. The arrested persons at the all-India level found a manifold higher incidence for males compared to females between 2005 and 2015. This is true for states throughout the reference period. It is interesting to note that Punjab ranked at the top in terms of female arrests during 2010 and 2015, followed by Tamil Nadu. The number of females arrested under NDPS in Punjab has gone up from 430 in 2010 to 698 in 2015. Punjab accounted for more than 46 percent of females arrested under the NDPS act in 2015.

The gender composition of arrested persons, in percentage terms, under NDPS from 2005 to 2015 is shown in Table 2.2A in annexure. At the all-India level, the share of male arrests during the reference period varied between 94.28 percent and 97.43 percent. Alternatively, the share of female arrests varied from 5.72 percent to 2.57 percent. With some exceptions, male arrests remained above 95 percent in most of the states over a period of ten years (2005 to 2015). Such a share was below 95 percent for Punjab and

*Table 2.2* Gender composition of arrested persons under the NDPS Act: 2005 to 2015

| *State* | *2005* | | | *2010* | | | *2014* | | | *2015* | | |
|---|---|---|---|---|---|---|---|---|---|---|---|---|
| | *Male* | *Female* | *Total* | *Male* | *Female* | *Total* | *Male* | *Female* | *Total* | *Male* | *Female* | *Total* |
| Andhra Pradesh | 817 | 38 | 855 | 653 | 67 | 720 | 1122 | 58 | 1180 | 1469 | 86 | 1555 |
| Assam | 218 | 30 | 248 | 208 | 31 | 239 | 375 | 10 | 385 | 278 | 4 | 282 |
| Bihar | 623 | 8 | 631 | 859 | 2 | 861 | 650 | 3 | 653 | 599 | 6 | 605 |
| Gujarat | 130 | 9 | 139 | 125 | 6 | 131 | 67 | 3 | 70 | 76 | 1 | 77 |
| Haryana | 1493 | 67 | 1560 | 1030 | 52 | 1082 | 1263 | 41 | 1304 | 2167 | 74 | 2241 |
| Himachal Pradesh | 270 | 9 | 279 | 705 | 27 | 732 | 787 | 24 | 811 | 747 | 28 | 775 |
| Jammu & Kashmir | 181 | 8 | 189 | 563 | 3 | 566 | 584 | 4 | 588 | 892 | 7 | 899 |
| Karnataka | 368 | 31 | 399 | 405 | 29 | 434 | 482 | 14 | 496 | 546 | 18 | 564 |
| Kerala | 505 | 25 | 530 | 872 | 21 | 893 | 2666 | 23 | 2689 | 4616 | 13 | 4629 |
| Madhya Pradesh | 1384 | 76 | 1460 | 1460 | 56 | 1516 | 1477 | 65 | 1542 | 1467 | 66 | 1533 |
| Maharashtra | 1968 | 90 | 2058 | 1861 | 106 | 1967 | 16223 | 67 | 16290 | 19916 | 80 | 19996 |
| Orissa | 159 | 5 | 164 | 235 | 5 | 240 | 695 | 5 | 700 | 737 | 0 | 737 |
| Punjab | 4836 | 472 | 5308 | 5986 | 430 | 6416 | 16301 | 783 | 17084 | 11473 | 698 | 12171 |
| Rajasthan | 1377 | 39 | 1416 | 1563 | 26 | 1589 | 1246 | 12 | 1258 | 1350 | 14 | 1364 |
| Tamil Nadu | 3722 | 701 | 4423 | 1550 | 192 | 1742 | 1505 | 245 | 1750 | 1606 | 262 | 1868 |
| Uttar Pradesh | 10965 | 82 | 11047 | 13456 | 19 | 13475 | 6267 | 45 | 6312 | 6975 | 9 | 6984 |
| West Bengal | 533 | 74 | 607 | 979 | 39 | 1018 | 1614 | 49 | 1663 | 1878 | 61 | 1939 |
| Total (States) | **30075** | **1823** | **31898** | **33001** | **1165** | **34166** | **53972** | **1516** | **55488** | **57532** | **1515** | **59047** |

*Source*: NCRB (Various Reports).

Tamil Nadu over the same period of time. For instance, it was 91.11 percent (2005) as compared to 94.27 percent in 2015 for Punjab.

### *2.1.3 Age-wise distribution of arrests under NDPS Act*

The age-wise information pertaining to the number of persons arrested under the NDPS Act across major states of India between 2005 and 2015 is presented in Table 2.3. It is clear that the majority of the persons arrested under the NDPS Act fall in the age group of 18 to 45 years at the national level during the reference period. Out of total arrested persons (33,895) at the all-India level in 2005, 45.17 percent fall in the age group 18 to 30 years and 39.54 percent in the age group 30 to 45 years (Table 2.3). The state-wise picture shows that in eight states (Bihar, Jammu and Kashmir, Madhya Pradesh, Maharashtra, Rajasthan, Tamil Nadu, Uttar Pradesh and West Bengal) the highest number of arrested persons was in the age group of18 to 30 years during 2005. In rest of the major states, the highest number of persons falls in the age group 30 to 45 years during 2005.

It is further seen from Table 2.3 that the trend did not change in 2012 as the greatest number of arrested persons remained in the age group 18 to 45 years. The number of states with the majority of arrested persons belonging to age group 18 to 30 years increased from eight to ten during 2005 and 2012 (Table 2.3). These states include Andhra Pradesh, Bihar, Gujarat, Jammu and Kashmir, Karnataka, Madhya Pradesh, Maharashtra, Sikkim, Uttar Pradesh and West Bengal. Further, it is interesting to note that Punjab accounted for the highest number of arrested persons in both the age groups in 2012 (Table 2.3). It is evident, as Punjab accounted for 26.04 percent of total arrested persons in the age group between 18 to 30 years and 32.27 percent in the age group between 30 to 45 years in 2015. Further, it is interesting to note that out of the total arrested persons in Punjab in 2012, 36 percent and 41 percent came from the age groups 18 to 30 and 30 to 45 years, respectively. This evidence clearly indicates that the greatest number of arrested persons under the NDPS Act is youth. The massive involvement of youth in the drug business does not go well with the sustainable growth and economic development of a nation. Besides reducing their direct contribution to normal economic activities, their involvement in such activities may cause social disturbance.

### *2.1.4 Incidence and rate of cases reported under the NDPS Act, 1985*

State-wise incidence of drugs reported under the NDPS Act from 1991 to 2020 is presented in Table 2.4. The share of each state with reference to all-India is portrayed in Table 2.3A in annexure. Data presented in Table 2.4 reveals that the incidence of drug related cases has increased from 20,944 (1991) to 24,377 (2001) and further reached to 59,806 in 2020. Tamil Nadu has dominated in incidence of drug cases in 1991 as compared to other states in absolute terms. However, Tamil Nadu was overtaken by Uttar Pradesh

*Table 2.3* Age-group of arrested persons under NDPS Act during 2005 and 2012

| *State* | *2005* | | | | | | *2012* | | | | | |
|---|---|---|---|---|---|---|---|---|---|---|---|---|
| | *Below 18 Years* | *Between 18–30 Years* | *Between 30–45 Years* | *Between 45–60 Years* | *Above 60 Years* | *Grand Total* | *Below 18 Years* | *Between 18–30 Years* | *Between 30–45 Years* | *Between 45–60 Years* | *Above 60 Years* | *Grand Total* |
| Andhra Pradesh | 2 | 243 | 346 | 215 | 49 | 855 | 4 | 408 | 368 | 116 | 21 | 917 |
| Assam | 0 | 95 | 122 | 31 | 0 | 248 | 3 | 64 | 91 | 22 | 0 | 180 |
| Bihar | 2 | 339 | 218 | 63 | 9 | 631 | 10 | 420 | 349 | 92 | 1 | 872 |
| Gujarat | 2 | 53 | 63 | 16 | 5 | 139 | 0 | 42 | 35 | 18 | 7 | 102 |
| Haryana | 19 | 564 | 671 | 282 | 24 | 1560 | 6 | 432 | 475 | 191 | 21 | 1125 |
| Himachal Pradesh | 0 | 92 | 129 | 46 | 12 | 279 | 8 | 288 | 239 | 82 | 22 | 639 |
| Jammu & Kashmir | 0 | 89 | 76 | 24 | 0 | 189 | 0 | 225 | 269 | 79 | 0 | 573 |
| Karnataka | 1 | 110 | 173 | 109 | 6 | 399 | 0 | 115 | 111 | 65 | 7 | 298 |
| Kerala | 1 | 185 | 231 | 100 | 13 | 530 | 2 | 281 | 387 | 152 | 17 | 839 |
| Madhya Pradesh | 12 | 660 | 581 | 187 | 20 | 1460 | 18 | 579 | 627 | 256 | 26 | 1506 |
| Maharashtra | 2 | 960 | 827 | 253 | 16 | 2058 | 7 | 2188 | 1999 | 493 | 47 | 4734 |
| Orissa | 0 | 70 | 88 | 6 | 0 | 164 | 0 | 118 | 155 | 75 | 3 | 351 |
| Punjab | 2 | 1957 | 2392 | 736 | 221 | 5308 | 8 | 4210 | 4791 | 2660 | 46 | 11715 |
| Rajasthan | 7 | 625 | 561 | 210 | 13 | 1416 | 9 | 630 | 682 | 197 | 11 | 1529 |
| Sikkim | 0 | 2 | 5 | 0 | 0 | 7 | 0 | 2 | 1 | 0 | 0 | 3 |
| Tamil Nadu | 19 | 1888 | 1644 | 802 | 70 | 4423 | 1 | 607 | 638 | 365 | 71 | 1682 |
| Uttar Pradesh | 2 | 5556 | 4151 | 1265 | 73 | 11047 | 5 | 4122 | 2545 | 520 | 0 | 7192 |
| West Bengal | 3 | 287 | 252 | 65 | 0 | 607 | 0 | 532 | 498 | 143 | 2 | 1175 |
| Total (States) | 90 | 14050 | 12750 | 4461 | 547 | 31898 | 89 | 15551 | 14471 | 5565 | 306 | 35982 |
| **All-India** | **94** | **15310** | **13403** | **4539** | **549** | **33895** | **92** | **16165** | **14848** | **5643** | **307** | **37055** |

*Source*: NCRB (Various Reports).

*Note:* Data is not available post 2012.

*Table 2.4* Incidence of drug reported under the NDPS Act: 1991 to 2020

| *State* | *1991* | *1995* | *2001* | *2005* | *2010* | *2013* | *2015* | *2020* |
|---|---|---|---|---|---|---|---|---|
| Andhra Pradesh | 135 | 571 | 651 | 563 | 455 | 553 | 718 | 866 |
| Assam | 110 | 113 | 146 | 125 | 180 | 266 | 210 | 983 |
| Bihar | 111 | 192 | 264 | 372 | 633 | 481 | 480 | 964 |
| Gujarat | 275 | 280 | 119 | 101 | 83 | 47 | 54 | 308 |
| Haryana | 814 | 1227 | 1322 | 1427 | 871 | 1129 | 1661 | 3060 |
| Himachal Pradesh | 85 | 84 | 229 | 242 | 596 | 531 | 622 | 1538 |
| Jammu & Kashmir | 45 | 51 | 111 | 192 | 421 | 390 | 588 | 1222 |
| Karnataka | 100 | 190 | 309 | 292 | 302 | 290 | 350 | 4054 |
| Kerala | 432 | 306 | 514 | 409 | 769 | 974 | 4103 | 4968 |
| Madhya Pradesh | 1116 | 1472 | 1107 | 1213 | 1170 | 1188 | 1096 | 3155 |
| Maharashtra | 4193 | 768 | 463 | 1365 | 1081 | 2714 | 18979 | 4714 |
| Orissa | 85 | 193 | 116 | 97 | 108 | 364 | 516 | 1179 |
| Punjab | 1303 | 1483 | 2231 | 4464 | 5508 | 14654 | 10159 | 6909 |
| Rajasthan | 939 | 649 | 705 | 973 | 1165 | 943 | 883 | 2743 |
| Tamil Nadu | 4638 | 2212 | 4237 | 4390 | 1467 | 1511 | 1522 | 5403 |
| Uttar Pradesh | 4426 | 8935 | 10213 | 10650 | 13295 | 6429 | 6505 | 10852 |
| West Bengal | 458 | 335 | 506 | 485 | 790 | 981 | 1292 | 1626 |
| Total | 19738 | 19736 | 23711 | 27838 | 29303 | 34101 | 50320 | 57600 |
| All-India | 20944 | 20194 | 24377 | 29421 | 29576 | 34668 | 50796 | 59806 |

*Source*: NCRB (Various Reports).

during the year 2020 (Table 2.4). Further, except Uttar Pradesh, all other states have witnessed an increase in terms of drug incidence reported under NDPS between 2010 and 2020. However, there is a considerable variation among the states which have recorded increases in drug incidence reported under the NDPS Act (Table 2.4).

The state wise data reveals that Tamil Nadu had a maximum incidence of drug cases in percentage terms (22.14 percent), followed by Uttar Pradesh (21.13 percent) and Maharashtra (20.02 percent) in 1991 (Table 2.3A in annexure). However, highest incidence of drug in percentage terms was in Uttar Pradesh (18.15 percent), followed by Punjab (11.55 percent) and Tamil Nadu (9.03 percent) during 2020. Out of five selected states for this study, in four states (Haryana, Himachal Pradesh, Jammu and Kashmir and Rajasthan) the incidence in terms of percentage remained below 6 percent from 1991 to 2020. In the case of Punjab, the incidence increased to 42.27 percent in 2013 from 6.22 percent in 1991, which came down to 11.55 percent in 2020 (Table 2.3A in annexure). This suggests that the situation in Punjab has worsened as compared to other selected states for study in the northwestern region. It would look even worse when comparing the size (in terms of population and geographical area) of Maharashtra and Uttar Pradesh with Punjab. The latter is much smaller than the other two states.

The information given, in terms of rate of persons arrested, by NCRB is also utilised for the purpose of study (Table 2.5). For India as a whole, the rate of persons arrested under the NDPS Act was 4.4 per lakh persons in 2018. The corresponding figure for the year 1991 was 2.5. It is important to

*Table 2.5* State-wise persons arrested under the NDPS Act (per lakh): 1991 to 2018

| *State* | *1991* | *1995* | *2001* | *2005* | *2010* | *2013* | *2015* | *2018* |
|---|---|---|---|---|---|---|---|---|
| Andhra Pradesh | 0.2 | 0.8 | 0.9 | 0.7 | 0.5 | 0.6 | 1.0 | 1.6 |
| Assam | 0.5 | 0.5 | 0.5 | 0.4 | 0.6 | 0.8 | 0.7 | 2.8 |
| Bihar | 0.1 | 0.2 | 0.3 | 0.4 | 0.5 | 0.4 | 0.3 | 0.8 |
| Gujarat | 0.7 | 0.6 | 0.2 | 0.2 | 0.1 | 0.1 | 0.1 | 0.4 |
| Haryana | 5.0 | 6.8 | 6.3 | 6.3 | 3.5 | 4.3 | 6.1 | 10.5 |
| Himachal Pradesh | 1.7 | 1.5 | 3.8 | 3.8 | 8.9 | 7.7 | 8.8 | 20.9 |
| Jammu & Kashmir | 0.6 | 0.6 | 1.1 | 1.7 | 3.2 | 3.2 | 4.8 | 9.2 |
| Karnataka | 0.2 | 0.4 | 0.6 | 0.5 | 0.5 | 0.5 | 0.6 | 6.1 |
| Kerala | 1.5 | 1.0 | 1.6 | 1.2 | 2.2 | 2.8 | 11.5 | 14.0 |
| Madhya Pradesh | 1.7 | 2.0 | 1.3 | 1.3 | 1.0 | 1.0 | 0.8 | 3.8 |
| Maharashtra | 5.3 | 0.9 | 0.5 | 1.3 | 1.0 | 2.3 | 15.9 | 3.8 |
| Orissa | 0.3 | 0.6 | 0.3 | 0.3 | 0.3 | 0.9 | 1.2 | 2.6 |
| Punjab | 6.4 | 6.9 | 9.2 | 17.3 | 20.2 | 51.6 | 35.1 | 22.9 |
| Rajasthan | 2.1 | 1.3 | 1.2 | 1.6 | 1.7 | 1.3 | 1.2 | 3.5 |
| Tamil Nadu | 8.3 | 3.8 | 6.8 | 6.8 | 2.2 | 2.2 | 2.2 | 7.1 |
| Uttar Pradesh | 3.2 | 6.0 | 6.0 | 5.7 | 6.5 | 2.9 | 2.8 | 4.7 |
| West Bengal | 0.7 | 0.5 | 0.6 | 0.6 | 0.9 | 1.1 | 1.4 | 1.7 |
| Total | 0.7 | 2.1 | 2.3 | 2.6 | 2.5 | 2.8 | 4.1 | 4.4 |
| **All-India** | **2.5** | **2.2** | **2.4** | **2.7** | **2.5** | **2.8** | **4.0** | 4.4 |

*Source*: NCRB (Various Reports).

note that the rate of drug incidence was much higher in Punjab as compared to other states and at the all-India level during 1995 and 2018. For instance, it was 6.9 per lakh persons in 1995 which increased to 51.6 per lakh persons in 2013 and declined to 22.9 in 2018. However, this rate was highest in Tamil Nadu (8.3) as compared to Punjab (6.4) in 1991. Amongst the five selected states for this study, the rate of arrested persons during 1991 were found to be highest in Punjab (6.4), followed by Haryana (5.0), Rajasthan (2.1), Himachal Pradesh (1.7) and Jammu and Kashmir (0.6). During 2018, Punjab still dominated at the rate of 22.9 per lakh followed by Himachal Pradesh (20.9), Haryana (10.5), Jammu and Kashmir (9.2) and Rajasthan (3.5).

### *2.1.5 Trends in recovery of drugs in selected states*

Details pertaining to the number of persons arrested and cases registered under the NDPS Act in Punjab, Haryana and Jammu division of J&K are presented in Table 2.6. Upward trends have been observed both in terms of persons arrested and cases registered under the NDPS Act from 2013 to 2018. The number of cases registered under NDPS increased more than two times (1,141 in 2013 to 2,587 in 2018) in the case of Haryana and about four times (158 in 2013 to 616 in 2018) in the case of Jammu from 2013 to 2018. Similarly, the persons arrested under the NDPS Act in Haryana and Jammu division have increased 2.4 times (1,379 in 2011 to 3,294 in 2018) and 3.9 times (185 in 2013 to 717 in 2018), respectively, in the reference

*Table 2.6* Number of cases registered and persons arrested under the NDPS Act

| *Year* | *Punjab* | | *Haryana* | | *Jammu division of J&K* | |
|---|---|---|---|---|---|---|
| | *Cases Registered* | *Persons Arrested* | *Cases Registered* | *Persons Arrested* | *Cases Registered* | *Persons Arrested* |
| 2013 | 14654 | 16821 | 1141 | 1379 | 158 | 185 |
| 2014 | 14483 | 17022 | 1020 | 1287 | 176 | 193 |
| 2015 | 10159 | 12181 | 1673 | 2184 | 275 | 307 |
| 2016 | 5906 | 7266 | 2063 | 2767 | 377 | 511 |
| 2017 | 12356 | 14230 | 2248 | 2817 | 611 | 770 |
| 2018 | 11653 | 14252 | 2587 | 3294 | 616 | 717 |
| CAGR* | –4.48 | –3.26 | 17.79 | 19.02 | 31.28 | 31.12 |

*Source*: State Crime Record Bureau.

* Refers to compound annual growth rate.

period. Opposite trends have been recorded in the case of Punjab wherein a decline was witnessed both in case of persons arrested and cases registered under the NDPS Act (Table 2.6). In absolute terms, the number of persons arrested and cases registered under the NDPS Act in Punjab remained 4.5 times and 4.3 times, respectively, from 2013 to 2018. This implies that the extent of the drug abuse problem in Punjab is more severe as compared to other selected states.

The drug-wise recovery in Punjab under the NDPS Act from 2013 to 2018 is presented in Table 2.7. It needs to be kept in mind that figures in the table show the quantity of each drug seized but there is the likelihood that the entire quantity may not have been seized. There is also a perception among people that concerned agencies may not provide the total quantity seized on record for reasons best known to the agencies. The people of other states also have a similar perception. This perception has been supported by Sahni (2019) when he wrote that, normally, seizures reflect a small fraction of the drugs in circulation, and the narcotics flowing across the border into Punjab would require manifold recoveries.

It is interesting to note that the quantity of all the drugs seized under the NDPS Act in the state has declined over the reference period. It is evident as the compound annual growth rate is negative across all the categories of drugs. The extent of decline is not uniform across all the drugs presented in Table 2.7. Considerable decline has been noticed in the case of drugs like smack, pseudo-ephedrine, the mixture to make ICE, intoxicant powder, etc. At the same time, other drugs like heroin, *charas*, opium, poppy, injection and other pharmaceutical drugs have been seized in large quantityies. The continuous availability of various types of drugs in a large quantity raises serious questions about the sources from where these drugs enter into Punjab.

Table 2.8 depicts the trends in recovery of various types of drugs in Haryana from 2013 to 2018. Unlike Punjab, the recovery of all types of illicit drugs

*Table 2.7* Recovery of drugs under the NDPS Act in Punjab

| *Type of drug* | *2013* | *2014* | *2015* | *2016* | *2017* | *2018* | *CAGR 2013 to 2018* |
|---|---|---|---|---|---|---|---|
| Heroin (Kgs) | 463.6 | 637.0 | 428.9 | 139.6 | 199.3 | 402.8 | –2.8 |
| Smack (Kgs) | 48.9 | 15.4 | 9.7 | 22.0 | 15.7 | 3.4 | –41.5 |
| Charas (Kgs) | 173.1 | 103.3 | 77.4 | 114.5 | 137.7 | 124.1 | –6.4 |
| Cocaine (Kgs) | 0.0 | 0.0 | 3.5 | 0.1 | 0.0 | 0.1 | 44.3 |
| Opium (Kgs) | 963.8 | 556.2 | 420.9 | 354.7 | 447.8 | 420.9 | –15.3 |
| Poppy Husk (Kgs) | 236639.2 | 98795.0 | 36052.4 | 33189.5 | 43749.9 | 46289.1 | –27.8 |
| Bhang (Kgs) | 529.0 | 777.4 | 1091.1 | 170.8 | 117.0 | 98.9 | –28.5 |
| Pseudo-ephedrine (Kgs) | 960.3 | 250.0 | 0.0 | 0.0 | 0.0 | 0.0 | –100.0 |
| Methamphe-tamine (Ice) (Kgs) | 14.3 | 0.8 | 1.6 | 2.2 | 3.0 | 0.0 | –75.7 |
| Ephedrine (Kgs) | 84.1 | 0.0 | 0.0 | 0.0 | 0.0 | 0.0 | –100.0 |
| Mixture to make ICE (Pseudoephedrine, Ephedrine & Metro phormine) (Kgs) | 542.4 | 1212.4 | 0.0 | 0.7 | 0.7 | 1.0 | –71.5 |
| Intoxicant Powder (Kgs) | 1617.9 | 974.5 | 582.2 | 181.3 | 204.5 | 147.8 | –38.0 |
| Injection (Nos.) | 323056 | 17837 | 16499 | 21382 | 36315 | 53738 | –30.1 |
| Pills/Capsules (Nos.) | 30652590 | 3643724 | 2265308 | 1958077 | 4491864 | 6017781 | –27.8 |

*Source*: State Crime Record Bureau.

*Table 2.8* Recovery of drugs under the NDPS Act in Haryana

| *Type of drug* | *2013* | *2014* | *2015* | *2016* | *2017* | *2018* | *CAGR 2013 to 2018* |
|---|---|---|---|---|---|---|---|
| Opium (kgs) | 76.2 | 37.9 | 128.7 | 118.1 | 86.1 | 105.7 | 6.8 |
| Charas/sulpha (kgs) | 354.3 | 97.4 | 1081.5 | 241.1 | 116.8 | 427.8 | 3.8 |
| Poppy husk (kgs) | 38782.3 | 20691.3 | 33568.8 | 10149.8 | 12081.2 | 10937.5 | –22.4 |
| Smack (kgs) | 15.5 | 4.2 | 10.9 | 25.2 | 111.2 | 21.1 | 6.3 |
| Ganja (kgs) | 296.4 | 1145.0 | 1665.3 | 2529.3 | 4376.2 | 5612.1 | 80.1 |
| Heroin (kgs) | 0.2 | 0.4 | 7.2 | 6.5 | 4.0 | 15.9 | 134.7 |
| | Pharmaceutical drugs | | | | | | |
| Tablets (Nos.) | 469010.0 | 92800.0 | 544021.0 | 696921.0 | 147025.0 | 724464.0 | 9.1 |
| Capsules (Nos.) | 31726.0 | 25390.0 | 24030.0 | 73119.0 | 2375.0 | 89877.0 | 23.2 |
| Injection (Nos.) | 735.0 | 1719.0 | 232.0 | 4104.0 | 3144.0 | 5220.0 | 48.0 |
| Syrup in bottles (Nos.) | – | 2964.0 | 7339.0 | 5515.0 | 2247.0 | 9368.0 | 33.3* |

* refers CAGR for the period 2014 to 2018.

*Table 2.9* Recovery of drugs under the NDPS Act in Jammu division of Jammu and Kashmir

| *Type of drug* | *2013* | *2014* | *2015* | *2016* | *2017* | *2018* | *CAGR 2013 to 2018* |
|---|---|---|---|---|---|---|---|
| Heroin (Kgs) | 6.9 | 58.2 | 15.0 | 64.1 | 65.3 | 89.9 | 67.4 |
| Smack (Gms) | 0.0 | 0.0 | 0.1 | 0.1 | 35.0 | 13.0 | 218.0 |
| Charas (Kgs) | 29.7 | 77.4 | 24.3 | 107.8 | 114.6 | 186.7 | 44.4 |
| Cocaine (Kgs | 0.0 | 0.0 | 0.0 | 0.0 | 0.0 | 0.0 | |
| Opium (Kgs) | 0.0 | 0.5 | 2.0 | 6.7 | 6.1 | 0.3 | |
| Poppy Husk (Kgs) | 1208.6 | 2010.9 | 1846.8 | 3268.9 | 7436.6 | 15915.8 | 67.5 |
| Ganja (Kgs) | 15.0 | 11.0 | 23.7 | 91.1 | 0.3 | 137.8 | 55.8 |
| Injection (Nos) | 0.0 | 95.0 | 0.0 | 0.0 | 91.0 | 0.0 | |
| Pills/capsules (Nos) | 109851.0 | 47040.0 | 148402.0 | 130055.0 | 88721.0 | 63489.0 | –10.4 |

*Source*: State Crime Record Bureau.

barring poppy husk in the state has significantly increased as depicted by the high CAGR. The highest increase has been observed in heroin as it increased from 0.2 kilograms in 2013 to 15.9 kilograms in 2018. Next in order was ganja and injection. The growing recovery implies that the supply of illicit drugs in Haryana is increasing rapidly. The drugs recovered in greatest magnitude include pharmaceutical drugs, poppy husk and ganja in the case of Haryana.

The recovery of almost all illicit drugs in Jammu division has increased during 2013 through 2018 (Table 2.9). It is visible in terms of a high compound annual growth rate of listed drugs. The most commonly available drugs in Jammu division during the reference period were heroin, *charas*, poppy husk and pharmaceutical drugs.

## 2.2. Main observations

Going by the data and information provided by the NCRB, the total number of persons arrested under the NDPS Act 1985 has increased more than two times between 2001 and 2017 for all of India. From the present study's point of view, this increase has been observed in all five states, namely Punjab, Himachal Pradesh, Jammu and Kashmir, Haryana and Rajasthan during the span of 17 years (2001 to 2017). The number of arrested persons in terms of percentages included an increase for Punjab, Himachal Pradesh and Jammu and Kashmir, whereas a decrease was recorded in the cases of Haryana and Rajasthan over the same period of time.

Gender-wise, the arrested persons for the overall situation were much higher in the case of male versus female in all the major states of India between 2005 and 2015.

The age-wise data suggests that the majority of the persons arrested under the NDPS Act fall in the age range of 18 to 30 years and 30 to 45 years in almost all the states of the country between 2005 and 2015. This implies that youth are largely involved in drug related incidences, which has far-reaching implications for the socio-economic development of the country.

Moreover, the data in terms of incidence of drug cases suggests that Punjab dominated in this regard as compared to four states (Haryana, Himachal Pradesh, Jammu and Kashmir and Rajasthan) from 1991 to 2020. Note that the rate of persons arrested was much higher in Punjab as compared to other states and the all-India level from 1995 to 2020.

Trends on recovery of drugs in selected states indicate that recovery of almost all types of drugs has declined in Punjab whereas it has increased in the cases of Haryana and Jammu. However, in absolute numbers, arrests and registered cases under the NDPS Act are much higher in Punjab as compared to the other states.

The information presented in this section is useful to understand the trends in various parameters pertaining to drugs at the macro-level across the major states in general and for the five selected states for the present study in particular. This data is also helpful in establishing some of the hypothesis which has been upheld by primary data in the study area.

# 3 Socio-economic profile of addicts and their households

Socio-economic characteristics of the addicts and their households is helpful to determine which socio-economic strata the addicts belong to. On the social front, we have discussed the gender composition, age, educational attainment, type and location of households and religion and caste of the households and the addicts. On the economic front, this chapter discusses their occupation, income, land holdings (of land-owning households), etc. All the statistics used in this chapter have been computed from the primary data collected during field survey.

## 3.1 Social profile

It has been found that out of 1,140 addicts, only seven (0.61 percent) were females. The low proportion of females is mainly for two reasons. One, the consumption of drugs among females in general is not very common, mainly because of socio-cultural reasons. Two, even if those females are addicts, they are not coming to drug de-addiction and rehabilitation centres because of socio-cultural taboos. During our interactions with various social groups, some people were of the view that there are some females, even young girls, who do take one or more intoxicants/drugs, but they refused to share the identity of the female addicts, mainly because of a bad reflection on the parents and may even reflect poorly on the matrimonial prospects of the unmarried girls. So, in the case of females, the first attempt is to conceal the identity. Very recently, a female doctor in one of the state universities did confide that some female students, particularly those who are studying in the five-year courses (joined after 12th class) and are residing in the hostel or in paying guest houses (PGs) are found taking liquor or some mild drugs. The main reasons behind such conduct seems to be their adolescent age and new liberty, away from the home and parents' eyes. It is very recently that one female drug de-addiction centre in Kapurthala district was established by the government of Punjab.

Nonetheless, we have done some case studies in which we interacted with female drug addicts. In the sampled de-addiction centres (DDCs), or even in rehabilitation centres, we came across seven female drug addicts. They were

DOI: 10.4324/9781003318019-3

mainly in Punjab (three), Haryana (three) and Rajasthan (one) (Table 3.1). Though in our sample of drug addicts, there is a negligible proportion of female addicts openly coming for de-addiction, yet in the perception of respondents (616 in all, 408 from Punjab and 208 each from other four states) from the control group (households not having any addict and selected from the same location to which belong the addicts), the proportion of female addicts is quite high. Interestingly, when we specifically asked about the number of female addicts, nearly all of them across all the states responded that there is no female addict. But in response to another question, they said both genders take drugs/intoxicants. Nearly 21 percent of them said that both genders are taking drugs. The break-up for the states is: Punjab, 20 percent; Haryana, 23 percent; Himachal Pradesh, 40 percent; J&K, 27 percent; and Rajasthan, 4 percent. The gender composition of household heads (HHs) of the addicts, however, shows that out of 950 households (the hidden drug addicts did not reveal the address of their parents), 197 (20.74 percent) were females. This percentage varied across the states. It varied from 16 percent in Himachal Pradesh to 27 percent in Jammu and Kashmir. A significantly large proportion of male-headed households varied from 73 percent in J&K to 84 percent in H.P. (Table 3.1).

*Table 3.1* Gender composition of addicts and their household heads across states

| *State* | *Addicts N=1,140* | | | *Household Heads N=950* | | |
|---|---|---|---|---|---|---|
| | *Male* | *Female* | *Total* | *Male* | *Female* | *Total* |
| Punjab | 657 (99.55) | 03 (0.45) | 660 (100.00) | 436 (79.27) | 114 (20.73) | 550 (100.00) |
| Haryana | 117 (97.50) | 03 (2.50) | 120 (100.00) | 77 (77.00) | 23 (23.00) | 100 (100.00) |
| H.P. | 120 (100.00) | 0 (0.00) | 120 (100.00) | 84 (84.00) | 16 (16.00) | 100 (100.00) |
| J&K | 119 (99.17) | 01 (0.83) | 120 (100.00) | 73 (73.00) | 27 (27.00) | 100 (100.00) |
| Rajasthan | 120 (100.00) | 0 (0.00) | 120 (100.00) | 83 (83.00) | 17 (17.00) | 100 (100.00) |
| Total | 1,133 (99.39) | 07 (0.61) | 1,140 (100.00) | 753 (79.26) | 197 (20.74) | 950 (100.00) |

*Notes*: 1. The total number of addicts is 1,140, which is the sum total of in-patient addicts (570), follow-up addicts (380) and hidden addicts (190). But the number of household heads is 950, as hidden addicts did not reveal the address and identity of their parents.

2. Figures in brackets indicate percentage share; being rounded up, they may not exactly add up to 100. This is applicable to all such tables in all the succeeding chapters unless mentioned otherwise.

3. H.P. stands for Himachal Pradesh and J&K for Jammu and Kashmir. At the time of collecting data, J&K was one unified state.

### *3.1.1 Age of the household heads of drug addicts*

The data reveals that nearly 59 percent of the household heads (HHs) were in the age group of 35 to 55 years (Table 3.2). This is the age group whose children are normally in the range of 10 to 20 years, which is the most gullible age group easily attracted towards intoxicants and even drugs. Between 18 to 35 years of age, only about 8 percent of HHs are there. The lower proportion in this age group is mainly because of the fact that in this age group, their children are in childhood and are not yet exposed to intoxicants. In the age group of 55 to 65 years, we have 23.26 percent of the HHs of addicts. Across the states, there is not much variation in the age group of HHs (Table 3.2). In the case of Punjab, the proportion of HHs in each age group nearly coincides with the average of all the five states. But the other states have some divergence from the average of all the states. In J&K, 51 percent of HHs were in the age group of 45 to 55 years and the corresponding proportion in H.P. was 43 percent. However, very high proportions of HHs in each state were in the age group of 35 to 65 years. Across states, the proportion of HHs in the age group of 35 to 65 years was 81 percent (Punjab), 77 percent (Haryana), 85 percent (H.P.), 89 percent (J&K) and 87 percent (Rajasthan). Parents in this age group are generally too busy in their careers and, hence, cannot find adequate time for their children. However, data suggests that it is in this age group of HHs that they would have to be more careful and communicative to their children so as to prevent them from indulging in any bad habit, including the use of intoxicants. In other words, work-life balance and finding time for children is very important to rear up good and balanced human beings.

*Table 3.2* Age of household heads of drug addicts across states

| *Age (Years)* | *Punjab* | *Haryana* | *H.P.* | *J&K* | *Rajasthan* | *Total* |
|---|---|---|---|---|---|---|
| 18–25 | 09<br>(1.64) | 02<br>(1.20) | 0<br>(0.00) | 01<br>(1.00) | 0<br>(0.00) | 12<br>(1.26) |
| 25–35 | 45<br>(8.18) | 12<br>(12.0) | 02<br>(2.0) | 03<br>(3.0) | 07<br>(8.0) | 69<br>(7.26) |
| 35–45 | 117<br>(21.27) | 17<br>(17.0) | 16<br>(16.0) | 16<br>(16.0) | 28<br>(28.0) | 194<br>(20.42) |
| 45–55 | 205<br>(37.27) | 39<br>(39.0) | 43<br>(43.0) | 51<br>(51.0) | 30<br>(30.0) | 368<br>(38.74) |
| 55–65 | 123<br>(23.36) | 21<br>(21.0) | 26<br>(26.0) | 22<br>(22.0) | 29<br>(29.0) | 221<br>(23.26) |
| 65 and above | 51<br>(9.27) | 9<br>(9.0) | 13<br>(13.0) | 07<br>(7.0) | 06<br>(6.0) | 86<br>(9.05) |
| Total | 550<br>(100.00) | 100<br>(100.00) | 100<br>(100.00) | 100<br>(100.00) | 100<br>(100.00) | 950<br>(100.00) |

*Note:* The upper limit of class interval includes the completed year. Thus, class interval 25 to 35 years means 25+ to up to 35 years.

### *3.1.2 Education level of drug addicts' household heads*

At the aggregate level, in all the five states, about 18.53 percent of the household heads (HHs) of drug addicts were illiterate. Nearly 30 percent had an education up to 8th standard. Another 37 percent were educated between 10th and 12th standard. Significantly, the incidence of drug addiction amongst the educated HHs is higher in the households whose heads have a 10th standard education. About 14 percent of HHs had some degree/diploma in higher education. Across states, Rajasthan had the highest proportion of illiterate HHs (31 percent). This corroborates with the lower overall literacy rate in Rajasthan among all the five states. It was followed by Punjab at 20.36 percent. This does not go well with the higher literacy rate in Punjab among the five states. In Punjab, nearly 30 percent of HHs were educated up to 8th standard, which is exactly equal to the average of states. In other states, the share varies from 28 percent (H.P.) to 39 percent (Haryana). The proportion of HHs with an education between 10th and 12th standard varied from 27 percent (Rajasthan) to 46 percent (H.P.). The proportion of HHs with higher degrees/diplomas was lowest (14 percent) in Rajasthan and highest in H.P. (22 percent). Thus, most of the drug addicts' HHs were either illiterate or low-educated (Table 3.3). Among all categories of education, the incidence of drug addiction is higher in those households whose HHs have secondary educations in Punjab, H.P. and Rajasthan. In Haryana, the incidence is higher in those households whose HHs is middle pass. Nonetheless,

*Table 3.3* Education level of household heads of drug addicts across states

| *Education* | *Punjab* | *Haryana* | *H.P.* | *J&K* | *Rajasthan* | *Total* |
|---|---|---|---|---|---|---|
| Illiterate | 112<br>(20.36) | 15<br>(15.0) | 04<br>(4.0) | 14<br>(14.0) | 31<br>(31.0) | 176<br>(18.53) |
| Primary | 87<br>(15.82) | 18<br>(18.0) | 13<br>(13.0) | 12<br>(12.0) | 13<br>(13.0) | 143<br>(15.05) |
| Middle | 77<br>(14.0) | 21<br>(21.0) | 15<br>(15.0) | 19<br>(19.0) | 15<br>(15.0) | 147<br>(15.47) |
| Secondary | 141<br>(25.64) | 18<br>(18.0) | 28<br>(28.0) | 18<br>(18.0) | 17<br>(17.0) | 222<br>(23.37) |
| Sr. Secondary | 67<br>(12.18) | 15<br>(15.0) | 18<br>(18.0) | 18<br>(18.0) | 10<br>(10.0) | 128<br>(13.47) |
| Diploma/Certificate | 14<br>(2.54) | 04<br>(4.0) | 09<br>(9.0) | 01<br>(1.0) | 0<br>(0.0) | 28<br>(2.95) |
| Graduate | 39<br>(7.09) | 07<br>(7.0) | 08<br>(8.0) | 13<br>(13.0) | 12<br>(12.0) | 79<br>(8.32) |
| Post-graduate | 13<br>(2.36) | 02<br>(2.0) | 05<br>(5.0) | 05<br>(5.0) | 02<br>(2.0) | 27<br>(2.84) |
| Total | 550<br>(100.00) | 100<br>(100.00) | 100<br>(100.00) | 100<br>(100.00) | 100<br>(100.00) | 950<br>(100.00) |

no clear-cut correlation is visible between educational attainment of household heads and prevalence of drug addicts.

### *3.1.3 Type and location of households of drug addicts*

It is significant to note that out of 1,140 households, 67.54 percent were nuclear families and the remaining 32.46 percent were joint families (Table 3.4). Across states, J&K had the highest proportion (82.5 percent) of nuclear families, while Punjab had the lowest proportion (62.58 percent) of nuclear families. The proportion of joint families varied from 17.5 percent (J&K) to 37.42 percent (Punjab). Clearly, the proportion of drug addicts is higher in nuclear families as it was found that the parents in such households have less time for their children as they are more absorbed in their occupation and household work. Nonetheless, the study suggests that parents in nuclear families will have to be more vigilant about the activities of their children, and this will be possible only if they are more friendly and communicative with them. On the other hand, in joint families there seems to be an inbuilt mechanism of observation and checks and balances which leads to a lower proportion of addicts. In regards to location, the aggregate share of rural-households was 52.46 percent and that of urban households was 47.54 percent. Among the states, J&K had the highest (60 percent) amount of rural households, followed by Rajasthan, Punjab, H.P. and Haryana. Paradoxically, the proportion of urban population is higher in Punjab than that of the other states. Though the proportion of rural households with drug addicts is higher, yet there may not be a significant difference between rural and urban

*Table 3.4* Classification of drug addicts according to family type and location

| *State* | *Family Type* | | *Location* | | *Total* |
|---|---|---|---|---|---|
| | *Nuclear* | *Joint* | *Urban* | *Rural* | |
| Punjab | 413<br>(62.58) | 247<br>(37.42) | 314<br>(47.58) | 346<br>(52.42) | 660<br>(100.00) |
| Haryana | 87<br>(72.50) | 33<br>(27.50) | 67<br>(55.83) | 53<br>(44.17) | 120<br>(100.00) |
| H.P. | 76<br>(63.33) | 44<br>(36.67) | 61<br>(50.83) | 59<br>(49.17) | 120<br>(100.00) |
| J&K | 99<br>(82.50) | 21<br>(17.50) | 48<br>(40.00) | 72<br>(60.00) | 120<br>(100.00) |
| Rajasthan | 95<br>(79.17) | 25<br>(20.83) | 52<br>(43.33) | 68<br>(56.67) | 120<br>(100.00) |
| Total | 770<br>(67.54) | 370<br>(32.46) | 542<br>(47.54) | 598<br>(52.46) | 1,140<br>(100.00) |

*Note:* In the previous three tables, the total sample is 950 as that sample does not include the households of the hidden drug addicts (190) who did not reveal the identity of their households because they take drugs in a concealed manner.

locations if we normalise the proportion with their respective rural-urban population. However, across states, the differences are quite perceptible in the case of J&K and Rajasthan, where the incidence is quite high in rural households. Nonetheless, Haryana and H.P. had a higher incidence of drug addiction in urban households.

### *3.1.4 Religion and caste of drug addicts across states*

Table 3.5 presents the religion-wise and caste-wise distribution of drug addicts. In view of the wide variation of religious following among states, we have not given the aggregate proportion of religion and caste among drug addicts. Punjab, being a predominantly Sikh religious state, has nearly 72 percent of addicts belonging to the Sikh religion, which is higher than their share in population, then comes the followers of the Hindu religion. Nearly 26 percent of drug addicts came from the Hindu religion in Punjab, which is lower than their proportion in the population. In Haryana, nearly 51 percent of drug addicts are from the Hindu religion, followed by Sikhs (49 percent) as the two districts (Ambala and Sirsa) have quite a substantial Sikh population. In H.P., almost all the drug addicts (99.17 percent) belong to the Hindu religion as it is mainly a Hindu state. In J&K also, 84.17 percent of drug addicts are from the Hindu religion, as the two districts (Jammu and Kashmir) have a very high proportion of Hindu population. However, the proportion of Muslims among the drug addicts was 11 percent in J&K. In Rajasthan also, the proportion of drug addicts from the Hindu religion was 72.5 percent, followed by 26.67 percent from the Sikh religion (as two districts, Ganganagar and Hanumangarh, have a substantial Sikh population).

In regards to the castes of drug addicts, there is quite a significant inter-caste variation both at the aggregate level and within the states. The proportion of general caste drug addicts in some of the states is mainly because of a higher proportion of general caste population in those states. J&K has 92.5 percent drug addicts from the general caste, followed by 76.67 percent in H.P. and 69.85 percent in Punjab. In Haryana and Rajasthan, the proportion of general caste drug addicts was 52.5 percent and 50.83 percent, respectively. There is quite a high proportion of drug addicts from backward castes in Rajasthan and Haryana, mainly because of their substantial presence in those populations. Punjab, having the highest proportion of SC population, has approximately 23 percent of its addicts from SCs, though lower as compared to their proportion in the total population of the state. Haryana and Rajasthan have 17 percent and 16 percent of drug addicts from SCs (Table 3.5). It is clear from the data that the incidence of drug addiction in Punjab is higher among followers of the Sikh religion than their proportion in the total population of the state. On the other hand, the incidence of drug addiction among the followers of the Hindu religion is lower than their proportion in the state's total population. In terms of caste, the incidence of drug addiction among the scheduled castes is lower than that of their

*Table 3.5* Distribution of drug addicts according to religion and caste

| *State* | *Religion* | | | | | *Caste* | | | |
|---|---|---|---|---|---|---|---|---|---|
| | *Sikh* | *Hindu* | *Muslim* | *Christian* | *Total* | *G.C.* | *SC* | *BC+OBC* | *Total* |
| Punjab | 473<br>(71.67) | 170<br>(25.76) | 10<br>(1.52) | 07<br>(1.06) | 660<br>(100.00) | 461<br>(69.85) | 151<br>(22.88) | 48<br>(7.27) | 660<br>(100.00) |
| Haryana | 59<br>(49.17) | 61<br>(50.83) | 0<br>(0.00) | 0<br>(0.00) | 120<br>(100.00) | 63<br>(52.50) | 20<br>(16.67) | 37<br>(30.83) | 120<br>(100.00) |
| H.P. | 01<br>(0.83) | 119<br>(99.17) | 0<br>(0.00) | 0<br>(0.00) | 120<br>(100.00) | 92<br>(76.67) | 13<br>(10.83) | 15*<br>(12.50) | 120<br>(100.00) |
| J&K | 05<br>(4.17) | 101<br>(84.17) | 13<br>(10.83) | 01<br>(10.83) | 120<br>(100.00) | 111<br>(92.50) | 05<br>(4.17) | 04*<br>(3.33) | 120<br>(100.00) |
| Rajasthan | 32<br>(26.67) | 87<br>(72.50) | 01<br>(0.83) | 0<br>(0.00) | 120<br>(100.00) | 61<br>(50.83) | 19<br>(15.83) | 40*<br>(33.33) | 120<br>(100.00) |

*Notes*: 1. * STs are included in BC+OBC.
2. G.C. – General Category; SC: Scheduled Caste; BC: Backward class; OBC: other Backward classes; ST: Scheduled Tribes.
3. In the previous three tables, the total sample is 950 as that sample does not include the households of the hidden drug addicts (190) who did not reveal the identity of their households because they take drugs in a concealed manner.
4. The predominance of Hindus in J&K is due to the fact that the entire sample is from Jammu division of J&K, where the overriding majority is Hindu.
5. The high proportion of Sikhs in the sample in Punjab is because of a higher proportion of Sikhs in that population.
6. The high proportion of Sikhs in the sample in Haryana is mainly because of the high proportion of the Sikh population in the two sampled districts, i.e., Sirsa and Ambala. Districts were selected because of their proximity to Punjab.

proportion in the total population. Across states, the incidence of drug addiction is higher among the people belonging to the general category than their proportion in the total population. This may be due to their relatively better economic position, but it certainly needs further probing and research.

### *3.1.5 Age of drug addicts across states*

Demographic dividends of a country depend on the quality and capabilities of its people especially that of its youth (Chandrasekhar et al., 2006). However, when youth is addicted to drugs it becomes a serious constraint on the socio-economic development of a country. In our study, approximately 73 percent of addicts were in the age group of 17 to 35 years (Table 3.6). Another 16 percent were in the age group of 35 to 45 percent. So, more than 89 percent of addicts are in the most productive age group, i.e., 17 to 45 years. Significantly, nearly 4 percent and 2.37 percent of addicts, respectively, were in the age group of 14 to 17 years and 56 to 65 years. Across states, in J&K, 24 percent of addicts are in the age group of 14 to 17 years, which is quite high given their age group. In the age group of 17– to 35 years, Punjab has the highest proportion (78.34 percent) of addicts. It was followed by H.P. (76 percent), Haryana (70 percent), Rajasthan (59.16 percent), and J&K (58.33 percent). The proportion of addicts in the age group of 35 to 45 years varies from 14.85 percent (Punjab) to 21.67 percent (Rajasthan). A very high proportion of addicts in the highly productive age group is not only a personal loss but also a societal as well as national loss. It must be a cause of serious concern and demands a proactive response from all the stakeholders. Drug-addiction in the age group of 14 to 17 years is another very serious concern.

*Table 3.6* Age-wise distribution of drug addicts across states

| *Age (Years)* | *Punjab* | *Haryana* | *H.P.* | *J&K* | *Rajasthan* | *Total* |
|---|---|---|---|---|---|---|
| 14–17 | 04 | 02 | 08 | 29 | 01 | 44 |
| | (0.61) | (1.67) | (6.67) | (24.17) | (0.83) | (3.86) |
| 17–25 | 210 | 39 | 46 | 40 | 28 | 363 |
| | (31.82) | (32.50) | (38.33) | (33.33) | (23.33) | (31.84) |
| 25–35 | 307 | 45 | 45 | 30 | 43 | 470 |
| | (46.52) | (37.50) | (37.50) | (25.00) | (35.83) | (41.23) |
| 35–45 | 98 | 25 | 19 | 19 | 26 | 187 |
| | (14.85) | (20.83) | (15.83) | (15.83) | (21.67) | (16.40) |
| 45–55 | 29 | 05 | 02 | 02 | 11 | 49 |
| | (4.39) | (4.17) | (1.67) | (1.67) | (9.17) | (4.30) |
| 55–65 | 12 | 04 | 0 | 0 | 11 | 27 |
| | (1.82) | (3.33) | (0.00) | (0.00) | (9.17) | (2.37) |
| Total | 660 | 120 | 120 | 120 | 120 | 1,140 |
| | (100.00) | (100.00) | (100.00) | (100.00) | (100.00) | (100.00) |

### *3.1.6 Educational attainment of drug addicts across states*

The data shows that the majority of the drug addicts had an education up to the senior secondary level. At the aggregate level, nearly 76 percent had an education up to 8th standard and 48 percent were 10th and 12th pass (Table 3.7). Only 11 percent were graduates and just 1.67 percent post-graduates. The proportion of illiterate drug addicts is merely 6.14 percent. It is quite evident that students in schools and those who have passed out of school have been the main victims of drugs. As a single category, senior secondary (12th) pass accounts for nearly 28 percent of drug addicts at the aggregate level. Across states, their proportion ranges from 28 percent (Punjab) to 36 percent (Himachal Pradesh). However, J&K and Rajasthan depict a different picture, as the highest share in these states is that of secondary (10th) pass. The share of drug addicts with a low level of education (5th and 8th standard) varies between 21 percent (H.P.) and 38 percent (Rajasthan). The data clearly reveals that school students and youth just passed out of school need to be under more observation, and they also need counselling. It also indicates that school-going students are more prone to be initiated into intoxicants and drugs. As such, the parents, teachers, civil society, police and the government must be more vigilant about the school-going children, especially in the middle and high schools, as this is a very gullible age and students get easily attracted towards intoxicants and drugs. This is the age group in which the adolescents are less aware about good and bad and are easily influenced by their peers. It has been found that drug suppliers and

*Table 3.7* Educational attainment of drug addicts across states

| *Educational Qualification* | *Punjab* | *Haryana* | *H.P.* | *J&K* | *Rajasthan* | *Total* |
|---|---|---|---|---|---|---|
| Illiterate | 41<br>(6.21) | 12<br>(10.00) | 03<br>(2.5) | 01<br>(0.83) | 13<br>(10.83) | 70<br>(6.14) |
| Primary | 96<br>(14.55) | 13<br>(10.83) | 07<br>(5.83) | 10<br>(8.33) | 21<br>(17.50) | 147<br>(12.89) |
| Middle | 97<br>(14.70) | 17<br>(14.17) | 18<br>(15.00) | 17<br>(14.17) | 24<br>(20.00) | 173<br>(15.18) |
| Secondary | 130<br>(19.70) | 24<br>(20.00) | 16<br>(13.33) | 33<br>(27.50) | 27<br>(22.50) | 230<br>(20.18) |
| Sr. Secondary | 188<br>(28.48) | 38<br>(31.67) | 43<br>(35.83) | 29<br>(24.17) | 18<br>(15.00) | 316<br>(27.72) |
| Diploma/Certificate | 29<br>(4.39) | 04<br>(3.33) | 13<br>(10.83) | 05<br>(4.17) | 03<br>(2.50) | 54<br>(4.74) |
| Graduate | 71<br>(10.76) | 10<br>(8.33) | 16<br>(13.33) | 22<br>(18.33) | 12<br>(10.00) | 131<br>(11.49) |
| Post graduate | 08<br>(1.21) | 02<br>(1.67) | 04<br>(3.30) | 03<br>(2.5) | 02<br>(1.67) | 19<br>(1.67) |
| Total | 660<br>(100.00) | 120<br>(100.00) | 120<br>(100.00) | 120<br>(100.00) | 120<br>(100.00) | 1,140<br>(100.00) |

peddlers take advantage of such a situation. Awareness and counselling are very important at this stage.

## 3.2 Economic profile of drug addicts and their households

Knowledge about the economic profile of drug addicts is important, as occupation and income are considered significant factors in shaping human behaviour, including a tendency towards drugs. This section, thus, discusses the economic characteristics of addicts and their households. This would give us information about the occupation and income of addicts and their households.

### *3.2.1 Primary occupation of household heads of drug addicts*

Table 3.8, reveals that addicts come from diverse types of economic strata, and they and their household members are engaged in various economic activities and occupations. The data highlights that as a single occupation, agriculture and allied agricultural activities account for the highest share of households (25 percent at the aggregate level) to which belong addicts. Nearly 28 percent of addicts come from households engaged in diverse (miscellaneous) types of economic activities. Approximately 10 percent of addicts belong to households headed by casual labourers. About 17 percent of households were headed by housewives (mostly widows) who did not have any specific occupations. Significantly, 8.21 percent of addicts belonged to households headed by persons in government jobs. The proportion of households being headed by persons in private jobs is about 11 percent, and the share of unemployed household heads was only 1.68 percent. Clearly, addicts are not confined to some particular types of households but belong to a varying strata of households. Across states, the share of agricultural households varies from 29 percent (Punjab) to 33 percent (Rajasthan) while J&K and H.P. had 4 percent and 8 percent, respectively. In regards to casual labour, J&K accounts for the highest proportion (20 percent) of such households. In other states, it varies from 8 percent to 13 percent. Significantly, H.P. accounted for the highest proportion (23 percent) of households whose heads are in government jobs, most of them in military and paramilitary forces. Their long absence from home may be responsible for their son(s) becoming victims of drug addiction. In regards to private jobs, J&K has the highest amount (29 percent) of such households. In regards to addicts coming from housewife-headed households, Punjab has the highest proportion (19.27 percent) of such households. In households headed by persons engaged in miscellaneous activities, Punjab has the highest proportion (26.91 percent). It is clear from the foregoing discussion that the incidence of drug addiction is not confined to any particular type of household but the occupation. Engaging in long hours and the uncertainty of employment and income do have an adverse impact on the parents' time to oversee their children.

*Table 3.8* Primary occupation of household heads of drug addicts across states

| *Occupation* | *Punjab* | *Haryana* | *H.P.* | *J&K* | *Rajasthan* | *Total* |
|---|---|---|---|---|---|---|
| Agriculture and allied activities | 161 (29.27) | 32 (32.00) | 8 (8.00) | 4 (4.00) | 33 (33.00) | 238 (25.05) |
| Casual labour | 44 (8.0) | 10 (10.00) | 9 (9.00) | 20 (20.00) | 13 (13.00) | 96 (10.11) |
| Govt. Job | 39 (7.09) | 2 (2.00) | 23 (23.00) | 11 (11.00) | 3 (3.00) | 78 (8.21) |
| Private Job | 43 (7.82) | 12 (12.00) | 7 (7.00) | 29 (29.00) | 12 (12.00) | 103 (10.84) |
| Miscellaneous activities | 148 (26.91) | 22 (22.00) | 42 (42.00) | 19 (19.00) | 25 (25.00) | 256 (27.95) |
| Housewife | 106 (19.27) | 18 (18.00) | 10 (10.00) | 17 (17.00) | 12 (12.00) | 163 (17.16) |
| Unemployed | 9 (1.64) | 4 (4.00) | 1 (1.00) | 0 (0.00) | 2 (2.00) | 16 (1.68) |
| Total | 550 (100.00) | 100 (100.00) | 100 (100.00) | 100 (100.00) | 100 (100.00) | 950 (100.00) |

### *3.2.1 Average annual income of drug addicts' households*

Households 'income' is an important determinant of the type of drugs being used by the addicts and the proportion of addicts belonging to that particular income range. But in this section, we shall focus only on the proportion of addicts in various income groups. Table 3.9 reveals that, on average, the household income of the addicts ranges from below Rs. 2 lakh to above Rs. 25 lakh. We have classified all 950 households into seven classes. The data reveals that drug addiction is prevalent among all income classes. At the aggregate level, households in the three income classes (up to Rs. 10 lakh per annum) account for 82.84 percent of the addicts. Within these three classes, the households with an annual income between Rs. 2 lakh to 5 lakh account for 34.42 percent of the addicts. In the other two classes (up to Rs. 2 lakh and between Rs. 5 lakh and 10 lakh), the share of addicts was 22.95 percent and 25.47 percent, respectively. The income class in the range of Rs. 10–15 lakh constitutes only 8.42 percent addicts and the range of Rs. 15–20 lakh account for 4.42 percent, respectively. This data must be viewed with a note of caution, as the higher proportion of addicts in the lower income classes may not be construed that there is a very high prevalence of drug addiction among these classes. But this is not the case, as the lower income households account for a very high proportion of total households. Thus, the normalisation of the share of drug addicts in each income class may reveal that the share of addicts may proportionately be the same across all income sources. However, for want of data about income classes in the total population, we could not do that exercise. Interestingly, the proportion of addicts in the upper income class (above Rs. 25 lakh) is 2.74 percent. It may look very low,

*Table 3.9* Average annual income of drug addicts' households across states (Rs.)

| *Income Range (Rs. lakh)* | *Punjab* | *Haryana* | *H.P.* | *J&K* | *Rajasthan* | *Total* |
|---|---|---|---|---|---|---|
| up to 2 | 96 | 29 | 21 | 38 | 34 | 218 |
| | (17.45) | (29.00) | (21.00) | (38.00) | (34.00) | (22.95) |
| 2–5 | 203 | 36 | 37 | 25 | 26 | 327 |
| | (36.91) | (36.00) | (37.00) | (25.00) | (26.00) | (34.42) |
| 5–10 | 144 | 18 | 28 | 23 | 29 | 242 |
| | (26.18) | (18.00) | (28.00) | (23.00) | (29.00) | (25.47) |
| 10–15 | 51 | 8 | 7 | 10 | 4 | 80 |
| | (9.27) | (8.00) | (7.00) | (10.00) | (4.00) | (8.42) |
| 15–20 | 28 | 4 | 6 | 2 | 2 | 42 |
| | (5.09) | (4.00) | (6.00) | (2.00) | (2.00) | (4.42) |
| 20–25 | 9 | 3 | – | 01 | 02 | 15 |
| | (1.64) | (3.00) | | (1.00) | (2.00) | (1.58) |
| Above 25 | 19 | 2 | 01 | 01 | 3 | 26 |
| | (3.45) | (2.00) | (1.00) | (1.00) | (3.00) | (2.74) |
| Total | 550 | 100 | 100 | 100 | 100 | 950 |
| | (100.00) | (100.00) | (100.00) | (100.00) | (100.00) | (100.00) |

but the share of very high-income households in the total households is also very low. It was found during the survey that addicts from the lower-income classes consume mainly less expensive drugs and also indulge in the peddling of drugs to get their daily dose, along with earning some cash. On the other hand, the addicts from the upper-income households mainly consume more expensive drugs. In one of the communications to us from a very responsible citizen, we were told that most of the drug peddlers are from the marginalised and poor households. Nonetheless, this does not mean that peddlers are not from other sections of the population.

Across the states, the picture is not the same as far as the proportion of addicts in each income class is concerned. In Punjab, the proportion of addicts from lower-income and lower-middle-income (up to Rs. 10 lakh) is 80.54 percent, which is lower than the average of the states under study. The proportion of addicts (14.36 percent) from the income class between Rs. 10–20 lakh, is, however, higher than the average of states. Similarly, the share of addicts (3.45 percent) from the very high-income class (above Rs. 25 lakh) is higher than the average of states in this income class. In Haryana, the proportion of addicts (83 percent) in the first three income classes (up to Rs. 10 lakh) is almost close to the average of states. Contrary to the average of states, H.P. has a higher proportion (86 percent) of addicts in the first three income classes than that of the average of states. Exactly similar is the story of J&K. However, in Rajasthan the proportion of addicts (89 percent) in the lower three income classes (up to Rs. 10 lakh) is higher than the average of states. But Rajasthan also depicted a higher share of addicts from the two very high-income classes (20 lakh and above), a higher proportion (5 percent) than the average of states. Punjab and Haryana, being in the category of upper per capita income, have a high proportion of addicts from the very high-income classes than that of the states' average. It is, thus, evident from the empirical evidence that drug addiction is prevalent across all the income classes, but the type of drugs varies across the income classes.

### *3.2.2 Ownership of land by addicts' households*

Though agricultural households constitute only 25 percent of all households, yet in order to know from which ownership holdings come most of the drug addicts, we classified them into five standard classes (Table 3.10). The aggregate data reveals that most of the addicts come from the first four classes (land holdings up to 25 acres). The percentage share varies from 21.31 percent (medium holdings) to 26.49 percent (small holdings). The households with large-sized holdings account for only 4.61 percent of the households. Across the states, the highest proportion (32.81 percent) of drug addicts belonged to the semi-medium landholding class. In comparison to this, the proportion of addicts from medium and small holdings in Punjab was 41.64 percent, whereas semi-medium and medium-sized holding households accounted for 55.52 percent of addicts. Large holdings accounted for 2.84 percent of addicts. By juxtaposing the data in Table 3.10 over the data in Table 3.1A (see appendix), one may find that a proportionately higher share of addicts belong to the marginal and small holdings than their share in the total land holdings. However, the share of addicts belonging to semi-medium and medium land holdings is lower than their share in total holdings. The share of drug addicts from large-sized land holdings, is, however, lower than their share in total land holdings. Significantly, the share of addicts coming from marginal holding households in Haryana and Rajasthan is significantly

*Table 3.10* Classification of agricultural households according to owned land holdings across states

| *Holding size (Acres)* | *Punjab* | *Haryana* | *H.P.* | *J&K* | *Rajasthan* | *Total* |
|---|---|---|---|---|---|---|
| Marginal (up to 2.5) | 42 | 8 | 37 | 30 | 3 | 120 |
| | (13.25) | (14.29) | (72.55) | (71.43) | (5.45) | (23.03) |
| Small (2.5 – 5.0) | 90 | 18 | 10 | 10 | 10 | 138 |
| | (28.39) | (32.14) | (19.61) | (23.81) | (18.18) | (26.49) |
| Semi-medium (5 – 10) | 104 | 10 | 2 | 1 | 11 | 128 |
| | (32.81) | (17.86) | (3.92) | (2.38) | (20.00) | (24.57) |
| Medium (10 – 25) | 72 | 14 | 1 | 1 | 23 | 111 |
| | (22.71) | (25.00) | (1.96) | (2.38) | (41.82) | (21.31) |
| Large (Above 25) | 9 | 6 | 1 | – | 8 | 24 |
| | (2.84) | (10.71) | (1.96) | | (14.55) | (4.61) |
| Total | 317 | 56 | 51 | 42 | 55 | 521 |
| | (100.00) | (100.00) | (100.00) | (100.00) | (100.00) | (100.00) |

lower than their share in total land holdings. In regards to H.P., the share of addicts from marginal land-holding households is approximately equal to their share in total land holdings. On the contrary, the share of addicts from the marginal holding-sized households is lower than their share in total land holdings in Rajasthan. As regards small holding households, in Haryana the share of addicts is significantly higher than their share in total land holdings. However, the share of addicts from semi-medium and medium land-holding households is lower than their share in total land holdings. The share of addicts from large land-holding households is very high when compared to their share in total land holdings. The combined share of addicts from semi-medium and medium land-holding households in H.P. is lower than their share of total land holdings. It seems that poor households (as per the size of land holdings) have a larger share of addicts in H.P. (Table 3.10 and 3.1A, given in the appendix).

In J&K, the share of addicts from semi-medium and medium land-holding households almost matches their share in total land holdings. However, Rajasthan depicts a different picture, with a significantly higher share of addicts from semi-medium and medium land-holding households than their share in total land holdings. Similarly, the share of addicts from large land-holding households is higher than their share of total land holdings (Table 3.10 and 3.1A). Though it is not possible to generalise the findings, yet two scenarios emerge very clearly from the data given in Table 3.10 and 3.1A. One, the bulk of addicts lies in the combined share of small, semi-medium and medium land-holding households in Punjab, Haryana and Rajasthan. Two, in H.P. and J&K, a very high proportion of drug addicts belong to marginal and small farmers. This is quite compatible with the proportion of such households in the respective total land holdings. However, the presence of addicts across various land holding sizes is quite significant.

### *3.2.3 Primary occupation of drug addicts*

Table 3.11 presents the data about the primary occupation of drug addicts. Out of 1,140 addicts, 26.40 percent come from agricultural households, just one percentage point higher than their share in households. This minor difference may be attributed to the inclusion of hidden drug addicts, which were not included in Table 3.8. An almost similar picture is visible from the share of casual labour (Table 3.8 and 3.11). When compared to household heads, the proportion of drug addicts in government jobs is higher (8.21 percent in the case of the latter and 3.51 percent in the case of the former). The proportion of drug addicts in private jobs, on the other hand, is lower than their respective HHs. But the proportionate engagement of addicts and their HHs in other/miscellaneous activities is nearly the same. It implies that there is hardly any occupational diversification from one generation to the next generation. However, the proportion of unemployed drug addicts is higher than that of their HHs (Table 3.8 and 3.11).

*Table 3.11* Primary occupation of drug addicts across states

| *Occupation* | *Punjab* | *Haryana* | *H.P.* | *J&K* | *Rajasthan* | *Total* |
|---|---|---|---|---|---|---|
| Agriculture and allied activities | 219 (33.18) | 38 (31.67) | 09 (7.50) | 0 (0.00) | 35 (29.17) | 301 (26.48) |
| Casual labour | 76 (11.52) | 11 (9.17) | 12 (10.00) | 04 (3.33) | 23 (19.17) | 126 (11.05) |
| Government job | 22 (3.33) | – | 05 (4.17) | 12 (10.0) | 01 (0.83) | 40 (3.51) |
| Private job | 90 (13.64) | 24 (20.00) | 36 (30.00) | 30 (25.00) | 22 (18.33) | 202 (17.72) |
| Other activities | 183 (27.73) | 26 (21.67) | 39 (32.5) | 35 (29.17) | 29 (24.17) | 312 (27.37) |
| Unemployed | 49 (7.42) | 09 (7.50) | 12 (10.00) | 21 (17.5) | 06 (5.00) | 97 (8.51) |
| Student | 19 (2.88) | 11 (9.17) | 07 (5.83) | 18 (15.00) | 04 (3.33) | 59 (5.18) |
| Housewife | 02 (0.30) | 01 (0.83) | – | – | – | 03 (0.26) |
| Total | 660 (100.00) | 120 (100.00) | 120 (100.00) | 120 (100.00) | 120 (100.00) | 1,140 (100.00) |

Across the states, the situation, by and large, is similar to that depicted in Tables 3.8 and 3.11. In Punjab, however, the share of drug addicts in agriculture is lower than that of their HHs. It may be mainly because of the fact that some of the addicts from agricultural households may not want to continue with their parent's occupation. The study by Ghuman and Sharma (2018) revealed that nearly 80 percent of agricultural households do not want their children to be in agriculture. In Haryana, the proportion of addicts and their HHs across the occupations is almost similar, indicating nearly no occupational diversification between the two generations. Strangely the proportion of drug addicts in government jobs is significantly higher than their HHs, maybe because of the educational attainment of the addicts. An almost similar situation is in the case of other/miscellaneous activities. In J&K, we did not come across any addict with agriculture as their primary occupation. However, the proportion of addicts engaged in casual labour is significantly lower than their HHs. Contrary to this, the proportion of addicts in casual labour is quite high in Rajasthan than that of their HHs. In government and private jobs, also, the share of addicts is very high as compared to that of their HHs (Table 3.8 and 3.11). The share of student addicts ranges from 3 percent (Punjab) to 15 percent (J&K), with perceptible variations across the states. Thus, addicts come from almost all the occupations, but there is a significant inter-state difference between the occupations. Agriculture, casual labour, private jobs, other activities and unemployed youth together account for 91.5 percent of addicts. Significantly, 8.51 percent of the addicts were unemployed (Table 3.11). It needs to be understood that a very high proportion of addicts are engaged in low-paid, under-employed, informal economic activities, which may be the cause of their frustration and, hence, their resorting to drug addiction and even to peddling.

### *3.2.4 Age of drug addicts at the time of entering into employment*

The majority of the addicts (58.23 percent) started working between the age group of 14 to 20 years, which is the legal age (14+). But 3.6 percent of the addicts started working between the age group of 7 to 14 years, i.e., as child labourers. Another 17.46 percent of addicts started working between the ages of 20 to 25 years. The proportion of addicts who started working beyond the age of 30 years was 15.88 percent, which is quite high. In other words, they were without employment up to the age of 30 years (Table 3.12), which is a serious concern. This also indicates the prevalence of very high youth unemployment. The National Sample Survey (NSSO) and Periodic Labour Force Surveys (PLFS) also show very high youth unemployment in India and across the states. Across states, Punjab and Rajasthan have a very high proportion of addicts (67 to 71 percent) who started working between the ages of 14 to20 years just to supplement their parents' income. The corresponding share in J&K was just 15 percent. In H.P. and Haryana, such a proportion was 46 and 55 percent, respectively. In J&K, 41.67 percent of addicts did not engage in any meaningful employment, in other words, they were unemployed. In the 20 to30 years age group, the proportion of addicts varied from 16 percent (Punjab and Rajasthan) to 35 percent (H.P.). The occupational classification of addicts does indicate that nearly 89 percent of addicts started working before the age of 25 years. So, it would not be fair to construe that they were unemployed and started consuming drugs due to unemployment. However, their earnings were quite low, and this may be one of the causes of their frustration leading to drug use. In other words, they may be working but still

*Table 3.12* Age of drug addicts at the time of entering into employment across states

| *Age (Years)* | *Punjab* | *Haryana* | *H.P.* | *J&K* | *Rajasthan* | *Total* |
|---|---|---|---|---|---|---|
| 7–14 | 19<br>(2.88) | 12<br>(10.00) | 03<br>(2.5) | 0<br>(0.00) | 07<br>(5.83) | 41<br>(3.60) |
| 14–20 | 440<br>(66.67) | 66<br>(55.00) | 55<br>(45.83) | 18<br>(15.0) | 85<br>(70.83) | 664<br>(58.23) |
| 20–25 | 104<br>(15.76) | 17<br>(14.17) | 34<br>(28.33) | 32<br>(26.67) | 12<br>(10.00) | 199<br>(17.46) |
| 25–30 | 17<br>(2.58) | 3<br>(2.5) | 8<br>(6.67) | 20<br>(16.67) | 07<br>(5.83) | 55<br>(4.82) |
| Above 30 | 80<br>(12.12) | 22<br>(18.33) | 20<br>(16.67) | 50<br>(41.67) | 9<br>(7.50) | 181<br>(15.88) |
| Total | 660<br>(100.00) | 120<br>(100.00) | 120<br>(100.00) | 120<br>(100.00) | 120<br>(100.00) | 1,140<br>(100.00) |

living in poverty and vulnerable economic conditions (Sengupta, Kannan, and Srivastava, 2009; Ghuman and Sharma, 2021).

### 3.3 Evidence from the case studies

In order to have a deep and detailed understanding of the socio-cultural and economic reasons behind drug addiction and abuse, we conducted 40 case studies spread over various selected districts of Punjab and some from J&K, Haryana and Rajasthan. The selection of the respondents was made from the sampled addicts. Out of the 40 case studies, only three pertain to the female addicts. Most of the respondents were from rural areas and the majority of them belonged to agricultural households and hence from Sikh families. The respondents were from all economic strata, i.e., upper-middle class (8), middle class (12), lower-middle class (16) and poor class (4). Most of them were also engaged in various economic activities, but addiction adversely impacted their work and, hence, their earnings. Some lost their jobs and businesses. Most of them spent huge amounts of money on drugs and treatment, running into lakhs of rupees. One such case (an engineer) told us that he had spent almost Rs. 50 lakh on his drugs and treatment and almost ruined the family. The daily expenses of most of the addicts for their daily dose of drugs ranged from Rs. 1000 to Rs. 5000. All of the respondents had received treatment in the drug de-addiction centres (DDCs), and the majority of them had to be admitted more than once because of relapsing. The relapsing happened mainly because of a lack of proper treatment, a lack of family, psychological and social support and a lack of willpower.

Apparently, peer pressure or company was the main reason for getting into addiction, but there were a host of other socio-cultural reasons in the background which created such circumstances that pushed them into the consumption of intoxicants and drugs. During one-on-one and heart-to heart conversations, the respondents confided in us that disharmonious relations among the family members (especially disrupted relations between their father and mother) were among the most important reasons for their getting into drugs. Failure in love relations, including non-acceptance of marriage proposals (by parents, especially that of girls), was also an important reason for their initiation into drugs. A feeling of neglect during childhood, parents' son preference, loneliness, nagging, stigma and curiosity were some other reasons. Unfulfilled aspirations and failure in life were also responsible for inciting them toward drugs. The desire to earn quick money, drug-peddling, theft and police cases were some of the other reasons stated by them. Family history of consuming intoxicants by their elders was also an important cause in developing their liking for drugs. Some of the respondents said that they emotionally blackmailed their mothers, being the child of a single mother (mainly divorced or whose husbands died), to get money for the purchase of drugs. As a matter of fact, the previously mentioned reasons were not mutually exclusive, rather, they were overlapping, and often there were multiple reasons for their entry into drug addiction and abuse. It also came to the fore that most of the addicts did enter into drugs because of uncongenial personal and/or family circumstances.

Significantly, all the respondents in our case studies were literate but for two (who were only primary school pass), all others were educated up to 10th standard. More than half of them were educated up to 12th class and the rest were either technical diploma holders, graduates or postgraduates. Significantly, three respondents were postgraduates and four were B. Tech. In regards to age, 26 (65 percent) were in the age group of 20 to 30 years, 8 (20 percent) were 30 to 40 years, and 6 (15 percent) were in the age group of 40 to 45 years. But 35 (87.5 percent) respondents were initiated into intoxicants between the age group of 12 to 20 years and 5 (12.5 percent) between the age group of 20 to 25 years. Most of them first started with soft (mainly licit) intoxicants such as cough syrup, tobacco and alcohol and then shifted to hard (illicit) drugs such as *bhukki*, *charas*, opium and heroin. Nearly 20 (50 percent) of the total 40 respondents started taking intoxicants while in school and the remaining 20 (50 percent) during diploma or college days.

It is clear from the foregoing discussion, data and empirical analysis that almost all the drug addicts were males. The proportion of female drug addicts is negligible, mainly because of low or non-usage of intoxicants by females. It needs to be acknowledged that in the male-dominated Indian socio-cultural system, evolved over the centuries, women in general do not consume intoxicants and drugs. The non-reporting or negligible reporting to the de-addiction centres by females consuming intoxicants is also due to social inhibitions and social taboos. Besides, even those females who are consuming intoxicants may not be subject to serious addiction. In regards to the gender composition of household heads (HHs), nearly 21 percent of households are being headed by females. Most of the addicts are from households whose heads were in the age group of 35 to 65 years. This is the age group when HHs are heavily busy with their commitment to economic and social responsibilities; their children are in the adolescent age and could be easily enticed towards intoxicants. It has also been found that a significant number of drug addicts belong to households whose heads are illiterate or just literate. The proportion of addicts from households whose heads are low educated is also very high. The majority of addicts come from nuclear families. In regards to the location of the households, the majority of the addicts are from rural households but the difference between rural and urban households is not significant. Given the higher proportion of a rural population, even this may lead us to the conclusion that the majority of addicts come from urban households. Among the social characteristics, religion is not the significant reason behind addiction, as addicts belong to all the religions practised in the states under study. In other words, the prevalence of drug addiction is nearly religion-neutral, but across the states, a higher proportion of addicts belongs to the religion which is being practised by the majority of the population. The age of drug addicts is a serious and worrisome concern since a very high proportion (73 percent) of the addicts were in the age group of 17 to 35 years, which is termed as youth-age. If we add the age group 35 to 45 years, then 88.47 percent of addicts fall in the age group of 17 to 45 years. Being a highly productive phase of one's life, this is a heavy loss to society and economy. Significantly, a sizeable majority of the addicts are educated up to senior secondary (12th standard) level.

In regards to economic characteristics of the addicts and their HHs, nearly one-fourth of addicts are from agricultural households. A similar proportion is from those households whose heads are engaged in low paid miscellaneous (informal) economic activities. A significant proportion of addicts belong to households that are being headed by housewives. The proportion of addicts from households whose heads are in government and private jobs is nearly one-fifth. One-tenth of the addicts are from households whose heads are doing casual work. Unemployment, on the face of it, does not seem to be the major cause of addiction, but under-employment and employment in low-paid informal economic activities (working poor) seem to be among the main reasons for drug addiction. Paradoxically, a very high proportion (57 percent) of addicts are from low-income households. With the addition of lower-middle-income households, the proportion of addicts from households with an annual income up to Rs. 10 lakh touches 83 percent. It may give the impression that the prevalence of drug addiction is very high among the low and lower-middle-income households. But once we factor in the proportion of different income groups in society, we find that the lower incidence of drug addiction among the high- and upper-income households is mainly due to their lower proportion in the total households.

Land-holding size also presents a peculiar picture as far as the proportion of addicts from each land-holding size is concerned. The data reveals that, in some states, the proportionate share of addicts from among the marginal and small land holdings is higher as compared to their share in the total land holdings, and in some states, it is the other way round. Punjab is the only state in the former category, whereas the other four states fall in the latter category. On the other hand, the proportion of drug addicts from agricultural households having semi-medium and medium sized land holdings is lower than their share in total landholdings. As compared to it, the share of addicts from the semi-medium and medium holdings is higher than their share in total holdings in Haryana and Rajasthan. However, it is lower in H.P. and J&K. This implies that in Punjab, Haryana, H.P. and J&K, the majority of addicts are from the households with marginal and small-sized land-holding households. However, in Rajasthan the proportion of addicts from the low land-holding households is significantly lower than their share in such land holdings. The reasons behind such behaviour need further investigation.

The occupational data of the addicts reveals that unemployment is not the main reason behind drug addiction. The majority of drug addicts are from agricultural households and households with low-paid miscellaneous economic activities. Most private jobs can also be clubbed with such activities. Significantly, a good number of workers in such activities are working poor. The low income, along with poverty (leading to frustration and economic distress), seems to be the defining factor behind youths becoming addicts. But this needs further research. Perhaps poverty and the low income of the households are behind the higher proportion (58 percent) of addicts starting work in the age group of 14 to 20 years, when most of them should be in schools and colleges. The high school drop-out rates may also be the reason for starting work at a young age. Significantly, 3.6 percent of the addicts started economic activity even before attaining the age of 14 years (the legal age of entering into the labour market). It is evident from the socio-economic profile of the addicts and their household heads that drug addiction may not be attributed to any specific social and economic class of the households. There may be multiple socio-economic reasons for youth falling prey to intoxicants and drugs. There is a need for further research to identify and address those reasons.

# 4 Growing up with intoxicants and drugs

## Revelations by households and drug addicts

It is an established understanding that addiction is a disease and addicts are patients. Accordingly, drug addiction and abuse needs to be viewed and addressed from this perspective. It is in this context that it is relevant to examine and understand the socio-cultural and politico-economic factors and circumstances which are inciting or pushing adolescents and youth towards intoxicants and drugs. According to medico-psychologists, drug use is affected by biological, social and cultural factors and human psyche is such that it gets more attracted towards negativities. It means that a person is at a higher risk to use drugs if he/she is growing up in a family/household in which use of intoxicants occurs quite often. People often under genetic predispositions develop dependence on drugs/intoxicants (Waraich, 2018).

This chapter, thus, discusses the influence of elders' consumption habits (especially intoxicants) on children, especially that of male members, besides examining the socio-economic factors behind the use of intoxicants and drugs eventually leading to drug addiction. The analysis and discussion is based on the revelations of drug addicts and members of their households. The discussion is mainly based on the quantitative data collected from the field survey.

### 4.1 Consumption of intoxicants by the household members of drug addicts

Children generally imbibe the value system and consumption habits of the elders in their household as they are the role model in the formative years of the child. Such an impact is often observed at the level of the conscious and subconscious mind. During their formative years, children often try to imitate their parents and elders in the family. In folk wisdom it is often said,

> "*Ma pur dhi, pita pur ghora;*
> *bahuta nahin tan thora, thora.*"

This means that the daughter often imbibes the conduct and habits of her mother and the son that of his father. The young minds also get impacted by the surrounding socio-cultural environment. It is in this context that we

DOI: 10.4324/9781003318019-4

decided to collect information about the consumption of intoxicants by the elders in the family/household. It has been often witnessed that if the elders in the household consume any intoxicants, the children do get influenced, maybe at the level of the subconscious mind. It might be equally true that the children may develop hate towards the intoxicants on witnessing the adverse consequences of their elders' consumption habits of intoxicants and drugs. Such detestation often develops when some elder(s) in the household get addicted to drugs and land in serious trouble. The information and observations from the field visits did support such an attitude and behaviour in the children. Nonetheless, it is an established fact that, in general, children, especially male children, are influenced by the conduct and behaviour of their parents and other elder members in the household, especially that of drug addiction and abuse. Perhaps this may be the prominent reason for very low or negligible incidence of intoxicant and drug consumption among the females in society, besides their socio-cultural contextualisation.

The primary data shows that there is a significant prevalence of intoxicants consumption in household across all the states except J&K (Table 4.1). At the aggregate level, about 77 percent of households have one or more members (mainly male) consuming one or more intoxicants. Across the states it varies from 75 percent in Haryana to 86 percent in Himachal Pradesh. In J&K it is only 35 percent.

The relationship of addicts with the household member(s) consuming intoxicants is presented in Table 4.2. It has been found that mainly it is the father of the addict who is in the habit of intoxicant consumption. At the aggregate level, 82.61 percent of fathers are consuming one or more intoxicants. Across the states, it ranges from 74.44 percent in Haryana to 93.2 percent in H.P. The high incidence in H.P. may be because of the cold weather and the high presence of serving and retired army personnel. In about 11 percent of households at the aggregate level, it is the uncles of the addicts who are consuming intoxicants. This lower incidence may be attributed to a lower proportion of joint families (see Table 3.4). Among the siblings, only 9.55 percent of households have an addict's brother consuming intoxicant(s).

*Table 4.1* Consumption of intoxicants by the household members of drug addicts

| *Response* | *Total* | *Punjab* | *Haryana* | *H.P.* | *J&K* | *Rajasthan* |
|---|---|---|---|---|---|---|
| Yes | 880<br>(77.19) | 553<br>(83.79) | 90<br>(75.00) | 103<br>(85.83) | 42<br>(35.00) | 92<br>(76.67) |
| No | 260<br>(22.81) | 107<br>(16.21) | 30<br>(25.00) | 17<br>(14.17) | 78<br>(65.00) | 28<br>(23.33) |
| Total | 1,140<br>(100.00) | 660<br>(100.00) | 120<br>(100.00) | 120<br>(100.00) | 120<br>(100.00) | 120<br>(100.00) |

*Note:* Figures in brackets indicate percentage share; this is applicable to all tables in this chapter, unless mentioned otherwise.

*Table 4.2* Addicts' relationship with household members consuming intoxicants

| *Household Member* | *Punjab* | *Haryana* | *H.P.* | *J&K* | *Rajasthan* | *Total* |
|---|---|---|---|---|---|---|
| Grandfather | 37 | 11 | 03 | 02 | 22 | 75 |
| | (6.69) | (12.22) | (2.91) | (4.76) | (23.91) | (8.52) |
| Father | 459 | 67 | 96 | 33 | 72 | 727 |
| | (83.00) | (74.44) | (93.20) | (78.57) | (78.26) | (82.61) |
| Uncle | 76 | 7 | 03 | 02 | 09 | 97 |
| | (13.74) | (7.78) | (2.91) | (4.76) | (9.78) | (11.02) |
| Brother | 64 | 5 | 01 | 05 | 09 | 84 |
| | (11.57) | (5.56) | (0.97) | (11.90) | (9.78) | (9.55) |
| Total respondents | 553 | 90 | 103 | 42 | 92 | 880 |
| | (100.00) | (100.00) | (100.00) | (100.00) | (100.00) | (100.00) |
| Total responses | 636 | 94 | 103 | 42 | 115 | 990 |
| | (115.01) | (104.44) | (100.00) | (100.00) | (125.00) | (112.50) |

The lower incidence of intoxicant consumption among the siblings may be attributed to a lesser number of siblings and that, too, the male siblings. It has also been found that only 8.52 percent of the grandfathers of the addicts consumed intoxicant(s). Again, the lower incidence may be because of fewer surviving grandfathers or those non-residing in the addicts' households. The higher number of responses (990) than the number of respondents (880) indicates that some of the households have more than one member consuming intoxicants. Such a phenomenon is higher in Punjab and Rajasthan (Table 4.2). It needs to be mentioned that alcohol is outside the purview of the NDPS Act and hence its use is not illicit. Further, alcohol is a socially acceptable intoxicant, though not encouraged, and the state governments in India collect significant revenue from the production and sale of alcohol.

### *4.1.2 Types of intoxicants consumed by household members*

Alcohol is the most commonly used intoxicant in the states under study. At the aggregate level, nearly 82 percent of those respondents who are consuming intoxicants are consuming alcohol. Across states, it varies from 78.57 percent (J&K) to 88.35 percent (Himachal). About 14 percent of respondents consume other intoxicants. Across states, it ranges between 7.14 percent in J&K and 16.64 percent in Punjab. In the case of other intoxicants, it is mainly those intoxicants that the possession and use of which is illegal under the NDPS Act. Tobacco is another intoxicant being used in these states. On average, the incidence of tobacco consumption among the intoxicant users is only 4.43 percent. Across states, this varies from 2.71 percent in Punjab to 14.29 percent in J&K (Table 4.3). The consumption of tobacco among the Sikh households is not visible because of the influence of the Sikh religion. In other households also, the consumption of tobacco is not very high, maybe

*Table 4.3* Type of intoxicants consumed by household members of drug addicts

| *Intoxicant* | *Punjab* | *Haryana* | *H.P.* | *J&K* | *Rajasthan* | *Total* |
|---|---|---|---|---|---|---|
| Alcohol | 446 (80.65) | 76 (84.44) | 91 (88.35) | 33 (78.57) | 75 (81.52) | 721 (81.93) |
| Tobacco | 15 (2.71) | 03 (3.33) | 12 (11.65) | 06 (14.29) | 03 (3.26) | 39 (4.43) |
| Any other | 92 (16.64) | 11 (12.22) | – | 03 (7.14) | 14 (15.22) | 120 (13.64) |
| Total respondents | 553 (100.00) | 90 (100.00) | 103 (100.00) | 42 (100.00) | 92 (100.00) | 880 (100.00) |

because of aggressive awareness campaigns by the governments, religious organisations and the NGOs against the ill effects of its use. However, such a campaign against the use of alcohol and other dugs perhaps is either not here or is not that effective.

### *4.1.3 Impact of intoxicant-consumption by elders on the children in the households*

Consumption of intoxicants by the elders in the household not only entices young minds towards the consumption of intoxicants but also weakens the moral authority of elders to curb such a tendency amongst adolescents and youth. Though 77 percent of the households have one or more than one (other than the addict) person consuming one or more intoxicants (Table 4.1), yet, 65 percent of the households admitted that it has induced their young members (who are now addicts) into consumption of intoxicants (Table 4.4). Across states, the proportion varies from 41 percent in Himachal Pradesh to 77 percent in Rajasthan. Compared to this, in the perception of 616 control group respondents (households not having any addict), about 42 percent of the addicts are influenced by the intoxicant consumption habits of the elders in the household. Across states, it varies from 35 percent in Himachal Pradesh to 64 percent in Rajasthan.

The respondents in our case studies revealed that, on the face of it, peer pressure or company seems to be the main reason for getting into addiction but there were a host of other socio-cultural reasons in the background which created such circumstances that pushed them to the consumption of intoxicants and drugs. A good number of case studies also support that family history of consuming intoxicants by the elders was also an important cause for developing their liking for drugs, though there are multiple other reasons for addicts' initiation into intoxicants and drugs discussed in detail in section 3.3 of Chapter 3.

It is significant to mention that medical experts and councillors dealing with drug de-addiction, during FGDs with them, are of the view that a

*Table 4.4* Influence of intoxicant consumption by elders in the household on drug addicts: Perception of households

| *Response* | *Punjab* | *Haryana* | *H.P.* | *J&K* | *Rajasthan* | *Total* |
|---|---|---|---|---|---|---|
| Yes | 359<br>(65.27) | 61<br>(61.00) | 41<br>(41.00) | 54<br>(54.00) | 77<br>(77.00) | 592<br>(62.32) |
| No | 191<br>(34.73) | 39<br>(39.00) | 59<br>(59.00) | 46<br>(46.00) | 23<br>(23.00) | 358<br>(37.68) |
| Total | 550<br>(100.00) | 100<br>(100.00) | 100<br>(100.00) | 100<br>(100.00) | 100<br>(100.00) | 950<br>(100.00) |

history of substance use in the family does influence youth and entices them to take intoxicants and drugs. Use of substance becomes attractive to the younger persons in the family as they get pleasure and they feel loneliness without drugs. This is a significant revelation and calls for a note of caution on all those household members who are consuming intoxicants. Significantly, 37.68 percent of respondents were of the opinion that consumption of intoxicants by elders in the family does not induce the youngsters towards intoxicants. Nonetheless, the fact is that a very high proportion of respondents admitted to the adverse impact of their habit of intoxicant consumption. Two reasons have been shared for such a revelation. One, there is a demonstrated effect on young minds. Two, when elders consume intoxicants their moral authority to advise children against the use of intoxicants gets eroded. In other words, they cannot be a good role model.

## 4.2 Initiation into intoxicant consumption

In view of the previous discussion, it has been found that young male children, mainly at the threshold of their adolescence, get attracted towards intoxicants and, hence, get initiated into intoxicant consumption. This section discusses the age of initiation into intoxicant use and intoxicant(s) consumed for the first time, etc.

### *4.2.1 Age of addicts at the time of initiation into intoxicants*

Though the sizeable majority (65 percent) of the addicts got initiated into intoxicant consumption between the age group of 14 to 20 years, yet children as young as in the age group of 7 to 14 years also got initiated into consumption of intoxicants. At the aggregate level, 10.26 percent of addicts got hooked on intoxicants as a teenager. The majority of them were school going or school drop-outs. Thus, up to 20 years of age, 75 percent of addicts started consuming intoxicants. About 18 percent of addicts got into intoxicant consumption between 20 to 25 years of age. Thus, up to the age of 25 years, more than 93 percent of the addicts entered into intoxicant consumption (Table 4.5). As per our case studies (40 in number), nearly 20 (50 percent) of

*Table 4.5* Age of drug addicts at the time of initiation into intoxicant consumption

| *Age (Years)* | *Punjab* | *Haryana* | *H.P.* | *J&K* | *Rajasthan* | *Total* |
|---|---|---|---|---|---|---|
| 7–14 | 45<br>(6.82) | 16<br>(13.33) | 19<br>(15.83) | 19<br>(15.83) | 18<br>(15.00) | 117<br>(10.26) |
| 14–20 | 443<br>(67.12) | 77<br>(64.17) | 76<br>(63.33) | 75<br>(62.50) | 69<br>(57.50) | 740<br>(64.91) |
| 20–25 | 126<br>(19.09) | 20<br>(16.67) | 17<br>(14.17) | 20<br>(16.67) | 21<br>(17.50) | 204<br>(17.89) |
| 25–30 | 31<br>(4.70) | 04<br>(3.33) | 05<br>(4.17) | 06<br>(5.00) | 08<br>(6.67) | 54<br>(4.74) |
| 30–35 | 07<br>(1.06) | 02<br>(1.67) | 01<br>(0.83) | – | 02<br>(1.67) | 12<br>(1.05) |
| 35–40 | 04<br>(0.61) | 01<br>(0.83) | – | – | – | 05<br>(0.44) |
| Above 40 | 04<br>(0.61) | – | 02<br>(1.67) | – | 02<br>(1.67) | 08<br>(0.70) |
| Total respondents | 660<br>(100.00) | 120<br>(100.00) | 120<br>(100.00) | 120<br>(100.00) | 120<br>(100.00) | 1,140<br>(100.00) |

the total 40 respondents started taking intoxicants while in school and the remaining 20 (50 percent) during diploma or college days.

It is ample evidence that the children and youth in transitional stage (from adolescence to adulthood) must be given special attention if we really want to address the issue and save our progeny from getting into consumption of intoxicants and drugs. This is a sine qua non to save them from drug addiction and abuse and, hence, to save our progeny.

Across states, the highest proportion (15.83 percent) of children (7 to 14 years) was in J&K and Himachal Pradesh and the lowest in Rajasthan. The proportion in the age group of 14 to 20 years varies from 57.5 percent in Rajasthan to 67.12 percent in Punjab. Similarly, Punjab has the highest proportion (19.09 percent) of those addicts who started consumption of intoxicants in the age group of 20 to 25 years. The lowest proportion (14.17 percent) of such addicts was in Himachal Pradesh. The proportion of such addicts in the age group of 25 to 30 years ranges between 3.33 percent in Haryana to 6.67 percent in Rajasthan. The statistics in the various age groups show that there is a very low probability for anyone to get hooked on intoxicants after the age of 30 years.

### *4.2.2 Intoxicants consumed for the first time by addicts*

Alcohol, tobacco and some others were the main intoxicants consumed by the addicts for the first time. At the aggregate level of all the five states, 38.25 percent of the addicts consumed alcohol as their first intoxicant. Across states, this proportion varies between 34.17 percent in Rajasthan and 41.67 percent in Punjab. In J&K, this proportion was 22.50 percent (Table 4.6). Significantly, alcohol is being consumed in a very high proportion of households

*Table 4.6* Intoxicants consumed for the first time

| *Intoxicant* | *Punjab* | *Haryana* | *H.P.* | *J&K* | *Rajasthan* | *Total* |
|---|---|---|---|---|---|---|
| Alcohol | 275<br>(41.67) | 48<br>(40.00) | 45<br>(37.50) | 27<br>(22.50) | 41<br>(34.17) | 436<br>(38.25) |
| Tobacco | 82<br>(12.42) | 12<br>(10.00) | 41<br>(34.17) | 31<br>(25.83) | 17<br>(14.17) | 183<br>(16.05) |
| Cough Syrup | 23<br>(3.48) | 01<br>(0.83) | – | 02<br>(1.67) | 02<br>(1.67) | 28<br>(2.46) |
| Others* | 280<br>(42.42) | 59<br>(49.17) | 34<br>(28.33) | 60<br>(50.00) | 60<br>(50.00) | 493<br>(43.25) |
| Total | 660<br>(100.00) | 120<br>(100.00) | 120<br>(100.00) | 120<br>(100.00) | 120<br>(100.00) | 1140<br>(100.00) |

* Including heroin, opium, cannabis, hashish/*charas*, marijuana, poppy husk, etc.

(81.93 percent) in the states under study (Table 4.3). In regards to tobacco, 16 percent of addicts consumed it for the first time. Across states, it was from 12.42 percent in Punjab to 34.17 percent in Himachal Pradesh (Table 4.6). The most worrisome is a very high consumption of other intoxicants which mainly includes heroin, opium, cannabis, hashish/*charas,* marijuana and poppy husk. Significantly, all these intoxicants are also banned under the NDPS Act. A little more than 43 percent of the addicts revealed that for the first time they consumed such intoxicants/drugs; thus committed a cognizable offence. Across states, the proportion of such addicts varies between 42.42 percent in Punjab and 50 percent in J&K and Rajasthan. In fact, Punjab is at fourth place from above. The case studies also revealed that most of them first started with soft (mainly licit) intoxicants such as cough syrup, tobacco and alcohol and then shifted to hard (illicit) drugs such as *bhukki*, *charas*, opium and heroin.

### 4.2.3 *Transition from traditional intoxicants to drugs covered under the NDPS Act*

Table 4.7 reveals the perception of addicts' households and households from the control group (households with no drug addict member) about the transition from traditional intoxicants to illicit drugs. It has been found that the majority of the addicts directly initiated into taking drugs. According to 58 percent of respondents in those households who have at least one addict, the addicts directly started consuming drugs. In other words, 42 percent of addicts from such households transitioned from traditional, mainly licit, intoxicants to drugs. The corresponding percentage shares according to control-group households are 86 percent and 14 percent, respectively. The situation in both cases is very worrisome as both categories of respondents think that the majority of addicts got directly into the consumption of illicit drugs.

*Table 4.7* Drug addicts' transition from traditional intoxicants to drugs: Percent of households

| *Household State* | *Addicts' household* | | | *Non-addict household* | | |
|---|---|---|---|---|---|---|
| | *Yes* | *No* | *Total* | *Yes* | *No* | *Total* |
| Punjab | 233 (42.36) | 317 (57.64) | 550 (100.00) | 59 (14.50) | 349 (85.50) | 408 (100) |
| Haryana | 45 (45.00) | 55 (55.00) | 100 (100.00) | 14 (26.90) | 38 (73.10) | 52 (100) |
| Himachal Pradesh | 11 (11.00) | 89 (89.00) | 100 (100.00) | – | 52 (100.00) | 52 (100) |
| J&K | 57 (57.00) | 43 (43.00) | 100 (100.00) | 2 (3.90) | 50 (96.10) | 52 (100) |
| Rajasthan | 55 (55.00) | 45 (45.00) | 100 (100.00) | 9 (17.30) | 43 (82.70) | 52 (100) |
| Total respondents | 401 (42.21) | 549 (57.79) | 950 (100.00) | 84 (13.60) | 532 (86.40) | 616 (100) |

*Note:* 1. As hidden drug addicts did not share the address of their parents, we have taken only 950 households.
2. The control group households (616) are those who do not have any drug addict person.

During the focus group discussions (FGDs) with social, religious and spiritual bodies, there was a strong opinion that earlier consumption of alcohol was very limited and confined to some social occasions or functions. But these days the use of alcohol has become very common, even among the youths, especially males. This habit leads to use of other drugs like *bhukki*, opium, heroin, bhang, *charas* and smack, etc. Even less costly drugs, such as chemical drugs, are becoming popular among the youth. Similar views were expressed during FGDs with medical experts who mentioned that previously the most common drugs were opium or *bhukki* but the trend has now shifted to hard drugs like heroin and pharmaceutical drugs. The main cause of increased use of chemical drugs is lower cost in comparison to other drugs and their easy availability. The use of chemical drugs is quite common among the economical weaker sections of the society.

## 4.3 Age of addicts at the time of starting consumption of drugs covered under the NDPS Act

In order to look deep into addicts' initiation into drugs (banned under the NDPS Act and, hence, possession and consumption is illegal) we also collected information about their initiation into drugs in various age groups. Table 4.8 reveals that 4.65 percent of addicts got into the consumption of drugs between 7 to 14 years of age. Across states, it ranges between 5 percent in Haryana to 8.33 percent in Himachal Pradesh. In Punjab, it is exceptionally low (1.06 percent) and in J&K it is exceptionally high (20.83 percent).

*Table 4.8* Age of addicts at the time of starting consumption of drugs

| *Age (Years)* | *Punjab* | *Haryana* | *H.P.* | *J&K* | *Rajasthan* | *Total* |
|---|---|---|---|---|---|---|
| 7–14 | 07<br>(1.06) | 06<br>(5.00) | 10<br>(8.33) | 25<br>(20.83) | 05<br>(4.17) | 53<br>(4.65) |
| 14–20 | 315<br>(47.73) | 66<br>(55.00) | 60<br>(50.00) | 49<br>(40.83) | 54<br>(45.00) | 544<br>(44.72) |
| 20–25 | 211<br>(31.97) | 32<br>(26.67) | 25<br>(20.83) | 29<br>(24.17) | 32<br>(26.67) | 329<br>(28.86) |
| 25–30 | 82<br>(12.42) | 09<br>(7.50) | 13<br>(10.83) | 08<br>(6.67) | 13<br>(10.83) | 125<br>(10.96) |
| 30–35 | 24<br>(3.64) | 05<br>(4.17) | 08<br>(6.67) | 06<br>(5.00) | 07<br>(5.83) | 50<br>(4.39) |
| Above 35 | 21<br>(3.18) | 02<br>(1.67) | 04<br>(3.33) | 03<br>(2.50) | 09<br>(7.50) | 39<br>(3.42) |
| Total | 660<br>(100.00) | 120<br>(100.00) | 120<br>(100.00) | 120<br>(100.00) | 120<br>(100.00) | 1,140<br>(100.00) |

The data also reveals that 47.72 percent of the addicts entered into drug consumption between the age group of 14 to 20 years. Across states, the highest proportion with 55 percent is in Haryana while the lowest (40.83 percent) is in J&K. Around 29 percent of the addicts got initiated into intoxicants with the consumption of drugs in the age group of 20 to 25 years. Thus, a very high proportion of addicts (78.23 percent) got their entry into drugs with the consumption of illicit drugs between the age of 7 to 25 years.

Across states, the proportion of addicts in the age group of 20 to 25 years varied from 20.83 percent in Himachal Pradesh to 31.97 percent in Punjab. Nearly 11 percent of the addicts revealed that they started their journey into drugs between the ages of 25 to 30 years. Across states, the proportion of such addicts varied between 6.67 percent in J&K to 12.42 percent in Punjab (Table 4.8). It is clear that Punjab has the lowest proportion of addicts below 14 years of age but in the latter three age groups the state has the highest proportion of addicts initiated into the consumption of intoxicants with drugs. In Punjab, 92.12 percent of the addicts revealed that they started consuming drugs in the age group of 14 to 30 years (the most youthful and productive age group) which is higher than the other four states. The data in Table 4.8 also reveals that the age group between 7 to 20 years is the most vulnerable age group as far as initiation into intoxicants is concerned. It, thus, needs to attract social vigilance and counselling. This also necessitates extra care and vigilance around the schools and colleges. Punjab government's counselling through its 'you are my buddy' programme may be of some use, but its effective outcome is yet to be seen. However, awareness campaigns in various states are being carried out by various agencies, government as well as private.

## 4.4 Factors responsible for addicts' initiation into drugs

In the FGDs conducted with the village panchayats, it emerged that, due to increasing consumerism, there is a constant decline in the moral fabric and community feeling in the society and yearning for an exuberant lifestyle has unnecessarily increased the cost of living. Increasing individualism and showing off beyond one's means has resulted in indebtedness. This has been further augmented by the unnecessary purchase of agricultural machinery, especially tractors. Besides augmenting indebtedness, it has also led to emotional crises at inter-and intra-personal relations. All this has led to the increasing use of alcohol, *bhukki*, cigarettes, *zarda* and other readily available intoxicants. The habit of using a wide range of habit-forming light drugs is also spreading fast. Increasing disconnects between parents and children are making the latter incline more towards their peer groups. The increasing trend of nuclear family structure owing to varied reasons, the increasing decline in norms of collective community interaction, collective living and sharing and an increasing sense of individualism is leading to a perceived sense of loneliness, and in turn leading to refuge in intoxicants.

Table 4.9 reveals that the most significant factor behind initiation into intoxicants, including drugs, is company and peer pressure. It, however, needs to be understood that peer pressure is not necessarily a bad thing; rather, it has both negative and positive influences. But peer or social pressure is mainly going with the crowd (herd behaviour) in order to be accepted among the peers. Thus, it all depends on the composition of the peer group. In general, the human psyche, especially that of adolescents and youth, is an easy prey to relatively bad influences as they seems to be an easy and enjoyable path. Teenagers are generally not in a position to seriously analyse the consequences of their conduct and activities as they are incapable of understanding the pros and cons of their acts and conduct. In general, they are more influenced by their peers rather than paying any heed to elderly advice

*Table 4.9* Factors responsible for initiation into drugs

| *Factors* | *Punjab* | *Haryana* | *H.P.* | *J&K* | *Rajasthan* | *Total* |
|---|---|---|---|---|---|---|
| Peer Pressure | 540 (81.82) | 94 (78.33) | 102 (85.00) | 113 (94.17) | 97 (80.83) | 946 (82.98) |
| Household environment | 42 (6.36) | 17 (14.17) | 03 (2.50) | 03 (2.50) | 13 (10.83) | 78 (6.84) |
| Surroundings/ Neighbourhood | 45 (6.82) | 02 (1.67) | 15 (12.50) | 03 (2.50) | 05 (4.17) | 70 (6.14) |
| TV/Media | 33 (5.00) | 07 (5.83) | – | 01 (0.83) | 05 (4.17) | 46 (4.04) |
| Total | 660 (100.00) | 120 (100.00) | 120 (100.00) | 120 (100.00) | 120 (100.00) | 1,140 (100.00) |

as they are less bothered about good and bad. At social get togethers and rave parties organised by the youth (especially by adolescents) the use and abuse of intoxicants and drugs is almost a fashion these days. At the night-clubs (late night social gatherings), mainly meant for enjoyment, the youth often display such conduct. Many serious happenings, including fatal accidents, are often the consequences of such activities.

The empirical data shows that approximately 83 percent of addicts got hooked on intoxicants and drugs under the peer pressure of classmates and friends. The addicts further revealed that in the beginning they started taking intoxicants and drugs mainly to have fun and draw pleasure but, in the process, they developed a liking for intoxicants. They never knew when their hobby led them to habit formation and in turn to drug addiction.

Across states, the proportion of addicts who got into drug consumption due to peer pressure varies from 78.33 percent in Haryana to 94.17 percent in J&K. More than 90 percent of the household members of the addicts also revealed that peer pressure was the single most important factor behind initiating their wards into intoxicants and drugs. Household environment and surroundings were the other factors which induced them towards intoxicants. At the aggregate level, 6.84 percent of the addicts revealed that they got into intoxicants and drugs because of an uncongenial household environment. Across states, the proportion of such addicts varied between 2.5 percent in H.P. and J&K to 14.17 percent in Haryana. The consumption of intoxicants in the neighbourhood and surroundings also influenced 6.14 percent of the addicts at the aggregate level. Across states it ranged from 2.5 percent in J&K to 12.5 percent in H.P.

The media and television (T.V.) were a very minor factor in inciting addicts to get into intoxicants and drugs. At the aggregate level, only 4.04 percent of the addicts revealed that they got into consumption of intoxicants because of T.V. and media. Weak willpower and a lack of awareness about the ill effects of intoxicants and drugs are also some of the minor contributory factors to push youth into consumption of drugs. Besides, emotional distress is another reason for drug addiction. H.P. has no such case while the proportion was merely 0.83 percent. In Punjab and Haryana, such a proportion was 5.0 percent and 5.8 percent, respectively.

In a nutshell, the consumption of intoxicants by elders, especially father, exerts a significant influence in inciting youth towards intoxicants and other drugs. This was supported by two-thirds of households of the addicts. Alcohol emerged as the single most dominant intoxicant consumed by the elders in the family. Most of the addicts confessed that they got initiated into intoxicants and drugs between 14 to 25 years of age. The age group of 7 to 14 years also accounted for about 10 percent of the addicts when they got hooked on intoxicants. Alcohol was the first-time consumed intoxicant by a sizeable proportion of addicts. However, heroin, opium, cannabis, hashish, marijuana and poppy husk were also among the first-time consumers of drugs among the addicts. Approximately 83 percent of the addicts revealed that peer pressure was the reason for their getting into consumption of intoxicants and drugs.

### 4.4.1 *Economic factors for addicts' initiation into drugs: Perception of household members*

Besides the previously mentioned social factors, there are certain important economic factors which are responsible for the spread of the drug menace. Unemployment and easy money (quick and ill-gotten money from illegal dealing in drugs) are the two prominent factors as is evident from Table 4.10. Out of 950 respondents, 39.79 percent hold unemployment as the factor behind initiation of their children into drugs. Across states, it varies from 37 percent (J&K) to 45 percent (Rajasthan). In H.P. only 27 percent of respondents are of the opinion that unemployment is a factor behind pushing youth into drugs (consuming and peddling). In the opinion of 41.47 percent of respondents, easy and quick money is the cause behind initiation into drugs. Across states, it varies from 38 percent in Haryana and Rajasthan to 41.27 percent in Punjab. In Rajasthan, 52 percent of respondents hold this as the most important factor. Low income of households is also responsible for pushing youth into drugs. As a matter of fact, the easy and quick earnings push youth from low-income households towards drugs. At the aggregate level, nearly 11 percent of respondents revealed that the low-income of their households pushed their wards into work at an early age and, in turn, to drugs. Across states, such a proportion varies from 3 percent (Haryana) to 10.55 percent in Punjab. H.P. is an exception, where 30 percent of the respondents are of the view that their wards have been pushed into drugs because of their low income.

Nearly 60 percent of the respondents in the control group (616 respondents from households with no addict), shared their perception that unemployment

*Table 4.10* Economic factors for drug addiction

| *Economic Factors* | *Punjab* | *Haryana* | *H.P.* | *J&K* | *Rajasthan* | *Total* |
|---|---|---|---|---|---|---|
| Unemployment | 225 (40.91) | 44 (44.00) | 27 (27.00) | 37 (37.00) | 45 (45.00) | 378 (39.79) |
| Easy money | 227 (41.27) | 38 (38.00) | 39 (39.00) | 52 (52.00) | 38 (38.00) | 394 (41.47) |
| Low income | 58 (10.55) | 03 (3.00) | 30 (30.00) | 09 (9.00) | 04 (4.00) | 104 (10.95) |
| Indebtedness | 28 (5.09) | 12 (12.00) | 01 (1.00) | 02 (2.00) | 07 (7.00) | 5 (5.26) |
| Miscellaneous | 12 (2.18) | 03 (3.00) | 03 (3.00) | 0 (0.00) | 06 (6.00) | 24 (2.53) |
| Total | 550 (100.00) | 100 (100.00) | 100 (100.00) | 100 (100.00) | 100 (100.00) | 950 (100.00) |

is a significant economic factor behind youth's initiation into intoxicants and addiction to drugs. Across states, this proportion varies from 63 percent in Punjab and Haryana to 77 percent in J&K. In H.P. and Rajasthan it is 32.7 percent and 42.3 percent, respectively. Low income of households, according to 24 percent of the control group respondents, is responsible for pushing youth into drugs. 17 percent of them opine that youth is allured to drugs due to easy and quick money. It is significant to mention that, according to drug addicts, unemployment is not a very important factor but, in the perception of the household members, it is a very important factor behind drug addiction and abuse.

Similar reasons also emerged during FGDs with village panchayat members and teachers and students from various educational institutions. Mechanisation of agricultural operations has given enough free time to the farming community. A large number of cultivators and labourers are being pushed out of agriculture due to shrinking employment opportunities therein. Ample free time due to unemployment (open as well as disguised) and underemployment is the major cause behind the high incidence of drugs among the youth, especially from the agricultural and rural sectors. With shrinking opportunities of suitable alternative employment in the non-agricultural sectors, the youth is frustrated and upset and is easily falling prey to the use of drugs. Yet, at the same time, youth, who have easy availability of money, spend it in clubs and parties where drugs are frequently used. In FGDs with police officials it was also revealed that generally, *bhang*, *bhukki* and medical drugs are used by the poor; opium, *bhukki* and *bhang* by the middle class and heroin, *charas* and cocaine by the upper class. The poor take drugs to enhance their performance at work while the rich to enhance their enjoyment level. Therefore, an approach to handle such people needs different strategies.

Besides, the previously mentioned social and economic factors, easy availability and supply of drugs (mainly because of Punjab's proximity to the international border) is also the main cause for initiation into drugs (Bhattacharji, 2019; The Tribune, April 27, 2022). Punjab, being the transit route of drug trafficking, is vulnerable to the drugs menace. The Border Security Force (BSF) seized 361 kg heroin in 2014, 244 kg 2015, 231 kg in 2016, and 278 kg in 2017, 221 kg in 2018 and 227 kg in 2019 in Punjab. So, the trend is on the decline (The Tribune, January 8, 2020). Drones are also used to smuggle arms and drugs from Pakistan (The Tribune, December 16, 2020). However, 102 kg of Afghan heroin (worth Rs 700 crore) was seized at the Integrated Check Post, Attari (Indo-Pak border), in April 2022 (The Tribune, April 25, 2022). The consignment was meant for a Delhi importer.

The Directorate of Revenue Intelligence (DRI) seized 2,988 kg of heroin (perhaps the biggest ever haul) at Mundra Port (Gujarat) in September 2021 (The Tribune, April 27, 2022). Again, 205.6 kg heroin (worth Rs. 1,439 crore) was seized by DRI from a Gujarat port on April 25, 2022 (The Tribune, April 26, 2022). The importer was arrested from a Punjab village in

Amritsar district (The Tribune, April 26, 2022). Besides the Golden Crescent (Iran, Afghanistan and Pakistan) route, heroin also enters Punjab from Uttar Pradesh and Rajasthan. Cultivation and sale of opium poppy husk is legal in Rajasthan and Madhya Pradesh and generally sent to the adjoining districts of Punjab (Arora and Kaura, *op. cit.*). On May 11, 2022, 62 kg heroin was caught from IGI Airport, Delhi (The Tribune, May 12, 2022). Punjab and Haryana High Court directed the Union Government to submit the report on fresh steps taken for controlling the increasing menace in cross border trade in drugs (The Tribune, May 13, 2022).

Thus, proximity to an international border is also an important factor in the availability of drugs and encouraging drug abuse and addiction. Table 4.1A (annexure) aptly highlights this fact. In the words of a retired IPS officer (Prakash Singh) and former Director General Border Security Force (BSF), "Punjab has always been vulnerable to smuggling, for there is market for it. During my tenure, gold was the main item of smuggling. Today, it is drug smuggling and it has gone up to horrific levels. The traffickers probably have protection from powerful people" (Quoted by Ranjan, 2019). According to Sahni (2019), the confiscation of more than 717 kilograms of heroin (including 532 kgs seized by customs and other enforcement agencies on June 30, 2019, The Hindu), is a reiteration of Pakistan's 'war of a thousand cuts' against India. Hence, this is a kind of warfare that transcends all boundaries and limits. This is akin to narco-terrorism-nexus between terrorism and drug trafficking. The border districts of Punjab are worst affected by heroin smuggled from Pakistan as the small district of Tarn Taran has the highest number of known drug users in rural areas while Amritsar tops among the state's urban areas. The drugs traveling through or consumed in India has many much deeper and serious implications for national security (Dikshit, 2019).

In a nutshell, the chapter described and analysed the circumstances which incites and pushes the youth towards the consumption of intoxicants and drugs. It has been found that there are multipronged factors responsible for youth's initiation into intoxicants and addiction to drugs. The younger children are adversely influenced by the elders' habit of consuming intoxicants. Numerous social and economic factors are responsible for children's initiation into drugs. They include peer pressure, family environment, unemployment, easy availability of money and drugs, etc. The initiation into intoxicants and drugs at an adolescent age and starting drug use at the time of such an initiation is a serious scenario. The analysis and discussion is mainly based on the revelations of the drug addicts, the members of their households, case studies and focus group discussions.

# 5 Pattern of drug addiction across states

This chapter dwells on commonly consumed drugs, sources of drug supply, post-consumption experiences and the incidence of relapsing among the addicts. The chapter has been divided into three sections. Section 1 discusses commonly consumed drugs, their sources of supply and methods of consuming drugs. Section 2 describes post-consumption experiences of drug addicts, and the incidence of relapsing is discussed in section 3. The duration of addiction to different drugs is the subject matter of the fourth section. The empirical evidence is based on the primary information and data collected from the respondents.

## 5.1 Commonly consumed drugs by addicts

There are nearly 10 major drugs commonly consumed in the states under study. The use of different drugs varies from state to state. Some of the drugs are more popular and some are less popular across the states. For example, heroin is more popular in Punjab and Jammu and Kashmir (J&K) than the other three states. The use of opium is higher in Punjab and Haryana. Poppy husk is a preferred drug in some regions in Punjab, Haryana and Rajasthan. Tramadol is more popular in Punjab. Tramadol is a synthetic opioid used to treat moderate to moderately severe pain. Even Punjab and Haryana High Court has taken a serious note of the heavy use of tramadol in Punjab and Haryana (The Tribune, March 31, 2022). The use of cannabis is higher in Himachal Pradesh (H.P.) and J&K. As compared to other states, the use of marijuana is higher in Haryana, Punjab and J&K. Buprenorphine is more popular in Punjab and Haryana. The use of codeine is higher in J&K. Cocaine is also used, though by a small number of addicts, in almost all the states, except Rajasthan (Table 5.1).

The fact that the number of responses (3,682) is much higher than the number of respondents (1,140) reveals that more than one drug is being used by an addict. On average, an addict uses more than three drugs. The incidence of using more than one drug was 3.46 times in Punjab and J&K. This was followed by 3.39 times in Haryana, 2.53 times in H.P. and 2.25 times in Rajasthan (Table 5.1). It is mainly because of the availability and

DOI: 10.4324/9781003318019-5

*Table 5.1* Commonly consumed drugs

| *Sr. No.* | *Drug* | *Punjab* | *Haryana* | *H.P.* | *J&K* | *Rajasthan* | *Total* |
|---|---|---|---|---|---|---|---|
| 1. | Heroin/Chitta/ brown sugar | 426 (64.55) | 45 (37.50) | 40 (33.33) | 76 (63.33) | 25 (20.83) | 612 (53.68) |
| 2. | Opium | 348 (52.73) | 76 (63.33) | 28 (23.33) | 52 (43.33) | 49 (40.83) | 553 (48.51) |
| 3. | Tramadol | 331 (50.15) | 55 (45.83) | 17 (14.17) | 06 (5.0) | 41 (34.17) | 450 (39.47) |
| 4. | Poppy husk/ Bhukki | 368 (55.76) | 68 (56.67) | 14 (11.67) | 46 (38.33) | 60 (50.0) | 556 (48.77) |
| 5. | Cannabis/ Bhang/Sukha | 215 (32.58) | 53 (44.17) | 99 (82.50) | 67 (55.83) | 33 (27.5) | 467 (40.96) |
| 6. | Marijuana/ Ganja/smack | 196 (29.70) | 47 (39.17) | 24 (20.0) | 44 (36.67) | 30 (25.00) | 341 (29.91) |
| 7. | Buprenorphine | 199 (30.15) | 36 (30.0) | 02 (1.67) | 09 (7.50) | 26 (21.67) | 272 (23.86) |
| 8. | Codeine | 124 (18.79) | 03 (2.5) | 10 (8.33) | 42 (35.0) | 03 (2.50) | 175 (15.35) |
| 9. | Hashish/ Charas | 68 (10.30) | 14 (11.67) | 60 (50.0) | 63 (52.50) | 03 (2.50) | 208 (18.25) |
| 10. | Cocaine | 11 (1.67) | 10 (8.33) | 09 (7.50) | 11 (9.17) | 0 (0.00) | 41 (3.60) |
| Total respondents | | 660 | 120 | 120 | 120 | 120 | 1140 |
| Total responses | | 2286 (346.4) | 407 (339.2) | 303 (252.5) | 416 (346.7) | 270 (225.0) | 3682 (323.0) |

*Note:* Figures in brackets indicate percentage share out of the total number of addicts in each state. This is applicable to all the tables in this chapter unless mentioned otherwise.

non-availability of a particular drug and the cost of the drug. In the event of non-availability of a particular drug, the addicts substitute other available (and also cheaper) drugs in order to satisfy their drug need. The reason is that some drugs are in higher use in some states/regions and also because of availability, price and socio-cultural factors. Thus, addicts' access to a particular drug and affordability are important factors for the use of a particular drug. The degree and intensity of addiction also plays an important role in the use of a particular drug. The transition from one type of drug to the other drug(s) is also reflected in the preferences of addicts towards particular drug(s). The use of crystal methamphetamine, popularly known as 'ice' and mainly used in parties, is also being used (The Tribune, June 29, 2022; July 4, 2022). The most important determinant, inter alia, is the demonstration effect which is reflected by the drug usage of peers.

The preference matrix of drug addicts (towards different drugs) is given in Table 5.1. At the aggregate level, the majority of the addicts have a preference for heroin (54 percent) and poppy husk (49 percent), followed by opium (49 percent), cannabis (41 percent), tramadol, marijuana, Buprenorphine, hashish/*charas*, codeine and cocaine. Across the states, more than

64.55 percent of addicts use heroin in Punjab. The corresponding proportion in J&K is 63.33 percent. This is followed by Haryana, H.P. and Rajasthan. The proportion of addicts using poppy husk is, however, higher in Haryana (56.67 percent), followed by Punjab, Rajasthan, J&K and H.P. With 63.33 percent of the addicts using opium, Haryana is ranked at number one, followed by Punjab (52.73 percent), J&K, Rajasthan and H.P. The proportion of tramadol users is higher (50.15 percent) in Punjab, followed by Haryana, Rajasthan, H.P. and J&K. In the use of cannabis, H.P. is at the top with 82.5 percent of addicts using this drug. It is followed by J&K (55.83 percent), Haryana, Punjab and Rajasthan. The proportion of addicts using marijuana varies from 20 percent in H.P. to 39.17 percent in Haryana. The corresponding proportion of Buprenorphine varies from 1.67 percent in H.P. to 30.15 percent in Punjab. With 35 percent of addicts using codeine, J&K has the topmost position. It is followed by Punjab, H.P., Haryana and Rajasthan. As regards Hashish, the majority of the addicts (50 to 52 percent) use it in H.P. and J&K. This is followed by Haryana, Punjab and Rajasthan. As stated before, the variation of use of different drugs is because of multiple reasons. Households' perception about the type of drugs being consumed by the addicts is given in Table 5.1A in annexure. 1.22 percent of respondents are of the perception that the addicts consume traditional drugs, with huge variation across states. For example, 85.53 percent of the respondents in Himachal Pradesh hold the view that addicts consume traditional drugs. At the aggregate level, 40.23 percent of respondents are of the view that addicts consume synthetic drugs, with the highest proportion in J&K, followed by Punjab. Another 37.74 percent of respondents said that drug addicts consume pharmaceutical drugs. Compared with Table 5.1, it seems very close to the ground reality as depicted by the addicts themselves.

## 5.2 Sources of drug supply

Demand creates supply or supply creates demand, is a complex phenomenon. As per Say's Law (economist J.B. Say), supply creates its own demand, though it is true in the case of drug supply, yet it is also demand-driven if we go by consumers' sovereignty. Drug suppliers do create demand for drugs by way of multiple channels. Quick and huge money from supply of drugs is perhaps the most important factor besides social and political reasons. Drug-financed terrorism (narco-terrorism) and gangsters are other reasons. The allurement for drugs and their utility to satisfy lust for drugs are important factors behind the demand for drugs which, in itself, depends on multiple socio-cultural and politico-economic factors. Thus, there is a peculiar relationship between demand for and supply of drugs. Supply creates demand and vice versa. The general law of supply states that supply is a function of price, if *ceteris paribus*. Thus, between demand and supply, price is a common factor. In the case of normal goods, advertisement plays an important role in creating demand, but it is not exactly the same in the case of demand for drugs, especially the illicit drugs. Rather, intoxicants in general are discouraged through advertisements and also by way of creating awareness of ill effects of drugs. Nonetheless, drug suppliers (manufactures and smugglers of drugs) have their own mechanism to generate demand for drugs. There is a strong network between drug suppliers and the consumers of drugs and there is a strong supply chain which has been discussed in the case studies and community perception. Often the main drug suppliers/smugglers seldom come into the picture; mainly because of the nefarious nexus between such suppliers/smugglers, political leaders and police officials (discussed in Chapter 7). However, right now, we are focusing on the apparent (on the screen and not behind the screen) sources of drug supply.

Table 5.2 reveals that the drug peddlers are the biggest sources of drug supply and there are layers and layers of supply chain behind the peddlers. The motive force, inter alia, behind this chain is huge and quick money. Nonetheless, it is an illusion that peddlers are the biggest source of drug supply as they are just the link between the drug suppliers and the consumers of drugs. This, along with allurement for drug consumption, is a strong motivator for the drug peddlers. Currently, women have also resorted to drug peddling which must be a cause of serious concern for society, security forces and the government. The cross border and internal drug suppliers are deliberately luring women (mainly unemployed) to evade suspicion of the security agencies (The Tribune, August 8, 2020; Watts, 2020; July 4, 2022). Besides peddlers, friends and chemists are the other sources of supply of drugs. The data in the table also reveals that drug addicts are not confined to one source; instead, they use multiple sources of supply. However, peddlers are the single most important mode of drug supply. This is the most important link in the supply chain, peddlers carrying the drugs to the end consumers. On average, 82.11 percent of the drug supply is through drug peddlers.

*Table 5.2* Sources of drug supply according to addicts

| *Source* | *Punjab* | *Haryana* | *H.P.* | *J&K* | *Rajasthan* | *Total* |
|---|---|---|---|---|---|---|
| Drug peddlers | 601<br>(91.6) | 75<br>(62.5) | 88<br>(73.33) | 89<br>(74.17) | 83<br>(69.1) | 936<br>(82.11) |
| Friends | 123<br>(18.18) | 39<br>(32.5) | 37<br>(30.83) | 45<br>(37.5) | 56<br>(46.67) | 300<br>(26.32) |
| Chemists | 114<br>(17.27) | 39<br>(32.5) | 02<br>(1.67) | 01<br>(0.83) | 34<br>(28.33) | 190<br>(16.67) |
| Others | 20<br>(3.03) | 03<br>(2.5) | 01<br>(0.83) | 05<br>(4.17) | 10<br>(8.33) | 39<br>(3.42) |
| Total respondents | 660<br>(100) | 120<br>(100) | 120<br>(100) | 120<br>(100) | 120<br>(100) | 1,140<br>(100) |
| Total responses | 858<br>(130.0) | 156<br>(130.0) | 128<br>(106.67) | 140<br>(116.67) | 183<br>(152.50) | 1,465<br>(128.51) |

*Note:* Figures in brackets indicate percentage share out of the total number of addicts in each state.

Friends supply 26.32 percent while chemists 16.67 percent. A meagre amount (3.42 percent) of drug supply is met through other sources. Across the states, the drug peddlers meet supply between 62.5 percent in Haryana and 91 percent in Punjab. The corresponding proportion of supply through friends (friends group of the addicts or peers of the addicts) ranges from 18.18 percent in Punjab to 46.67 percent in Rajasthan. The chemists are the important source of drug supply in Rajasthan (28.33 percent) and in Haryana (32.5 percent). They, however, play a marginal role in J&K and H.P., while in Punjab 17.27 percent of addicts get drugs from the chemists. Paradoxically, there are secret codewords for different drugs with all the sources of supply.

Looking at the total sample of drug addicts (1,140) and the responses of the respondents (1,465) to source their drug, it is evident that, on average, a drug addict uses 1.29 sources. It is the highest (1.53) in Rajasthan and lowest (1.07) in H.P. In Punjab and Haryana, it is 1.3 times (Table 5.2). According to household members of the addicts, peddlers are also the main source of supply of drugs (Table 5.2A in annexure). Out of 950 respondents, 66.63 percent are of the view that addicts get the drugs through peddlers. Across states, it varies from 50 percent in Rajasthan to 76.36 percent in Punjab. On the other hand, 18.32 percent of the respondents say that the addicts get the supply through their friends, who are also drug addicts. Another 10.84 percent of the respondents are of the view that chemists also supply drugs. They mainly supply synthetic drugs. Only 4.21 percent of respondents said that there are some other sources of drug supply. Among the respondents from the control group households, 72.9 percent said that the addicts get their supply from local sources, i.e., from within their own state and their vicinity. But they don't know the original source of supply. Nevertheless, 17.4 percent of respondents are of the view that drug supply comes from national sources. Another 12.3 percent of respondents said that drug supply comes from international sources.

Many participants in some of the FGDs pointed out the role of specific communities and villages involved in the drug trade, especially in Punjab. It was revealed by the participants during FGDs with village panchayats and Urban Local Bodies (ULBs) that some families from the border districts are traditionally engaged in drug smuggling and peddling. Areas around railway stations are also frequently used by the drug suppliers and drug peddlers. Due to the rush of passengers, it often becomes difficult to detect the illegal activities of drug peddlers. The locations such as railway stations are a permanent stay for homeless, unemployed and mendicants. Most of them consume or sell drugs. Some people, mainly youngsters, also buy drugs from them. The General Railway Police (GRP) could not prevail upon them because of resistance from the local NGO's working with the Human Rights Commission.

FGDs with ULBs, police officials and medical experts revealed that some colonies in the urban areas are infamous for drug problems. The communities living in these areas generally belong to lower castes like Scheduled Castes,

Sansis, Sikligars, Rai Sikhs and others. Mostly they are landless, unemployed, under-employed and illiterate and do petty activities to earn their livelihood. The use of locally brewed alcohol of poor quality, medical drugs, *zarda*, *bhukki*, cigarettes/*beedi* and other cheap intoxicants and drugs are very common in such localities and recently they have also started trading hard drugs like heroin. The participants were of the view that state governments have not created any mechanism whereby such vulnerable sections of society living in such congested *mohallas* and slums could be engaged in positive economic activities and rehabilitated. The respondents further shared that even the dance girls and boys performing in social functions are also involved in drug use to strengthen and maintain their stamina. This habit leads them to become regular users and eventually indulge in other anti-social activities. This makes them vulnerable to HIV and other serious health problems.

## 5.3 Methods of consuming drugs by addicts

Mainly three methods of taking drugs are popular among the addicts. These are oral consumption, injecting and inhaling. It has been revealed by the addicts that they use more than one method. This is evident from the 1,472 responses by 1,140 respondents. On average, each addict uses 1.29 methods of consuming drugs. Across the states, it varies from 1.14 in Rajasthan to 1.43 in Haryana (Table 5.3). At the aggregate level, 51.05 percent of the respondents revealed that they do oral consumption of drugs. This is followed by inhaling the drugs (44.65 percent). Injecting method comes at number three with 33.42 percent of respondents resorting to this method. Across states, 83.33 percent of the addicts in Rajasthan take drugs orally. The respective proportion in Haryana and J&K is 73.33 percent and 55 percent present. Punjab (46.52 percent) and H.P. (17.5 percent) come next. In H.P. the most popular method of taking drugs is through inhaling, followed by Haryana (49.17 percent) and J&K (46.67 percent). Nearly 41 percent of addicts in

*Table 5.3* Methods of drugs consumption

| *Method* | *Punjab* | *Haryana* | *H.P.* | *J&K* | *Rajasthan* | *Total* |
|---|---|---|---|---|---|---|
| Oral consumption | 307<br>(46.52) | 88<br>(73.33) | 21<br>(17.50) | 66<br>(55.00) | 100<br>(83.33) | 582<br>(51.05) |
| Inhaling | 271<br>(41.06) | 59<br>(49.17) | 101<br>(84.17) | 56<br>(46.67) | 22<br>(18.33) | 509<br>(44.65) |
| Injecting | 286<br>(43.33) | 25<br>(15.83) | 16<br>(13.33) | 39<br>(32.50) | 15<br>(12.5) | 381<br>(33.42) |
| Total respondents | 660<br>(100) | 120<br>(100) | 120<br>(100) | 120<br>(100) | 120<br>(100) | 1,140<br>(100) |
| Total responses | 864<br>(130.91) | 172<br>(143.33) | 138<br>(115.0) | 161<br>(134.17) | 137<br>(114.17) | 1,472<br>(129.12) |

Punjab take drugs through inhaling. However, the injecting (drugs) method is more popular in Punjab as shared by 43.33 percent of respondents, followed by J&K (32.5 percent), Haryana, H.P. and Rajasthan (12.5 percent). Sharing the same syringe by two or more addicts is quite normal across the states, and this leads to certain serious ailments such as HIV among the addicts. Even oral consumption and inhaling is shared by two or more addicts who often transmit disease(s) from the one who is already suffering from some disease(s).

## 5.4 Post consumption experiences narrated by drug addicts

The drug addicts, by satisfying their lust for drugs, do fulfil certain objectives by way of using drugs. In economics, it means drugs do have utility for the addicts and after consuming drug(s) they do draw satisfaction, so drugs have a satisfying power as well. This is the famous law of utility (demand satisfying power of a commodity). But the type and degree of satisfaction varies from person to person as it is mainly subjective even though more than one person can consume the same commodity, here drugs. Paradoxically, the use of drug(s) is not subject to the law of diminishing marginal utility. The utility (here lust for drugs) rather increases with more and more use of drugs. This satisfaction or post-consumption experience has been classified into three categories, viz. pleasure, relaxing and energy (Table 5.4). All the three categories can be clubbed into biochemical happiness which is also the number one cause of crime in the world (Harari, 2015). At the aggregate level, 53.16 percent of respondents revealed that they draw pleasure after consuming the drug(s).

Across the states, the proportion of such addicts varies from 44.17 percent in H.P. to 80 percent in J&K. Another 27.54 percent of the 1,140 addicts shared that they feel relaxed after consuming drug(s). Across the states, the share of such addicts varies from 21.67 percent in Rajasthan to 44.17 percent in H.P. In J&K, only 13.33 percent of the addicts said that they feel relaxed after consuming the drug(s). It, however, may not be construed that

*Table 5.4* Post consumption experience of drug addicts

| *Experience* | *Punjab* | *Haryana* | *H.P.* | *J&K* | *Rajasthan* | *Total* |
|---|---|---|---|---|---|---|
| Pleasure | 314<br>(47.58) | 63<br>(52.50) | 53<br>(44.17) | 96<br>(80.0) | 80<br>(66.67) | 606<br>(53.16) |
| Relaxation | 182<br>(27.58) | 37<br>(30.83) | 53<br>(44.17) | 16<br>(13.33) | 26<br>(21.67) | 314<br>(27.54) |
| Energetic | 164<br>(24.85) | 20<br>(16.67) | 14<br>(11.67) | 08<br>(6.67) | 14<br>(11.67) | 220<br>(19.30) |
| Total respondents | 660<br>(100) | 120<br>(100) | 120<br>(100) | 120<br>(100) | 120<br>(100) | 1,140<br>(100) |

(as a proxy) a significant number of addicts are under some tensions and so they consume drugs for relaxation. Nonetheless, it cannot be ruled out that the consumption of drug(s) gives them temporary relief from tension(s). It is equally true that most other persons passing through similar circumstances may not be taking refuge in drugs. It depends on their willpower and the family and social support mechanism. There are some addicts who use drugs as a source of energy (a feeling of masculinity). At the aggregate level, the proportion of such addicts is 19.30 percent. Across states, it varies from 6.67 percent in J&K to 24.85 percent in Punjab. All the respondents, however, forget to acknowledge that all the post-consumption experiences are a temporary phenomenon and in order to have the same feelings they get trapped (a vicious circle) in the habit of taking drug(s). Once they become habitual to drug consumption, they get addicted to drug(s). And once they get addicted, they develop a strong urge to consume drug(s), then, in the absence of drug(s), their behaviour becomes abnormal; often they start behaving inhumanly and resort to abuse. In such a situation they simply cannot do without a drug and can go to any extent to get the drug. They even forget their social relations as their animal spirit overpowers them. Our case studies do support such a behavioural change. Many times, the addicts resort to violence and even forget respect for and emotional attachment to relations. A number of respondents in our case studies shared that the addicts have resorted to slapping and beating even their mothers, fathers, wives and children.

## 5.5 Incidence of relapsing

Relapsing is a serious problem with the majority of addicts who get treatment in the de-addiction centres (government as well as private). We could get responses from the 950 addicts (taking treatment as in-patient or follow-up addicts) out of 1,140 as it does not apply to 190 hidden addicts. Table 5.5 shows that 65.89 percent of the addicts (who underwent treatment) again got into drug consumption. This is a very high proportion by any stretch of imagination. It, inter alia, implies two things: one, addicts in the de-addiction and rehabilitation centres do lack in completing the entire process/course of de-addiction and rehabilitation. Two, after getting de-addiction

*Table 5.5* Incidence of relapsing among the addicts

| *Response* | *Punjab* | *Haryana* | *H.P.* | *J&K* | *Rajasthan* | *Total* |
|---|---|---|---|---|---|---|
| Yes | 353<br>(64.18) | 60<br>(60.40) | 73<br>(73.00) | 75<br>(75.00) | 65<br>(65.00) | 626<br>(65.89) |
| No | 197<br>(35.82) | 40<br>(40.00) | 27<br>(27.00) | 25<br>(25.00) | 35<br>(35.00) | 324<br>(34.11) |
| Total | 550<br>(100) | 100<br>(100) | 100<br>(100) | 100<br>(100) | 100<br>(100) | 950<br>(100) |

and rehabilitation treatment, the addicts again start using drugs once they are back to the socio-cultural and economic conditions (which pushed them towards drugs), mainly because of weak willpower and the lack of emotional and psychological support from their household members. This means that, even after getting a good de-addiction treatment and completing the so-called rehabilitating course, the compatible social support and socio-economic mechanism is missing in the system. This means, along with de-addiction and rehabilitation, the socio-cultural and politico-economic system must be in place to save the addicts from getting into the same rut. This, in turn, means that the system would have to address all those socio-cultural and politico-economic circumstances which pushed the normal person into the drug trap. Significantly, almost in all the states under study, the rehabilitation mechanism is hardly in place. Lack of rehabilitation centres and mechanisms, inter alia, is also one of the main causes of relapsing.

Table 5.6 reveals the entire range of reasons/factors which lead to the de-addicted and rehabilitated persons again using drugs, i.e., back to the square one that is relapsing. Out of the 626 cases of relapsing, 284 (45.37 percent) happened due to the company and pressure of peers. Across states, it varies from the 35 percent in Haryana to 49.23 percent in Rajasthan. It suggests that after the de-addiction is done and the addict is in the process of rehabilitation, there is a need to wean away and protect the de-addicted person from

*Table 5.6* Causes for relapsing

| *Sr. No.* | *Cause* | *Punjab* | *Haryana* | *H.P.* | *J&K* | *Rajasthan* | *Total* |
|---|---|---|---|---|---|---|---|
| 1. | Peer Pressure | 172 (48.73) | 21 (35.00) | 28 (38.36) | 31 (41.33) | 32 (49.23) | 284 (45.37) |
| 2. | Curiosity | 67 (18.98) | 08 (13.33) | 31 (42.47) | 30 (40.00) | 15 (23.08) | 152 (24.28) |
| 3. | Pleasure | 17 (4.82) | 10 (16.67) | 0 (0.00) | 10 (13.33) | 02 (3.08) | 39 (6.23) |
| 4. | Avoid fatigue | 25 (7.08) | 03 (5.0) | 0 (0.00) | 0 (0.00) | 04 (6.15) | 32 (6.23) |
| 5. | Tragedy in Family | 05 (1.42) | 05 (8.33) | 01 (1.37) | 0 (0.00) | 02 (3.08) | 13 (2.08) |
| 6. | Escaping from withdrawal symptoms | 18 (5.09) | 07 (11.67) | 05 (6.85) | 0 (0.00) | 0 (0.00) | 30 (4.79) |
| 7. | Deficiency in de-addiction and rehabilitation | 17 (4.82) | 0 (0.00) | 0 (0.00) | 01 (1.33) | 01 (1.54) | 19 (3.04) |
| 8. | Miscellaneous | 31 (8.78) | 06 (10.00) | 08 (10.96) | 03 (4.00) | 09 (13.85) | 57 (9.11) |
| Total cases of relapsing | | 353 (64.18) | 60 (60.00) | 73 (73.00) | 75 (75.00) | 65 (65.00) | 626 (65.89) |
| Total addicts | | 550 (100) | 100 (100) | 100 (100) | 100 (100) | 100 (100) | 950 (100) |

peer pressure so that he can be saved from relapsing. The second important reason for relapsing is the curiosity to take drug(s). At the aggregate level, 24.28 percent of cases of relapsing occurred due to curiosity among the de-addicted persons. H.P. and J&K witnessed 42.47 percent and 40 percent of cases of relapsing due to curiosity for drugs. In other states, it varied from 13.33 percent (Haryana) and 23.08 percent in Rajasthan. About 5 percent of de-addicted patients revealed that they got into drug(s) again just to avoid fatigue. Then there are withdrawal symptoms, which push the de-addicted patients again into drug use. Only 3 percent of the de-addicted cases revealed that relapsing occurred owing to deficiency in the treatment. Around 9 percent of the relapsing cases occurred due to a bunch of other reasons. Whatever may be the causes, the high incidence of relapsing is a serious challenge. All the stakeholders such as government, society, households, state and civil society would have to accept this challenge as a collective whole. In other words, the challenge would have to be addressed by the system and that, too, with a systemic approach, because drug addiction and abuse is embedded in the socio-cultural and politico-economic system. Unfortunately, there is no systemic approach to deal with the drug menace.

## 5.6 Duration of addiction to various drugs

The varying proportion of addicts addicted to the use of different drugs and for short and long durations may be of some help to the policy makers, doctors and councillors at the de-addiction centres. Those who are in addiction for short duration may give greater success in de-addiction, rehabilitation and lower incidence of relapsing. On the other hand, the prevalence of long duration addiction may involve far more effort. There is, thus, a need to approach the councillors and medical experts in the initial stages of addiction. However, the delay in consulting the doctors and councillors is a general practice of society. Such a practice may be due to multiple reasons ranging from ignorance, lack of awareness, and shortage of finances to concealing the addiction because of social stigma, etc. This needs to be addressed and the primary responsibility is that of the parents, other household members and the department of social justice. They must take the addict to the councillors and doctors at the initial stage instead of ignoring or postponing the phenomenon. It needs to be acknowledged that the initial days, weeks and months of addiction are very crucial to treat the patient in an effective manner. With the passage of time, the addict becomes almost a slave to his/her habit of addiction.

As discussed earlier (Table 5.1) and also shown in Table 5.7, there are mainly nine drugs which are being used by the addicts in the states under study. It is also clear from Table 5.7 to 5.11 that there were more responses than the number of addicts. In Punjab, 304 addicts used heroin (Table 5.7). It is followed by tramadol, poppy husk, opium, marijuana, buprenorphine and codeine. The information of duration of addiction to various drugs is

*Table 5.7* Duration of addiction to various drugs in Punjab (months)

| *Sr. No.* | *Drug/Duration* ↓ → | *up to 12* | *12–24* | *24–36* | *36–48* | *48–60* | *Above 60* | *Total* |
|---|---|---|---|---|---|---|---|---|
| 1. | Heroin | 80 (26.32) | 46 (15.13) | 55 (18.09) | 32 (10.53) | 30 (9.87) | 61 (20.07) | 304 (100) |
| 2. | Opium | 117 (68.02) | 22 (12.79) | 09 (5.23) | 06 (3.49) | 03 (1.74) | 15 (8.72) | 172 (100) |
| 3. | Tramadol | 102 (54.55) | 26 (13.90) | 20 (10.70) | 15 (8.02) | 09 (4.81) | 15 (8.02) | 187 (100) |
| 4. | Poppy Husk | 65 (39.08) | 18 (10.34) | 15 (8.62) | 09 (5.17) | 11 (6.32) | 56 (32.18) | 174 (100) |
| 5. | Cannabis/ Bhang/Sukha | 45 (48.39) | 10 (10.75) | 08 (8.60) | 10 (10.75) | 06 (6.45) | 14 (15.05) | 93 (100) |
| 6. | Marijuana/ Ganja/ Smack | 41 (37.96) | 16 (14.81) | 15 (13.88) | 07 (6.48) | 09 (8.33) | 20 (18.52) | 108 (100) |
| 7. | Buprenorphine | 72 (80.00) | 07 (7.78) | 04 (4.44) | 03 (3.33) | 0 (0.00) | 04 (4.44) | 90 (100) |
| 8. | Cocaine | 35 (59.32) | 06 (10.17) | 03 (3.33) | 05 (8.47) | 03 (3.33) | 07 (11.86) | 59 (100) |
| 9. | Hashish/ Charas | 26 (37.50) | 05 (12.50) | 07 (17.50) | 03 (7.50) | 03 (7.50) | 07 (17.50) | 40 (100) |
| Total | | 572 (46.62) | 156 (12.71) | 136 (11.08) | 90 (7.33) | 74 (6.03) | 199 (16.22) | 1227 (100) |

important from the de-addiction and rehabilitation standpoint. If the addiction is not very old, then perhaps the de-addiction process, inter alia, may be less cumbersome and less expensive. The data in Table 5.7 shows that, at the time of data collection, 46.62 percent of the addicts in Punjab revealed that they were using drugs for less than a year. The proportion of addicts as per duration of addiction varies from 12 to 24 months (12.71 percent), 24 to 48 months (11.08 percent) 36 to 48 months (7.33 percent), 48 to 60 months (6.03 percent) and beyond 60 months (16.22 percent) in Punjab. Addiction to various drugs also varies from less than 12 months to beyond 60 months. The proportion of addicts in addiction to various drugs up to 12 months varied from 37.5 percent (hashish) to 80 percent (buprenorphine). The proportion of the addicts being in addiction beyond 60 months varies from 4.44 percent (buprenorphine) to 32.18 percent (poppy husk).

Table 5.8 presents the proportion of addicts and their duration of addiction to various drugs in Haryana. Out of the 401 responses, it has been found that 59.1 percent of the addicts were addicted to drugs for less than 12 months. Among the various drugs, the proportion of addicts with a duration of up to 12 months varies from 34.33 percent (poppy husk) to 77.78 percent (buprenorphine). The proportion of addicts in the duration of 12 to 24 months varies from 3.85 percent (cannabis) to 23.26 percent (heroin). The corresponding proportion for 24 to 36 months duration varies

*Table 5.8* Duration of addiction to various drugs in Haryana (months)

| *Sr. No.* | *Drug/Duration* ↓ → | *Up to 12* | *12–24* | *24–36* | *36–48* | *48–60* | *Above 60* | *Total* |
|---|---|---|---|---|---|---|---|---|
| 1. | Heroin | 25 (58.14) | 10 (23.26) | 01 (2.33) | 02 (4.65) | 02 (4.65) | 3 (6.98) | 43 (100) |
| 2. | Opium | 45 (59.21) | 06 (7.89) | 03 (3.95) | 06 (7.89) | 2 (2.63) | 14 (18.42) | 76 (100) |
| 3. | Tramadol | 38 (69.10) | 03 (5.45) | 03 (5.45) | 03 (5.45) | 02 (3.64) | 06 (10.97) | 55 (100) |
| 4. | Poppy Husk | 23 (34.33) | 07 (10.45) | 06 (8.96) | 09 (13.43) | 04 (5.97) | 18 (26.87) | 67 (100) |
| 5. | Cannabis/ Bhang/Sukha | 38 (73.08) | 02 (3.85) | 03 (5.77) | 02 (3.85) | 01 (1.92) | 06 (11.54) | 52 (100) |
| 6. | Marijuana/ Ganja/Smack | 26 (55.32) | 06 (12.77) | 08 (17.02) | 0 (0.00) | 02 (4.26) | 05 (10.64) | 47 (100) |
| 7. | Buprenorphine | 28 (77.78) | 03 (8.33) | 02 (5.56) | 02 (5.56) | 01 (2.78) | 0 (0.00) | 36 (100) |
| 8. | Cocaine | 05 (45.45) | 02 (18.18) | 01 (9.09) | 02 (18.18) | 0 (0.00) | 01 (9.09) | 11 (100) |
| 9. | Hashish/Charas | 09 (64.29) | 0 (0.00) | 01 (7.14) | 0 (0.00) | 0 (0.00) | 04 (28.57) | 14 (100) |
| Total | | 237 (59.10) | 39 (9.73) | 28 (6.98) | 26 (6.48) | 14 (3.49) | 57 (14.21) | 401 (100) |

from 2.33 percent (heroin) to 9.09 percent (codeine). In the case of 36 to 48 months duration the proportion varies from 3.85 percent (cannabis) to 18.18 percent (codeine). The proportion of addicts in the duration period of 48 to 60 months varies from 1.92 percent (cannabis) to 5.97 percent (poppy husk). Beyond 60 months duration, the proportion of addicts to different drugs varies from 6.98 percent (heroin) to 28.57 percent (hashish). Thus, the majority of the addicts fall in the duration period of less than a year and beyond the duration of 5 years. This is quite similar to Punjab.

In the case of Himachal Pradesh (H.P.) also, the majority of the addicts are in the duration of less than 12 months and beyond 60 months. Together, these two durations account for 63.75 percent of the addicts (Table 5.9). The proportion of addicts in other durations varies from 7.08 percent (48 to 60 months) to 11.67 percent (23 to 46 months). Among the various drugs, the proportion of addicts falling in the duration up to 12 months, ranges from 18.75 percent (marijuana) to 77.78 percent (poppy husk). In the case of 12 to 24 months duration, the proportion varies from 5.26 percent (hashish) to 42.86 percent (opium). In the case of 24 to 36 months' duration, the proportion of addicts addicted to various drugs ranges between 7.02 percent (hashish) to 21 percent (heroin). The corresponding proportion for 36 to 48 months varies from 2.63 percent (heroin) to 16.67 percent (tramadol). For 48 to 60 months duration, the proportion of addicts varies from 5.26 percent (hashish) to 12.5 percent (marijuana). Beyond 60 months, the proportion of

*Table 5.9* Duration of addiction to various drugs in Himachal Pradesh (months)

| *Sr. No.* | *Drug/Duration* ↓ → | *up to 12* | *12–24* | *24–36* | *36–48* | *48–60* | *Above 60* | *Total* |
|---|---|---|---|---|---|---|---|---|
| 1. | Heroin | 16 (42.11) | 05 (13.16) | 08 (21.05) | 01 (2.63) | 03 (7.89) | 05 (13.16) | 38 (100) |
| 2. | Opium | 03 (42.86) | 03 (42.86) | 01 (14.29) | – | – | – | 07 (100) |
| 3. | Tramadol | 04 (66.67) | – | 01 (16.67) | 01 (16.67) | – | – | 06 (100) |
| 4. | Poppy Husk | 07 (77.78) | 01 (11.11) | 01 (11.11) | – | – | – | 09 (100) |
| 5. | Cannabis/ Bhang/Sukha | 25 (27.17) | 07 (7.61) | 09 (9.78) | 09 (9.78) | 09 (9.78) | 33 (35.87) | 92 (100) |
| 6. | Marijuana/ Ganja/Smack | 03 (18.75) | 03 (18.75) | 02 (12.50) | 02 (12.50) | 02 (12.50) | 04 (25.00) | 16 (100) |
| 7. | Cocaine | 11 (73.33) | 01 (6.67) | 02 (13.33) | 01 (6.67) | – | – | 15 (100) |
| 8. | Hashish/ Charas | 10 (17.54) | 03 (5.26) | 04 (7.02) | 05 (8.78) | 03 (5.26) | 32 (56.14) | 57 (100) |
| Total | | 79 (39.92) | 23 (9.58) | 28 (11.67) | 19 (7.92) | 17 (7.08) | 74 (30.83) | 240 (100) |

addicts to various drugs ranges between 13.16 percent (heroin) to 56.14 percent (hashish). As compared to Punjab and Haryana, the use of a number of drugs is almost missing in H.P. The proportion of addicts in some durations and addiction to certain drugs is also very low as compared to Punjab and Haryana. This may mainly be due to locally available drugs.

The situation is not much different in J&K as far as the duration of addiction to various drugs is concerned. Like other states, the proportion of addicts in duration up to 12 months (34.81 percent) and beyond 60 months (22.84 percent) is higher than other time-periods. The proportion of addicts in 12 to 24 months duration is 18.63 percent, in 24 to 36 months 11.09 percent, and in 36 to 48 months 8.87 percent. The corresponding proportion in 48 to 60 months duration is 3.77 percent. Beyond 60 months, the proportion is 22.84 percent. Amongst various drugs, the proportion of addicts to different drugs and different duration varies a lot (Table 5.10). Prevalence of addiction up to 12 months is highest (66.67 percent) for Buprenorphine, followed by codeine (51.43 percent), cannabis (45.45 percent), poppy husk (43.45 percent), marijuana (41.86 percent), opium (35.56 percent) and heroin (31.08 percent). Clearly, the duration to all these drugs is not very old but reveals quite a high preference of addicts for these drugs. In the 12 to 24 months duration, heroin has 28.38 percent of addicts followed by opium and poppy husk, opium, marijuana and codeine. The highest proportion of addicts in the 24 to 36 months duration is for marijuana (23.26 percent). It is followed by heroin (14.86 percent), poppy husk (14.58 percent), cannabis

*Table 5.10* Duration of addiction to various drugs in Jammu and Kashmir (months)

| *Sr. No.* | *Drug/Duration* ↓ → | *Up to 12* | *12–24* | *24–36* | *36–48* | *48–60* | *Above 60* | *Total* |
|---|---|---|---|---|---|---|---|---|
| 1. | Heroin | 23 (31.08) | 21 (28.38) | 11 (14.86) | 08 (10.81) | 06 (8.11) | 05 (6.76) | 74 (100) |
| 2. | Opium | 16 (35.56) | 09 (20.0) | 04 (8.89) | 09 (20.0) | 03 (6.67) | 04 (8.89) | 45 (100) |
| 3. | Tramadol | 18 (51.43) | 06 (17.14) | 2 (5.71) | 03 (8.57) | 0.1 (2.81) | 05 (14.29) | 35 (100) |
| 4. | Poppy Husk | 21 (43.75) | 10 (20.83) | 07 (14.58) | 05 (10.42) | 0 (0.00) | 05 (10.42) | 48 (100) |
| 5. | Cannabis/ Bhang/Sukha | 30 (45.45) | 10 (15.15) | 08 (12.12) | 05 (7.58) | 02 (3.03) | 11 (16.67) | 66 (100) |
| 6. | Marijuana/ Ganja/Smack | 18 (41.86) | 08 (18.60) | 10 (23.26) | 05 (11.63) | 01 (2.33) | 01 (2.33) | 43 (100) |
| 7. | Buprenorphine | 12 (66.67) | 02 (11.11) | – | – | 01 (5.56) | 03 (16.67) | 18 (100) |
| 8. | Cocaine | 06 (10.0) | 01 (1.67) | – | – | – | 53 (88.33) | 60 (100) |
| 9. | Hashish/Charas | 13 (20.97) | 17 (27.42) | 08 (12.90) | 05 (8.06) | 03 (4.84) | 16 (25.81) | 62 (100) |
| Total | | 157 (34.81) | 84 (18.63) | 50 (11.09) | 40 (8.87) | 17 (3.77) | 103 (22.84) | 451 (100) |

(12.12 percent) and opium (8.89 percent). In the next higher duration (36 to 48 months) the highest proportion of addicts is for opium (20 percent) followed by marijuana (11.63 percent), heroin (10.81 percent), poppy husk (10.42 percent), codeine (8.57 percent) and cannabis (7.58 percent). In the 48 to 60 months duration, the proportion of addicts addicted to heroin is highest (8.11 percent). It is followed by opium and Buprenorphine. Beyond 60 months' duration of addiction, 88.33 percent of addicts are addicted to cocaine, followed by hashish, cannabis, Buprenorphine, codeine, poppy husk and opium and heroin (Table 5.10).

Rajasthan also presents the highest share of addicts for the duration of addiction up to 12 months (46.36 percent) (Table 5.11). It is followed by 21.84 percent in the duration of beyond 60 months and 14.18 percent in 12 to 24 months duration. The proportion of addicts in other three durations varies from 4.60 percent (48 to 60 months) and 6.90 percent (24 to 36 months). Amongst different drugs, cannabis (with the exception of hashish) accounts for 78.13 percent of addicts in up to 12 months' category of addiction. It is followed by Buprenorphine (62.50 percent), tramadol (53.66 percent), heroin (47.83 percent), opium (40.82 percent), marijuana (34.48 percent) and poppy husk (23.73 percent). In the 12 to 24 months duration, the highest proportion is for addiction to marijuana (27.59 percent). It is followed by opium (18.37 percent), Buprenorphine (16.67 percent), tramadol (14.63 percent) and heroin (13.04 percent). Buprenorphine accounts for the highest

*Table 5.11* Duration of addiction to various drugs in Rajasthan (months)

| *Sr. No.* | *Drug/Duration* ↓ → | *Up to 12* | *12–24* | *24–36* | *36–48* | *48–60* | *Above 60* | *Total* |
|---|---|---|---|---|---|---|---|---|
| 1. | Heroin | 11 (47.83) | 03 (13.04) | 02 (8.70) | 03 (13.04) | 01 (4.35) | 03 (13.04) | 23 (100) |
| 2. | Opium | 20 (40.82) | 09 (18.37) | 02 (4.08) | 02 (4.08) | 03 (6.12) | 13 (26.53) | 49 (100) |
| 3. | Tramadol | 22 (53.66) | 06 (14.63) | 01 (2.44) | 08 (19.51) | 02 (4.88) | 02 (4.88) | 41 (100) |
| 4. | Poppy Husk | 14 (23.73) | 04 (6.78) | 04 (6.78) | 02 (3.39) | 04 (6.78) | 31 (52.54) | 59 (100) |
| 5. | Cannabis/ Bhang/Sukha | 25 (78.13) | 03 (9.38) | 01 (3.13) | 0 (0.00) | 01 (3.13) | 02 (6.25) | 32 (100) |
| 6. | Marijuana/ Ganja/Smack | 10 (34.48) | 08 (27.59) | 02 (6.90) | 02 (6.90) | 01 (3.44) | 06 (20.69) | 29 (100) |
| 7. | Buprenorphine | 15 (62.50) | 04 (16.67) | 04 (16.67) | 01 (4.17) | – | – | 24 (100) |
| 8. | Hashish/ Charas | 04 (100) | – | – | – | – | – | 04 (100) |
| Total | | 121 (46.36) | 37 (14.18) | 16 (6.13) | 18 (16.90) | 12 (4.60) | 57 (21.84) | 261 (100) |

proportion of addicts (16.67 percent) in 24 to 36 months' addiction. It is followed by heroin (8.70 percent), marijuana (6.90 percent) and poppy husk (6.67 percent). In the 36 to 48 months duration, the highest proportion is for tramadol (19.51 percent), followed by 13.04 percent for heroin, 6.9 percent for marijuana and 4.08 percent for opium. It ranges from 3.13 percent for cannabis to 6.78 percent for poppy husk in the 48 to 60 months duration. In the addiction beyond 60 months duration, 52.54 percent of addicts are for poppy husk, followed by 26.53 percent of addicts for opium. It is followed by marijuana (20.69 percent), 13.04 percent for heroin, 6.25 percent for cannabis and 4.88 percent for tramadol.

It is evident from the foregoing discussion that most of the commonly used drugs are chemically prepared synthetic drugs (mostly opioids), but natural drugs are also in use. These drugs are being mainly supplied by peddlers, followed by 'friends' of the addicts and chemists. Oral consumption, inhaling and injections are the major modes of drug consumption. The addicts mainly use drugs for pleasure, relaxing and getting energy. Despite getting treatment at drug de-addiction centres and rehabilitation centres, the incidence of relapsing is very high; almost two-thirds of de-addicted persons again get back to the use of drugs, mainly because of peer pressure and out of curiosity. Significantly, the incidence of relapsing is higher among the addicts with a longer duration of drug consumption. It necessitates that the concerned agencies and stakeholders will have to be pro-active in dealing with the problem of drug addiction and abuse. They will have to follow the proverbial phrase 'catch them young' and 'nip the evil in the bud,' otherwise, as the duration of addiction increases, it becomes more and more difficult to help the addicts in de-addiction and rehabilitation. Ironically, the drug-smugglers follow the policy of 'catch them young,' i.e., they invariably focus on the teenagers. Paradoxically, the government and its agencies, including political parties, do not get sensitised to the issues until and unless they take the form of a menace, and the same is applicable to the drug menace. The political parties are generally interested in keeping the issue alive rather than finding a durable solution.

Significantly, at the time of survey, a very high proportion of addicts were in drug consumption for less than 12 months. However, this varied from state to state. Addiction to various drugs also varied from state to state. In Punjab, heroin, opium, tramadol, poppy husk and marijuana were the major drugs being used for the last (at the time of survey) 60 months. In Haryana, opium, poppy husk, tramadol, cannabis and heroin were the main drugs in such a category. In Himachal Pradesh cannabis (bhang), hashish and heroin were the main drugs being used for a long time. Heroin, cannabis, cocaine, poppy husk, opium and marijuana were the major drugs in this category. In Rajasthan, poppy husk, opium, tramadol, cannabis, marijuana and heroin were the main drugs in this category. Pharmaceuticals and synthetic drugs account for a large share of the drugs.

# 6 Socio-economic costs of drug addiction and abuse

Drug addiction and abuse is a very complex and multidimensional socio-cultural problem and has multi-pronged socio-economic implications and repercussions for the individual as well as for society, the economy and polity. Nobody is immune to the adverse effects of drug addiction and abuse. As a matter of fact, the cost of drug addiction and abuse is reflected in the economic, social, health-care and law-enforcement burden of the community and on the country's natural and financial resources. Being a social problem, drug addiction is every individual's problem, which often impacts the psyche of the addict and has serious ramifications for the addict's family, society and the economy. Many times, addiction and abuse inculcate a feeling of guilt, inability and incapacitation in the mind of the drug addict. This, in turn, has an adverse impact on the addict to lead a healthy and full life which is very unfortunate for the family, society and economy. This, in turn, impairs the self-esteem and dignity of the addict as well as the family and household members. Widespread drug use and abuse also puts an uncalled-for financial burden on law and order, governance and prisons. Thus, addiction is a potential social disease that affects all aspects of a person's life as well as that of society, the economy and polity. Even the social cost of drug addiction and abuse has implications for economic costs and vice-versa. In fact, drug addiction and abuse is a serious drag on socio-cultural and economic development. As a matter of fact, the drug menace anywhere is a threat to socio-cultural and politico-economic stability everywhere (global narco-terrorism is a stark example), just as poverty anywhere is a threat to prosperity everywhere.

The broad objective of this chapter, however, is to discuss various aspects of the social and economic costs of drug addiction, both for the family of the addict and society as a whole. The social cost of drug addiction manifests in terms of social evils which arise due to drug addiction and abuse and threatens peace and harmony in the family as well as in society. Further, it affects the family of the drug addict as addiction not only disturbs the addict's personal life but also negatively impacts the education of addicts' children and overall social image and well-being of the family in the form of broken/constrained relations with relatives and friends. Besides the social

DOI: 10.4324/9781003318019-6

cost, drug addiction also has immense economic costs for the family, society and the country. Economic costs of drug addiction are visible in the form of spending on drug consumption, loss of earnings, expenditure on treatment, loss of productive life, and an adverse impact on work, etc. However, the entire social costs cannot be measured in monetary terms. Nonetheless, it is a drag on finances and slows downs the overall growth and development of the family. It is also not possible to quantify the total economic cost of drug addiction and abuse as it has multi-pronged dimensions which relate to the future economic potentialities of the addict, his/her family members and his/her children, though some researchers have tried to generate crude estimates.

We have tried to measure the social and economic costs of drug addiction by using a series of indicators, including loss of business, work-life, education, spending on drug addiction, spending on treatment, repercussions for the addicts in various ways, etc. These issues have been discussed and analysed from the perspective of both drug addicts and their families. All issues have been segregated under the following broad heads: the first part outlines the discussion on the social costs of drug addiction and abuse for the drug addicts, family and society. The second part of the chapter focuses on the economic costs of drug addiction and abuse for the economy, society and for the drug addicts. The third part aims at discussing the issues which have both social and economic repercussions.

## 6.1 Social costs for addicts' households

The social costs of drug addiction can be defined in terms of its negative implications for the peace and harmony of the society on the one hand and family-life disturbances in terms of violence in the family, intra-family trust deficiency, loss of social status of the family, self-esteem of the family and the addict, health problems of the drug addict, impact on the life of drug addicts' children and so on. Many times it ruins the family. Such social costs may have long-lasting implications for the social and economic development of the individual household and the country. Any kind of violence can derail the socio-economic development of the family, just like the economy gets derailed from the development path by disturbances in the country. In this context, it is critical to understand various forms of social costs for drug addicts, family and society as a whole. The total estimation and quantification of the social impact and the cost of the drug menace may not be possible but some crude qualitative impacts can be captured.

The adverse impact of drug addiction on the family's image is the most serious effect, as the family's self-esteem is very important for socio-economic development. Often it casts its shadow on the matrimonial prospects of the children. In many cases, during our empirical work and case studies, we observed that the adverse social impact transits from one generation to the next. As per the data, 72.53 percent of the drug addicts' households revealed

*Table 6.1* Social impact on addicts' households

| *State→* *Impact↓* | *Punjab* | *Haryana* | *H.P.* | *J&K* | *Rajasthan* | *Total* |
|---|---|---|---|---|---|---|
| Loss of social image | 396 (72.0) | 85 (85.0) | 65 (65.0) | 75 (75.0) | 68 (68.0) | 689 (72.53) |
| Social isolation | 154 (28.0) | 15 (15.0) | 35 (35.0) | 25 (25.0) | 32 (32.0) | 261 (27.47) |
| Total | 550 (100) | 100 (100) | 100 (100) | 100 (100) | 100 (100) | 950 (100) |

*Source*: Field survey.

*Note:* Figures in brackets indicate percentage share. This is applicable to all the tables in this chapter unless mentioned otherwise.

that they are suffering from deterioration in their social-image due to the drug addiction of the family member(s). Across states, it varies between 65 percent and 85 percent (Table 6.1). The remaining 27.47 percent of households shared that they are undergoing social isolation because of the drug addiction of their family members. Across states, it varies between 15 percent and 32 percent. As a matter of fact, the household members of the addicts are the victim of both types of adverse effects of drug addiction. It was revealed by a majority of the unmarried addicts' parents that they were finding it difficult to find a suitable match for their addicted son with a variety of social repercussions for the family. It has even adversely impacted the matrimonial prospects of other unmarried siblings of the addict. Such treatment by society is causing immense tension in the households, which, in turn, is resulting in numerous intra-family social tensions and often disturbs the mental balance of the family members. The drug addiction in the family is a drag on other family members' time, capabilities and economic productivity.

### 6.1.1 *Adverse impact on health of addicts as revealed by the household members*

There is immense social cost of drug addiction and abuse in terms of adverse impact on the health of the drug addicts, which, in turn, impacts an addict's capacity to lead a healthy life and reap the full benefits of the productive years of their life-cycle. An adverse impact on health has social as well as economic costs. Often, it leads to many serious ailments, including psychological, functional and structural alterations in an individual's brain. According to psychologists and medical experts, drug addiction is a mental disease, and, hence, the addict needs to be treated as a patient. Serious ailments such as HIV, hepatitis A and hepatitis C have other major adverse impacts on the addict's health (Institute for Social Development Studies, n.d.). Depression, anxiety, panic disorders, aggression, hallucinations and paranoia are other ill effects of drug addiction and abuse. The premature death caused by such ailments has both social and economic ramifications for the parents, wife and children. The potential social and economic loss due to premature death can never be truly monetised as it is just not possible to gauge the socio-economic potentialities of a prematurely dead person. The first and foremost victims of such happenings are addicts' parents and siblings. In fact, adverse consequences of drug addiction impact the behaviour pattern of three generations: parents, self and children of the addicts. Their very initiative in life gets severely beaten up by the addict's behaviour and conduct. If the addict is married and has children, then both his/her spouse and children are the most serious sufferers, and it is just not possible to estimate their future potential contribution to the family, society and economy.

The addict is a patient and needs to be treated as a patient. Table 6.2 reveals the health impact as revealed by the household members. More than 35 percent of the respondents said that their addict family members, mainly son(s), are suffering from serious physical ailments. Across states, it varies from 32 percent (Punjab) to 43 percent (Haryana). About 32 percent of respondents said that their addict members are suffering from mental ailments. Across states, it ranges between 30 percent (H.P.) and 34 percent (Haryana). Besides, 33.16 percent of the respondents revealed that the addicts are suffering from various other ailments. Across states, it varies from 23 percent (Haryana) and 37 percent in Punjab. It is clear that the addicts are suffering from various types of ailments which are causing immense pain to the family members besides putting a heavy financial burden on the family. In fact, the families are suffering from a double whammy: economic loss and additional financial burden. They are losing the earnings/productivity of the addicted members as well as what is spent on their daily drug doses and health issues. Even the productivity of the family members is negatively impacted as they have to attend to the addict at the cost of their health and productivity.

*Table 6.2* Impact on health of addicts

| *State→*<br>*Impact↓* | *Punjab* | *Haryana* | *H.P.* | *J&K* | *Rajasthan* | *Total* |
|---|---|---|---|---|---|---|
| Physical ailment | 177<br>(32.18) | 43<br>(43.0) | 36<br>(36.0) | 38<br>(38.0) | 41<br>(41.0) | 335<br>(35.36) |
| Mental ailment | 168<br>(30.55) | 34<br>(34.0) | 30<br>(30.0) | 35<br>(35.0) | 33<br>(33.0) | 300<br>(31.58) |
| Other impacts* | 205<br>(37.27) | 23<br>(23.0) | 34<br>(34.0) | 27<br>(27.0) | 26<br>(26.0) | 315<br>(33.16) |
| Total | 550<br>(100) | 100 | 100 | 100 | 100 | 950<br>(100) |

* Physical as well as mental ailments.

It is significant to mention that drug addiction in itself is a serious mental ailment that leads to multiple physical ailments. All this eventually adversely impacts the physical and mental health of other members of the household and family.

### *6.1.2 Adverse impact on addicts' relations with household members*

The adverse impact of addiction is not only confined to social image and health issues; it has multi-pronged social repercussions for the addict's relation with the other members in the household, especially within the nuclear family. Unfortunately, a distressed and helpless mother had to tie her 23-year-old son (addicted to drugs for over six years) with iron chains just to prevent him from taking drugs (The Tribune, July 4, 2022). Perhaps, we simply cannot imagine how painful it would have been for that hapless mother. There are numerous tragic stories of young wives who divorced their drug-addict husbands, even leaving behind young children.

Some such implications and repercussions have been presented in Table 6.3. Distrust and suspicion within family members, quarrels and emotional distress are some of the main ramifications for the intra-family relations. There were 2,006 responses by 1,140 respondents revealing various types of problems that had surfaced among the family members. More than 83 percent of the respondents revealed that there is a serious trust-deficit for the addict (Table 6.3). Nobody in the family trusts the addict and loss of trust is a serious social problem as mutual trust is the substrate of all social relations. Across states, between 75 percent (Haryana) 87 percent (Rajasthan) respondents revealed trust-loss of the addict. Quarrel in the family is the

*Table 6.3* Adverse impact on addicts' family relations

| *State→*<br>*Impact↓* | *Punjab* | *Haryana* | *H.P.* | *J&K* | *Rajasthan* | *Total* |
|---|---|---|---|---|---|---|
| Mistrust | 518<br>(78.48) | 90<br>(75.0) | 100<br>(83.33) | 100<br>(83.33) | 103<br>(86.67) | 911<br>(82.52) |
| Quarrel | 341<br>(51.67) | 70<br>(58.33) | 21<br>(17.50) | 52<br>(43.33) | 70<br>(58.33) | 554<br>(48.60) |
| Emotional distress | 211<br>(31.97) | 19<br>(15.83) | 15<br>(12.50) | 57<br>(47.50) | 33<br>(27.50) | 335<br>(29.39) |
| Broken marital relations | 55<br>(8.33) | 21<br>(17.50) | 07<br>(5.83) | 03<br>(2.50) | 19<br>(15.83) | 105<br>(9.21) |
| Impact on children* | 45<br>(6.82) | 16<br>(13.33) | 02<br>(1.67) | 11<br>(9.17) | 27<br>(22.50) | 101<br>(8.86) |
| Total respondents | 660<br>(100) | 120<br>(100) | 120<br>(100) | 120<br>(100) | 120<br>(100) | 1,140<br>(100) |
| Total responses | 1170<br>(177.3) | 216<br>(180.0) | 145<br>(120.8) | 223<br>(185.8) | 252<br>(210.0) | 2,006<br>(175.96) |

* Education, psychological, etc.

next in order as 48.6 percent of the respondents said that, due to the drug addiction, there are frequent incidents of quarrels with the addict and family members. Across states, this proportion varies from 44.33 percent in J&K to 58.33 percent in Haryana and Rajasthan. H.P. is an exception with 17.5 percent. Another 29.39 percent of the respondents shared that drug addiction by the family member(s) is a cause of psychological and emotional distress and disturbance among the family members. Across states, it varies from 27.5 percent in Rajasthan to 47.56 percent in J&K. In H.P. and Haryana this proportion is quite low. Broken marital relations are also told by 9.21 percent of respondents. Across states, this proportion varies from 2.5 percent in J&K to 17.5 percent in Haryana. Children of married addicts are also suffering from adverse impacts in terms of their loss of childhood, education and life, according to 8.86 percent of the respondents. Across states, the proportion varies from 6.82 percent in Punjab to 22.5 percent in Rajasthan; H.P. has the lowest proportion (.167 percent) in this category. Significantly, every respondent had 1.76 percent responses of various adverse impacts for the family members. This means that the addict and his/her family members are victims of multiple issues because of the problem of drug addiction in the family.

## 6.2 Repercussion of addiction for drug addicts as revealed by the addicts

Besides health and relationship issues, the addicts get entangled in a number of anti-social activities. However, health issues of the addict and other family members have emerged as the main issue as told by the addicts. About 50 percent of respondents (addicts) revealed that they are suffering from multiple health issues because of their habit of drug addiction and abuse (Table 6.4). The proportion is highest (56.97 percent) in Punjab; followed by Haryana (49.17 percent), then H.P., J&K and Rajasthan (35 percent). Drug-induced violence in the home is another serious fall out of addiction. Nearly 24 percent of the respondents revealed that because of their drug addiction and abuse, there are often violent incidences (both by them and sometimes by the family members as a reaction). Asking for money for purchase of drugs and creating social problems are the main reasons for violence in the family. Across states, this proportion varies from 15.83 percent in J&K to 28.33 percent in H.P. Arrest by the police owing to anti-social and illegal activities by the addict has also been reported by 15 percent of the respondents. Across states, the proportion ranges between 13.64 percent in Punjab and 20.83 percent in H.P. However, conviction and imprisonment has been reported by 9.3 percent of the respondents. Across states, this proportion varies between 5 percent in Rajasthan and 10.91 percent in Punjab. Drug peddling (mainly to arrange doses and/or earn some money) has also been reported by 7.89 percent of the respondents, varying from 5 percent in Haryana to 10 percent in J&K. Nearly 7 percent of the respondents revealed that

*Table 6.4* Repercussions for drug addicts

| *State→* *Repercussion↓* | *Punjab* | *Haryana* | *H.P.* | *J&K* | *Rajasthan* | *Total* |
|---|---|---|---|---|---|---|
| Health issues | 376 (56.97) | 59 (49.17) | 57 (47.50) | 38 (31.67) | 42 (35.00) | 571 (50.09) |
| Violence at home | 166 (25.15) | 32 (26.67) | 34 (28.33) | 19 (15.83) | 23 (19.17) | 274 (24.04) |
| Arrest by police | 90 (13.64) | 21 (17.50) | 25 (20.83) | 18 (15.00) | 17 (14.17) | 171 (15.0) |
| Conviction and imprisonment | 72 (10.91) | 11 (9.17) | 11 (9.17) | 07 (5.83) | 06 (5.00) | 106 (9.30) |
| Drug peddling | 51 (7.71) | 06 (5.00) | 11 (9.17) | 12 (10.00) | 10 (8.33) | 90 (7.89) |
| Theft | 39 (5.91) | 09 (7.50) | 10 (8.33) | 07 (5.83) | 11 (9.17) | 76 (6.67) |
| Other ill effects | 130 (19.70) | 13 (10.83) | 15 (12.50) | 24 (20.00) | 20 (16.67) | 202 (17.72) |
| Total respondents | 660 (100) | 120 (100) | 120 (100) | 120 (100) | 120 (100) | 1,140 (100) |
| Total responses | 924 (140) | 151 (125.83) | 167 (139.17) | 124 (103.33) | 129 (107.50) | 1,495 (131.14) |

they have been involved in theft to meet the expenses of drug purchasing. Across states, this proportion varies from 5.83 percent in J&K to 8.33 percent in H.P. Besides, 17.72 percent of the respondents admitted their involvement in other anti-social and illegal activities. Significantly, all the 1,140 respondents came up with 1,495 responses, implying that the addicts are engaged in more than one uncalled-for activity owing to their drug addiction and abuse.

### 6.2.1 *Impact of addiction on the addict's personal life as revealed by addicts*

The habit of drug addiction and abuse causes a serious (often irreparable) personal loss to the addict in terms of self-image, work, and family-life as well as studies (Table 6.5). Out of all the 1,140 respondents, 78.42 percent admitted an adverse impact of drug addiction on their personal image in society. Across states, this proportion varies from 68.33 percent in J&K, 91.67 percent in H.P., 90.45 percent in Punjab, 45 percent in Haryana and 42.5 percent in Rajasthan. 30.35 percent of respondents admitted that they are suffering from image loss (also in terms of relations) in the neighbourhood and in friend circles. This proportion varies from 11.67 percent in Rajasthan to 39.39 percent in Punjab. An adverse impact of addiction on work has been admitted by 63.77 percent of the respondents, varying from 54.17 percent in J&K to 67.5 percent in H.P. Disturbance in family life (many times leading

*Table 6.5* Adverse impact of addiction on addicts' personal life

| *State→*<br>*Impact↓* | *Punjab* | *Haryana* | *H.P.* | *J&K* | *Rajasthan* | *Total* |
|---|---|---|---|---|---|---|
| Self-image | 597<br>(90.45) | 54<br>(45.0) | 110<br>(91.67) | 82<br>(68.33) | 51<br>(42.5) | 894<br>(78.42) |
| Work life | 426<br>(64.55) | 77<br>(64.17) | 81<br>(67.5) | 65<br>(54.17) | 78<br>(65.00) | 727<br>(63.77) |
| Family life | 496<br>(75.15) | 61<br>(50.83) | 76<br>(63.90) | 74<br>(61.67) | 44<br>(36.67) | 751<br>(65.00) |
| Studies | 79<br>(11.97) | 30<br>(25.00) | 22<br>(18.33) | 30<br>(25.00) | 13<br>(10.83) | 174<br>(15.26) |
| Neighborhood and friends | 260<br>(39.39) | 21<br>(17.50) | 20<br>(16.67) | 31<br>(25.83) | 14<br>(11.67) | 346<br>(30.35) |
| Total respondents | 660<br>(100) | 120<br>(100) | 120<br>(100) | 120<br>(100) | 120<br>(100) | 1,140<br>(100) |
| Total responses | 1,858<br>(281.52) | 243<br>(202.5) | 309<br>(257.5) | 282<br>(235.0) | 200<br>(166.67) | 2,892<br>(253.68) |

to serious consequences, even leading to constrained matrimonial relations and emotional disturbance to children) has been reported by 65.88 percent of the respondents. Across states, this proportion varies from 36.67 percent in Rajasthan to 75.15 percent in Punjab. An adverse impact on studies (according to those who are students) has also been revealed by 15.26 percent of the respondents. Across states, it varies from 11 percent in Rajasthan to 25 percent in Haryana and J&K. Significantly, the addicts, on average, are suffering on more than two counts as 1,140 respondents revealed 2,892 (2.54 times) responses (Table 6.5).

### 6.2.2 *Social cost in terms of social and emotional support to addicts as revealed by the addicts*

Parents, siblings and relatives of the addicts have to bear an uncalculated social cost in terms of lending social and emotional support to their addict family member(s). To analyse this issue, we classified the addicts into two groups: married and unmarried. It was found that the parents of the addict are the main source of social support. Table 6.6 shows that 76.51 percent of the married addicts are banking on their parents for social and emotional support. Compared to this, 23.49 percent of respondents revealed that they draw such support from their siblings and relatives, including wives. Across states, the proportion of respondents banking upon parental support varies from 66.25 percent in Rajasthan to 97.92 percent in J&K. The proportion in the case of support by siblings and relatives ranges between 2.08 percent in J&K to 33.75 percent in Rajasthan. In the case of unmarried addicts, the data shows that they are getting social and emotional support from their parents.

*Table 6.6* Social and emotional support to addicts

| *State→* *Source of support↓* | *Punjab* | *Haryana* | *H.P.* | *J&K* | *Rajasthan* | *Total* |
|---|---|---|---|---|---|---|
| Married addicts (579) | | | | | | |
| Parents | 255 (75.0) | 41 (71.93) | 47 (87.04) | 47 (97.92) | 53 (66.25) | 443 (76.51) |
| Siblings, wives and other relatives | 85 (25.0) | 16 (28.07) | 07 (12.96) | 01 (2.08) | 27 (33.75) | 136 (23.49) |
| Total | 340 (100) | 57 (100) | 54 (100) | 48 (100) | 80 (100) | 579 (100) |
| Unmarried Addicts (561) | | | | | | |
| Parents | 320 | 63 | 66 | 72 | 40 | 561 |
| Grand Total | 660 | 120 | 120 | 120 | 120 | 1140 |
| % age of married | 51.52 | 47.50 | 45.0 | 40.0 | 66.67 | 50.79 |
| % age of unmarried | 48.48 | 52.50 | 55.0 | 60.0 | 33.33 | 49.21 |

## 6.3 Economic cost of drug addiction and abuse as revealed by addicts

The calculation and estimation of the economic cost of drug addiction and abuse is a complex phenomenon. However, we have tried to lay our hands on some of the factors which can give some idea of the economic cost of drug addiction and abuse. These are mainly the daily expenses of purchasing drugs by the addicts, expenditures on treatment, premature deaths and sources of money for the purchase of drugs and treatment. The age group of the premature deaths is another major economic cost for the family, society and the economy. It was found during the survey that more than 97 percent of addicts experienced financial loss due to their habit of drug addiction and abuse.

### *6.3.1 Expenses on drugs and treatment as revealed by the addicts*

Mainly two types of expenses, purchase of drugs and treatment, have been studied by us, though there are some other expenditure heads. We have not studied expenditure on rehabilitation, but we have taken into account the expenses incurred by the addicts and their family members in de-addiction and rehabilitation centres. As a matter of fact, the effective mechanism and process of rehabilitation is almost missing in all the states under study.

#### *Expenses on drugs*

Table 6.7 presents the expenses on purchase of drugs by the addicts. 34.74 percent of addicts were spending (at the time of survey) up to Rs. 200

*Table 6.7* Average daily expenditure on drugs

| *State→* *Expenditure↓* *(Rs.)* | *Punjab* | *Haryana* | *H.P.* | *J&K* | *Rajasthan* | *Total* |
|---|---|---|---|---|---|---|
| up to 200 | 186 (28.18) | 53 (44.17) | 63 (52.5) | 19 (15.83) | 75 (62.5) | 396 (34.74) |
| 200–400 | 64 (9.70) | 18 (15.0) | 15 (12.50) | 19 (15.83) | 14 (11.67) | 130 (11.40) |
| 400–600 | 75 (11.36) | 13 (10.83) | 09 (7.50) | 18 (15.0) | 08 (6.67) | 123 (10.79) |
| 600–800 | 59 (8.94) | 06 (5.0) | 06 (5.0) | 13 (10.83) | 01 (0.83) | 85 (7.46) |
| 800–1,000 | 118 (17.88) | 07 (5.83) | 08 (6.67) | 17 (14.17) | 8 (6.67) | 158 (13.86) |
| 1,000–2,000 | 114 (17.27) | 11 (9.17) | 14 (11.67) | 19 (15.83) | 08 (6.67) | 166 (14.56) |
| 2,000 and above | 44 (6.67) | 12 (10.0) | 05 (4.17) | 15 (12.50) | 06 (5.0) | 82 (7.19) |
| Total respondents | 660 (100) | 120 (100) | 120 (100) | 120 (100) | 120 (100) | 1,140 (100) |

to have their daily dose of drugs. Across states, this proportion varies between 15.83 percent in J&K to 62.5 percent in Rajasthan. Another 11.4 percent of the addicts were spending between Rs. 200–400 a day to have their daily dose of drug. It ranges from 9.7 percent in Punjab to 15.83 percent in J&K and to 62.5 percent in Rajasthan. 10.79 percent of addicts were spending between Rs. 400–600 per day, on average, on their daily dose of drugs. Across states, the proportion varies from 6.67 percent in Rajasthan to 11.36 percent in Punjab. In the range of Rs. 600–800 for a daily expenditure on drugs, the proportion of addicts is 7.46 percent. Barring Rajasthan, this proportion varies from 5 percent in H.P. and Haryana to 10.83 percent in J&K.

The proportion of addicts spending Rs. 800–1,000 on their daily dose is 13.86 percent, ranging from 5.83 percent in Haryana to 17.88 percent in Punjab. 14.56 percent of addicts were spending between Rs. 1,000–2,000 to purchase their daily dose of drugs. The proportion varies from 6.67 percent in Rajasthan to 17.27 percent in Punjab. There were 7.19 percent of addicts spending above Rs. 2,000 to get their daily dose. Across states, the proportion varies from 4.17 percent in H.P. to 12.5 percent in J&K. The data reveals that, as we move towards a higher range of expenditure, the proportion of addicts was higher in Punjab but for the expenditure exceeding Rs. 2,000. This can mainly be attributed to the consumption of costly (synthetic and heroin) drugs. Punjab also figures high in the higher range of peak daily expenses on purchase of a daily dose of drugs. The annual estimates of expenditure on the purchase of drugs can be generated from the previously stated figures; the longer the duration of addiction the higher would be the expenses. Similarly, costly drugs like heroin costs more than the other drugs.

*Table 6.8* Expenditure on treatment of addicts

| *State→* *Expenditure↓ (Rs.)* | *Punjab* | *Haryana* | *H.P.* | *J&K* | *Rajasthan* | *Total* |
|---|---|---|---|---|---|---|
| Up to 5,000 | 180 (32.83) | 45 | 15 | 41 | 34 | 315 (33.16) |
| 5,000–20,000 | 150 (27.27) | 21 | 20 | 30 | 37 | 258 (27.16) |
| 20,000–60,000 | 146 (26.55) | 18 | 47 | 23 | 20 | 254 (26.74) |
| 60,000–100,000 | 48 (8.73) | 06 | 14 | 02 | 05 | 75 (7.89) |
| 100,000–200,000 | 26 (4.73) | 10 | 04 | 04 | 04 | 48 (5.05) |
| Total respondents | 550 (100) | 100 | 100 | 100 | 100 | 950 (100) |

*Expenses on treatment of addicts as revealed by the addicts*

In this section we have tried to focus on the average expenses of treatment (mainly on de-addiction) of the addicts. In all, there were 950 addicts (respondents) as 190 hidden addicts have not been taken into account as they are not undergoing any treatment. The average per addict expenditure on treatment ranges from Rs. 5,000 to Rs. 2 lakh (Table 6.8).

On an average, more than 60 percent of the addicts have spent up to Rs. 20,000 on their treatment. Out of them, 33.16 percent spent up to Rs. 5,000, mainly in government run de-addiction and rehabilitation centres. Across states, it ranges from 32.73 percent in Punjab to 45 percent in Haryana. The proportion is just 15 percent in H.P. Another 27.16 percent of addicts spent between Rs. 5,000–20,000 on treatment. The proportion across states varies between 20 percent in H.P. to 37 percent in Rajasthan. At the aggregate level, 26.74 percent of addicts spent Rs. 20,000–60,000 on treatment, ranging from 18 percent in Haryana to 26.55 percent in Punjab. The proportion of addicts who spent between Rs. 60,000–100,000 is 7.89 percent at the aggregate level. Across states, it ranges between 2 percent in J&K and 14 percent in H.P. Only 5 percent of addicts spent between Rs. 100,000–2 00,000, on average, on treatment, ranging from 4 percent and 10 percent across states. The higher expenditure incurred on treatment is mainly in the private de-addiction centres. However, money spent on the treatment of drug addicts is tantamount to saving a lot in terms of health costs and savings on criminal litigation and on prisons, besides curbing absenteeism (studies and work) among the addicts.

## 6.4 Sources of money for the purchase of drugs

There are multiple sources of money for purchasing drugs, ranging from self-financing to drug-peddling. The most important source of money, as revealed by 71.84 percent of the addicts, is from self-earnings. The proportion varies from 67.67 percent in Haryana to 85 percent in Rajasthan (Table 6.9). This implies that quite a high number of addicts are engaged in economic activities and finance their expenditure on drugs by way of self-earnings. Pocket money, as a source of purchasing drugs, has been revealed by 42.37 percent addicts. The proportion ranges from 25.83 percent in Rajasthan to 47.12 percent in Punjab. This is an indication that these addicts were mainly students and/or unemployed. Approximately 21 percent of addicts revealed that they get money to purchase drugs by way of emotional blackmailing their parents. The proportion ranges from 13.33 percent in H.P. to 31.67 percent in Haryana. Our field survey revealed that these addicts are mainly from women-headed families (mainly widows). The only-son-family is also the cause behind emotional blackmailing of parents. It was also found that some addicts were using coercive methods to extract money from their parents to purchase drugs. Stealing and selling family goods and articles was also revealed by 8.86 percent of the addicts. Across states, it varies from 3.33 percent in H.P. and Haryana to 12.42 percent in Punjab. In Rajasthan, such an incidence is just among 0.83 percent of the addicts. About 6.23 percent of the addicts said that they also take money from their friends. Drug peddling is also an important source of money to purchase drugs, as 10 percent of the addicts admitted this fact (Table 6.9). Across states, the proportion varies from 5.83 percent in Rajasthan to 10.83 percent in Haryana. Significantly, the addicts, on average, have 1.6 sources of money to purchase drugs. Across states, the proportion ranges between 1.38 in Rajasthan to 1.67 in Punjab. Paradoxically, pocket money and money got through coercive methods and emotional blackmailing of parents were tantamount to the same thing. This

*Table 6.9* Sources of money to purchase drugs

| *State→*<br>*Source↓* | *Punjab* | *Haryana* | *H.P.* | *J&K* | *Rajasthan* | *Total* |
|---|---|---|---|---|---|---|
| Self-earnings | 460<br>(69.70) | 80<br>(67.67) | 92<br>(76.67) | 85<br>(70.83) | 102<br>(85.0) | 819<br>(71.84) |
| Pocket money | 311<br>(47.12) | 48<br>(40.0) | 44<br>(36.67) | 49<br>(40.83) | 31<br>(25.83) | 483<br>(42.37) |
| Emotional black-mailing | 138<br>(20.91) | 38<br>(31.67) | 16<br>(13.33) | 24<br>(20.0) | 23<br>(19.17) | 239<br>(20.96) |
| Selling family goods | 82<br>(12.42) | 04<br>(3.33) | 04<br>(3.33) | 10<br>(8.33) | 01<br>(0.83) | 101<br>(8.86) |
| Friends | 47<br>(7.12) | 10<br>(8.33) | 04<br>(3.33) | 08<br>(6.67) | 02<br>(1.67) | 71<br>(6.23) |
| Drug-peddling/ crime | 65<br>(9.85) | 13<br>(10.83) | 16<br>(13.33) | 13<br>(10.83) | 07<br>(5.83) | 114<br>(10.0) |
| Total respondents | 660<br>(100) | 120<br>(100) | 120<br>(100) | 120<br>(100) | 120<br>(100) | 1,140<br>(100) |
| Total responses | 1,103<br>(167.12) | 193<br>(160.83) | 176<br>(146.67) | 189<br>(157.5) | 166<br>(138.33) | 1,827<br>(160.26) |

*Table 6.10* Financing of treatment of drug addicts

| *State→* *Source↓* | *Punjab* | *Haryana* | *H.P.* | *J&K* | *Rajasthan* | *Total* |
|---|---|---|---|---|---|---|
| Family | 406 (73.82) | 73 | 91 | 63 | 67 | 700 (73.68) |
| Self | 120 (21.82) | 18 | 03 | 31 | 27 | 199 (20.95) |
| Relatives, etc. | 24 (4.36) | 09 | 06 | 06 | 06 | 51 (5.37) |
| Total respondents | 550 (100) | 100 | 100 | 100 | 100 | 950 |

means nearly 63 percent of the addicts get money to purchase drugs through these two sources.

*Source of financing treatment of addicts*

Family is the most important source of incurring expenditure on treatment. About 74 percent of the addicts revealed that their treatment expenses are being borne by their family, mainly parents (Table 6.10). Across states, the proportion varies from 63 percent in J&K to 91 percent in H.P. Only 21 percent of the addicts bear the treatment expenses on their own, varying from 18 percent in Haryana to 27 percent in Rajasthan, whereas in H.P., only 3 percent of addicts bore out the expenses of their treatment on their own. The proportion of addicts whose treatment expenses were borne by relatives and friends was 5.37 percent. Thus, the financial burden (cost) on addicts' treatment falls mainly on the family. Such an expenditure could have been spent on some meaningful purpose had there been no drug victim in the family. It was found during the field survey that most of the families (particularly poor and lower-middle-class families) have to resort to loans (incurring a debt burden) and exhausting savings or selling some family valuables to meet the treatment expenses of the addict. Most of the families revealed that they spent their past savings on the treatment. Significantly, a good number of households revealed that they had to raise a loan for the treatment of their addicted family member and also had to sell some land or other assets of the family. Our case studies have revealed such incidences amply. The study, however, has not calculated the expenditure on treatment of ailments cropping up due to long term drug addiction. Nonetheless, many respondents and case studies revealed that they are spending a huge amount on the treatment of ailments happening due to drug addiction.

## 6.5 Untimely and premature deaths of addicts and its impact

It is a matter of serious concern that a number of premature deaths have taken place due to drug addiction and abuse. A premature death due to any reason is not only a loss to the family but also a national loss. It is all the more painful if the premature death is due to drug addiction and abuse. There are numerous hapless old parents (who wished their sons could be a support to them in their old age) whose young sons have been hooked on drugs and died in the prime of their lives due to overdoses of drugs. A full page of the newspaper is devoted to highlighting stories of such hapless young wives, distressed young children and unfortunate old parents broken down under the unbearable dead weight of the untimely demise of their husbands, fathers and sons. Sisters have lost their young brothers. Their hopes to lead a good life have been dashed to the ground and they are left with no choice but to endure the burden of life for no fault of theirs. Significantly, coverage in the media has documented the tragic deaths (with drug overdose) of seven young men between 21 and 32 years of age (out of them, three were married and had small children). These reported deaths happened in six districts of Punjab, namely, Amritsar, Tarn Taran, Bathinda, Faridkot, Ludhiana and Jalandhar (Hindustan Times, July 4, 2018a). This media coverage highlighted that the then-Health Minster of Punjab claimed that only two drug overdose deaths were confirmed per official records.[8]

We tried to generate estimates of drug-related deaths on the basis of information shared by the sampled drug addicts. Out of 1,140 sampled addicts, 511 revealed that they knew a total of 1,059 drug addicts who died prematurely due to drug addiction and abuse. Thus, on average, each of our respondents knew two such deaths. Out of them, nine were female, five in Punjab, three in J&K and one in Haryana. Unfortunately, 56.47 percent of such deaths were in the age group of 15 to 25 years (Table 6.11). Amongst them, 22.38 percent of the deaths occurred in the age group of 15 to 20 years, the age yet to start life. Across states, this proportion ranges between 15.91 percent in Rajasthan to 56.63 percent in J&K. The proportion of deaths in the age group of 20 to 25 years was 34 percent; between 22 percent in Rajasthan and between 34 to 35 percent in Punjab and Haryana. About 24 percent of deaths occurred in the age group of 25 to 30 years, ranging from 23.26 percent in H.P and 29.55 percent in Rajasthan (in J&K, it was 6 percent). The proportion of deaths in the age range of 30 to 35 years was 10.58 percent. Across states, the proportion varied between 6 percent in J&K to 12.12 percent in Rajasthan. The aggregate proportion of deaths in the age group of 15 to 35 years comes out to be 91 percent, which is very disturbing. This age group is considered

8 The denial mode was despite the then-President of Punjab State Congress' public promise (in the run-up to Legislative Assembly elections in 2017, who later became Chief Minister) to break the backbone of the drug menace in Punjab within a few months after forming the government. Notably, even our request to get permission to conduct the survey in 2017 was not dealt with for over six months (despite our frequent personal visits to the concerned department and numerous phone calls to the health Minister's office) by the Directorate of Health, Punjab (Dainik Bhaskar, 2017). Contrary to this, all the remaining four states (Haryana, Himachal Pradesh, J&K and Rajasthan) were very quick to grant permission to conduct the study in their states.

*Table 6.11* Age-group of addicts died due to drug addiction

| *State→*<br>*Age group↓*<br>*(years)* | *Punjab* | *Haryana* | *H.P.* | *J&K* | *Rajasthan* | *Total* |
|---|---|---|---|---|---|---|
| 15–20 | 114<br>(18.66) | 48<br>(25.26) | 07<br>(16.28) | 47<br>(56.63) | 21<br>(15.91) | 237<br>(22.38) |
| 20–25 | 229<br>(37.48) | 62<br>(32.63) | 15<br>(34.88) | 26<br>(31.33) | 29<br>(21.97) | 361<br>(34.09) |
| 25–30 | 150<br>(24.55) | 49<br>(25.79) | 10<br>(23.26) | 05<br>(6.02) | 39<br>(29.55) | 253<br>(23.89) |
| 30–35 | 69<br>(11.29) | 17<br>(8.95) | 05<br>(11.63) | 05<br>(6.02) | 16<br>(12.12) | 112<br>(10.58) |
| Above 35 | 49<br>(8.02) | 14<br>(7.37) | 06<br>(13.95) | – | 27<br>(20.45) | 96<br>(9.07) |
| Total responses | 611<br>(100) | 190<br>(100) | 43<br>(100) | 83<br>(100) | 132<br>(100) | 1,059<br>(100) |

the most productive one. This means we are losing our youth (due to drug addiction) in the prime of their age and, hence, a productive force in the range of 30 years to 50 years.

Many fatal accidents happen under the influence of intoxicants/drugs (no data is available for accidents occurring under the influence of drugs or smuggling related drugs) in which some innocent persons also die. As per the media reports, while trying to evade policemen, drug smugglers killed two youths (19 and 22 years, on a motorbike) with their speeding car (The Tribune, July 11, 2022). Significantly, Punjab, perhaps, is infamous for the highest amount of fatal road accidents (per one lakh population) and many accidents might be happening under the influence drugs/intoxicants while driving, but it is difficult to say anything in the absence of data.

Despite social loss, there is an immense economic loss to the households, society and the country. Due to non-availability of actual and entire data, we could not generate the exact number of such deaths. Only a census survey can provide such an information. Another method is to generate estimates from living addicts, but, again, their actual number is not available. In such a situation, data can be generated from all the addicts who are taking treatment in all the drug de-addiction and rehabilitation centres and other addicts taking out-patient treatment in the designated health centres. They may provide information about the drug-related deaths, as they are expected to have knowledge about such deaths in their known circles. This method, in the absence of a census survey, can also be used for generating estimates of the extent of drug addiction. We tried this method to generate some crude estimates about the number of addicted persons (though it was not within the scope of this study). The 1,140 sampled addicts in our study revealed that

*Table 6.12* Marital status of addicts who died due to drug addiction

| *State→* *Marital status↓* | *Punjab* | *Haryana* | *H.P.* | *J&K* | *Rajasthan* | *Total* |
|---|---|---|---|---|---|---|
| Married | 223 (36.50) | 68 (35.79) | 11 (25.58) | 28 (33.73) | 78 (59.09) | 408 (38.53) |
| Unmarried | 388 (63.50) | 122 (64.21) | 32 (74.42) | 55 (66.27) | 54 (40.91) | 651 (61.47) |
| Total | 611 (100) | 190 (100) | 43 (100) | 83 (100) | 132 (100) | 1,059 (100) |

they know 20,997 more addicts; on average, a sampled addict knew 18 to 19 other addicts (Table 6.1A in annexure).

Table 6.12 highlights that 38.53 percent of the prematurely deceased addicts were married. A calculation of the socio-economic cost to the wife and children is beyond comprehension, and computation is just not possible to quantify the socio-economic agony the young widows may be undergoing. The children's career prospects are worst affected by the premature death of their father, as they could never reach the full potential of their career in the absence of a father. Table 6.12 also reveals that 61.47 percent of the prematurely deceased persons were unmarried. The calculation of the economic cost for the parents, society and the country is not an easy task, as who knows what could have been their socio-economic contributions to the family, society and the country?

### *Occupation of addicts deceased due to drug addiction*

Though occupation is not explicitly related to social and economic loss, yet the age and occupation of addicts does help to generate an understanding of future economic loss due to premature deaths. Table 6.13 shows the occupation of such addicts. At the aggregate level, 27.86 percent of such addicts were from the agricultural sector. Across states, the proportion varies between 25 percent in Rajasthan and 35.68 percent in Punjab. In J&K and H.P., the proportion of such addicts was 3.61 percent and 6.98 percent, respectively. Another 19 percent of addicts who met with a premature death due to drug addiction belonged to the category of casual labour. Across states, the proportion varies from 14.89 percent in Punjab to 46.21 percent in Rajasthan, while H.P. and J&K had 4.65 percent and 9.64 percent, respectively. The proportion of such addicts employed in government job was just 1.79 percent at the aggregate. However, such a proportion in private jobs was 7.37 percent, varying between 5.79 percent in Haryana and 16.28 percent in H.P. The proportion of unemployed addicts who died prematurely was 14.73 percent, which is quite high. Across states, this varied from 15.71 percent in Punjab

*Table 6.13* Occupation-wise distribution

| *State→* *Occupation↓* | *Punjab* | *Haryana* | *H.P.* | *J&K* | *Rajasthan* | *Total* |
|---|---|---|---|---|---|---|
| Agriculture and allied activities | 218 (35.68) | 38 (20.00) | 03 (6.98) | 03 (3.61) | 33 (25.00) | 295 (27.86) |
| Casual labour | 91 (14.89) | 40 (21.05) | 02 (4.65) | 08 (9.64) | 61 (46.21) | 202 (19.07) |
| Government job | 13 (2.13) | 01 (0.53) | 02 (4.65) | – | 03 (2.27) | 19 (1.79) |
| Private job | 39 (6.38) | 11 (5.79) | 07 (16.28) | 13 (15.67) | 08 (6.06) | 78 (7.37) |
| Unemployed | 96 (15.71) | 40 (21.05) | 09 (20.93) | 05 (6.02) | 06 (4.55) | 156 (14.73) |
| Student | 54 (8.84) | 23 (12.11) | 10 (23.26) | 24 (28.92) | 19 (14.39) | 190 (17.94) |
| Other informal activities | 100 (16.37) | 37 (19.47) | 10 (23.26) | 24 (28.92) | 19 (14.39) | 190 (17.94) |
| Total | 611 (100) | 190 (100) | 43 (100) | 83 (100) | 132 (100) | 1,059 (100) |

to 21.05 percent in Haryana, whereas it was 4.55 percent in Rajasthan and 6 percent in J&K. Significantly, students accounted for 11.24 percent of such deaths, which is quite a disgusting situation as there does not seem to be any valid reason for students to meet such an unfortunate death, but it was mainly due to drug addiction and abuse. Nearly 18 percent of addicts were engaged in other miscellaneous economic activities.

It is clear from the previous discussion that nearly 88 percent of premature deaths of addicts were from the informal and unorganised sector. A very high proportion of informal sector employment is witnessing low wages and earnings, lack of social security and sub-human working conditions. A very high proportion of them are in the category of working poor subject to multidimensional poverty and vulnerability (Ghuman, 2012). Such a scenario leads to financial constraints, economic hardships and a feeling of depression. Significantly, nearly 93 percent of the Indian workforce is engaged in informal employment. Though it cannot be construed from this that more premature deaths of addicts are due only to economic distress and insecurity (low wages in the informal sector resulting into working poor) but drug addiction might be due to economic distress and socio-economic insecurity. However, it does not mean that youths from the relatively well-off sections do not get hooked on drug addiction.

In a nutshell, drug addiction and abuse is a very complex socio-cultural and politico-economic phenomenon and needs a multidimensional inquiry and multipronged mechanism to address the menace. Nonetheless, drug addiction and abuse does have a huge socio-economic cost to all the stakeholders and often many such costs are beyond accounting and estimation. Thus, there is utter justification to generate authentic data about the extent of drug addiction, premature deaths and socio-economic and other costs to sensitise the stakeholders and formulate meaningful policies to address the drug menace. The existing literature and our study have generated enough justification for addressing the drug menace on a war footing and in a missionary mode so that society and the economy can be saved from undue costs and violence.

# 7 Prevalence and prevention of drug menace

## Community perception

The institutions of governance, elected bodies, political parties, NGOs, religious organisations and civil society often claim that they are making many efforts to spread awareness about the ill effects of drugs. Some of them, often backed by the law, also take persuasive, preventive and coercive measures to dissuade people from taking drugs, and rightly so, as it is what society expects from them. However, often there are gaps between their claims and ground reality. It is in this context that we tried to have a community's perception/view/opinion about the claims and role of the institutions, as community is considered the mirror through which we can see the ground realities. The people and civil society also mirror their expectations through their perceptions, opinions and views. This chapter, thus, dwells on the community's perception about the role of various social and religious institutions and that of the government and its various agencies. The discussion and analysis are based on the perceptions and views of respondents from the sampled households (those of addicts and non-addicts), focus group discussions (FGDs), our field observations and case studies. The chapter is divided into seven sections. Section 7.1 discusses the community perception about the efficiency and efficacy of awareness activities of the said institutions against the ill effects of drugs. Influence of youth icons and folk-culture is discussed in section 7.2. Section 7.3 reveals the role of religious organisations in the campaign against drugs. The following section examines the community perception about the role of rural local bodies (village elected bodies) and Urban Local Bodies in spreading awareness and curbing the spread of drugs. Section 7.5 discusses the government's role in addressing the drug menace. The role of police is discussed in section 7.6. The last section dwells on the role of political leadership in addressing the issue of the drug menace.

### 7.1 Community perception about the awareness activities

Civil society and various institutions of government are supposed to spread awareness about the ill effects of intoxicants and drugs. We tried to learn about the awareness activities of these institutions from different

DOI: 10.4324/9781003318019-7

groups of respondents, including from households, focus group discussions (FGDs) and the in-depth case studies of some of the sampled drug addicts. The responses of the respondents are given in Table 7.1. Out of the 950 respondents from the addicts' households, 22.74 percent revealed that some sort of awareness activities are being carried out by the concerned institutions and organisations. Across states, it varies from 16 percent in J&K to 23.82 percent in Punjab. Nearly 18 percent of the respondents did not have any knowledge of any awareness activity. Across states, it varies between 14.36 percent in Punjab and 31 percent in Rajasthan. Significantly, 58.95 percent of the respondents answered that no awareness activities are being carried out. Across states, the proportion varies from 47 percent in Rajasthan to 61.82 percent in Punjab. Out of 616 respondents in the control group (households having no addict), nearly 43.51 percent were of the view that awareness activities are being carried out. Across states, the proportion ranges between 15.38 percent in J&K and 50 percent in H.P. Approximately 49 percent of the respondents did not agree. Across states, the proportion of such responses varied from 36.54 percent in Haryana to 78.85 percent in J&K. Nearly 7.31 percent of respondents expressed their ignorance about any awareness activities by the concerned institutions and organisations. Significantly, out of all the households, a majority of the households were of the opinion that no meaningful awareness activities are being conducted against the drug menace.

*Table 7.1* Households' opinion about the awareness activities

| *Response→* *State↓* | *Addicts' households (950)* | | | | *Non-addict households (616)@* | | | |
|---|---|---|---|---|---|---|---|---|
| | *Yes* | *No* | *Don't know* | *Total* | *Yes* | *No* | *Don't know* | *Total* |
| Punjab | 131 (23.82) | 340 (61.82) | 79 (14.36) | 550 (100) | 197 (42.65) | 187 (45.83) | 24 (5.88) | 408 (100) |
| Haryana | 19 (19.00) | 61 (61.00) | 20 (20.00) | 100 | 20 (38.46) | 19 (36.54) | 13 (25.00) | 52 (100) |
| H.P. | 28 (28.00) | 57 (57.00) | 15 (15.00) | 100 | 26 (50.00) | 26 (50.00) | 0 (0.00) | 52 (100) |
| J&K | 16 (16.00) | 55 (55.00) | 29 (29.00) | 100 | 8 (15.38) | 41 (78.85) | 3 (5.78) | 52 (100) |
| Rajasthan | 22 (22.00) | 47 (47.00) | 31 (31.00) | 100 | 17 (32.69) | 30 (57.69) | 5 (9.62) | 52 (100) |
| Total | 216 (22.74) | 560 (58.94) | 174 (18.32) | 950* | 268 (43.51) | 303 (49.19) | 45 (7.31) | 616 (100) |

* Does not include hidden (190) households
@ Households having no addict
*Note:* Figures in brackets indicate percent share. This is applicable to all the tables in this chapter unless mentioned otherwise.

*Table 7.2* Types of awareness activities being carried out

| *Response→* *State↓* | *Addicts' household* | | | | | *Non-addict households* | | | | |
|---|---|---|---|---|---|---|---|---|---|---|
| | *Awareness camp* | *Rallies* | *Nukar Natak* | *Police-public meeting* | *Total* | *Awareness camp* | *Rallies* | *Nukar Natak* | *Police-public meeting* | *Total* |
| Punjab | 89 (67.94) | 29 (22.14) | 4 (3.05) | 9 (6.67) | 131 (100) | 81 (41.12) | 95 (48.32) | 12 (6.09) | 09 (4.57) | 197 (100) |
| Haryana | 16 (84.21) | 02 (10.53) | 0 (0.00) | 1 (5.26) | 19 (100) | 6 (30.00) | 7 (35.00) | 4 (20.0) | 3 (15.0) | 20 (100) |
| H.P. | 24 (85.71) | 4 (14.28) | 0 (0.00) | 0 (0.00) | 28 (100) | 22 (84.6) | 02 (7.7) | – | 02 (7.7) | 26 (100) |
| J&K | 12 (75.0) | 03 (18.75) | 0 (0.00) | 00 (6.253) | 16 (100) | 04 (50.0) | 04 (50.0) | – | – | 08 (100) |
| Rajasthan | 16 (72.73) | 04 (18.18) | 02 (9.10) | 0 (0.00) | 22 (100) | 13 (76.47) | 04 (23.53) | – | – | 17 (100) |
| Total | 157 (72.69) | 42 (19.44) | 06 (2.78) | 11 (5.09) | 216 (100) | 126 (47.01) | 112 (41.79) | 16 (5.97) | 14 (5.22) | 268 (100) |

### *7.1.1 Types of awareness activities*

We divided all respondent households into two groups, viz., the households having drug addicts and the households having no drug addict (control group households) as there is a wide variation between the perceptions of the two groups. For example, 73 percent of the respondents in addicts' households revealed that an awareness campaign against the ill effects of drugs by way of preaching is being carried out whereas the proportion of such respondents in the control group is 47 percent. The respective proportion in the former group varies from 67 percent in Punjab to 86 percent in H.P. In the latter group, such a proportion varies from 30 percent in Haryana to 85 percent in H.P. On the contrary, 42 percent of respondents in the latter group were of the view that the concerned institutions spread awareness by holdings rallies. The proportion varies from 10.53 percent in Haryana to 19 percent in J&K in the former group of respondents. In the latter group, it varies from 7.7 percent in H.P. and 50 percent in J&K. *Nukar Nataks* (street-corner plays) and police-public meetings are the other modes of spreading awareness among the people. But the proportion of respondents from the addicts' households is just 2.78 percent and that from the control group is 6 percent. The proportion of respondents revealing police-public joint awareness meetings is 5 percent and 16 percent in the former and latter groups, respectively (Table 7.2). Thus, not only the perception of respondents varies a lot in the two groups but actors state there is wide variation.

The kind of awareness activities wanted by those households who said no awareness activities are being carried out (Table 7.1) are enlisted in Table 7.3. The respondents are from both the groups of households. Out of the total respondents, 924 (46 percent) want meaningful awareness activities to focus on the ill effects of drugs, carried out in an effective manner. Across states, it varies from 27 percent in Rajasthan to 77 percent in H.P. About 20 percent of respondents are of the view that mass awareness campaigns should be launched. Nearly the same proportion of respondents want to have *nukar nataks* for spreading awareness against drugs as they exert direct impact on the minds of the viewers.

Women participants during FGDs in Himachal Pradesh suggested that the Mahila Mandals' role needs to be activated because the women are quite effective in reforming society by tackling various social evils. Citing an example in one of the FGDs conducted in Himachal Pradesh, the female participants informed us that two women councillors are enrolled in community policing institutions. This is supposed to work for checking various social evils, including the drug problem. This has become increasingly important these days, especially for girl students who live away from their homes as paying guests and in hostels. During discussion in FGD in Haryana with Bisnoi community, the participants informed us that their community generally organises events in which emphasis is laid on highlighting the social evils including that of the ill effects of drugs. The community organises "*Charitar*

*Table 7.3* Types of awareness activities expected by households*

| *State→* *Activity ↓* | *Punjab* | *Haryana* | *H.P.* | *J&K* | *Rajasthan* | *Total* |
|---|---|---|---|---|---|---|
| Awareness camps | 284 (48.30) | 23 (28.75) | 64 (77.11) | 33 (34.38) | 21 (27.27) | 425 (46.0) |
| Mass campaign | 128 (21.77) | 11 (13.75) | 06 (7.23) | 25 (26.04) | 11 (14.29) | 181 (19.59) |
| Joint mass campaign by health and police departments | 104 (17.69) | 43 (53.75) | 03 (3.61) | 03 (3.13) | 29 (37.66) | 182 (19.70) |
| Nukar-Natak | 58 (9.86) | 02 (2.5) | 09 (10.84) | 09 (9.38) | 13 (16.88) | 91 (9.85) |
| Others | 14 (2.38) | 01 (1.25) | 01 (1.20) | 26 (27.08) | 03 (3.90) | 45 (4.87) |
| Total responses | 588 (100) | 80 (100) | 83 (100) | 96 (100) | 77 (100) | 924 (100) |

* Also indicates control group households.
*Note:* The responses in the table are from those households who said no awareness activities are being done in their areas.

*Nirman Shiver"* (character-building camps) and also *"Drug Free Day"* to spread awareness among society. The District Legal Service Authority of Kullu, Himachal Pradesh, is also a part of "*Sehbhagita,*" It is a noble initiative to check the rising illegal use and misuse of various drugs in the district. This initiative was taken by a female Superintendent of Police (S.P.) of Kullu, a young IPS officer. She was coordinating efforts of youth from Nehru Yuva Kendra, District Social Welfare department, Red Cross Society, Village Panchayat, Municipal Committees, district police and other religious bodies. In Rajasthan, the civil and police administration, jointly with the health department, started an initiative in 1992 aimed at spreading awareness about the harmful effects of drug use. Since then, such awareness initiatives are a continuum exercise. During this campaign, workshops are arranged in schools and in villages to educate people to desist from the use of drugs. We were told that the campaign is quite effective and successful in generating awareness among the adolescents and youth. It is being claimed by the organisers that, as a result, almost half of the drug using youth in these districts have stopped taking drugs. However, it is difficult to sustain this exercise and permanently stop their relapsing. Similar efforts have been initiated in some areas of Punjab by the youth with the People's Welfare Society and Friends Welfare Society. Mr. Mohan Sharma, former Director of the Drug De-addiction Centre (DDC) of the Red Cross Society District Sangrur district of Punjab, needs a special mention. He has been associated with this centre for about 16 years and did counselling for nearly 10,000 drug addicts. According to him, medical treatment alone is not sufficient for de-addiction. It needs to be supplemented by dedicated counselling based on a comprehensive understanding of the root cause for an addict's addiction. This required level of motivation and dedication is mainly missing in the government and private DDCs. The concerned staff in government DDCs is mainly interested in routine duty and the private DDCs are interested in money. The Government of Punjab constituted an anti-drug special task force (STF) in April 2017. The STF prepared comprehensive action against drug abuse (CADA) in August 2018. The STF, under CADA, in collaboration with Punjabi University, Patiala, launched the Buddy ("you are my buddy, I am your buddy") programme to spread awareness against drug use and abuse in Punjab, especially among the students in schools, colleges and universities. In order to involve the general public in the campaign against drugs, the government also launched the DAPO (Drug Abuse Prevention Officer) programme (under KADA) in March 2018. These programmes were launched with much enthusiasm and fanfare, but, at the time of the field survey and FGDs (2017–2019), we found that not many people were aware about the activities of these programmes. Currently, there is not much community presence of the Buddy and DAPO programmes, and, hence, they are much less effective.

## 7.2 Influence of icons, folk-songs and media on youth as revealed by non-addicts' households

Icons of youth exert a significant influence on the minds and psyche of the youth, especially teenagers and adolescents. And when the use and abuse of drugs is highlighted by their icons, it directly influences their young minds. Media, cinema and icons often promote what is saleable in the market, so it is a two-way street: one, media, cinema and icons generate the demand (just like the advertisement industry), and, two, over a period of time there comes the demand. It is in this context that we got the response of households of addicts and that of control group households. Besides, we conducted a number of FGDs with numerous stakeholders such as village panchayats, Urban Local Bodies, teachers and students, religious and spiritual organisations, medical experts, police officials, etc. Most of them shared that the promotion of gun culture, drugs and vulgarities (through songs, social media, movies, and even on some T.V. channels) is a powerful tool to entice youth towards many social ills, including drug addiction and abuse. At least five (out of a total of 40) respondents revealed that they started taking drugs under the influence of some songs and movies. One of the case study respondents (female) from a poor family, married to an addict, revealed that she started taking drugs after joining an orchestra group.

In such a socio-cultural environment, many times the lumpen culture overshadows the real and healthy culture of the region. And such a culture even gets tacit support in the market-driven neo-liberalism from interested parties. Such a scenario often leads to erosion of healthy socio-cultural values and ethics. Punjab has been facing the challenge of such a scenario for more than the last three decades. Unfortunately, the socio-cultural organisations, institutions of governance, and the polity did not awaken to the occasion. Many case studies, conducted by us, do support even pious human relations become victims of drug addiction and abuse. Social scientists and activists have been trying to focus on the issue of the burgeoning gun culture in Punjab for more than a decade, but the situation has gone from bad to worse. Gill (2013), in his article, highlighted that the burgeoning gun culture in Punjab is mainly because of the partisan role of the police and the police administrations' overarching subservience to the full-time politicians, resulting in a politician-criminal nexus. The murder of a deputy superintendent of police (DSP) by mining mafia (by crushing him under the dumpster signalled to stop during a raid to check illegal mining) in Haryana on July 19, 2022 is a stark example of such an unholy nexus (The Tribune, July 20, 2022).

Table 7.4 reveals the responses of 1,566 households (950 addicts' households and 616 control group households) regarding the influence of icons on youth in instigating them to the use and abuse of drugs. There were three types of responses. At the aggregate level, 82.44 percent of the respondents have the perception that youth icons (only those who implicitly or explicitly try to promote the gun and drug culture) do influence the youth to use and abuse intoxicants and drugs. Across states, this proportion varies from 73.68 percent in Haryana to 92.11 percent in Rajasthan. Punjab is often quoted and discussed for such a scenario, but in J&K and Rajasthan, higher proportion of respondents have the perception that icons exert a great influence on young minds. However, 14.24 percent of respondents said that icons do not entice youth towards drugs. Across states, this varies from 2.63 percent in Rajasthan to 21 percent in Haryana. Only 3.32 percent of respondents expressed their neutrality. Nonetheless, it has been prominently highlighted that icons do exert influence on the gullible minds of adolescents and youth and the negative impact often outweighs the positive impact.

*Table 7.4* Influence of icons on youth

| *State→ Response↓* | *Punjab* | *Haryana* | *H.P.* | *J&K* | *Rajasthan* | *Total* |
|---|---|---|---|---|---|---|
| Yes | 792 (82.67) | 112 (73.68) | 115 (75.66) | 132 (86.84) | 140 (92.11) | 1,291 (82.44) |
| No | 146 (15.24) | 32 (21.05) | 27 (17.76) | 14 (9.21) | 04 (2.63) | 223 (14.26) |
| Don't know | 20 (2.09) | 08 (5.26) | 10 (6.58) | 06 (3.95) | 08 (5.26) | 52 (3.32) |
| Total | 958 (100) | 152 (100) | 152 (100) | 152 (100) | 152 (100) | 1,566 (100) |

## 7.3 Role of religious and spiritual organisations as revealed by non-addicts households

Religious and spiritual organisations have an enormous amount of impact on people all over the world. This is more-so in India. Any edict/advice by the religious organisations is carefully adhered to by the people. It is in this context that we had interactive sessions with representatives of some religious organisations to know about the efforts being made by them to make people aware of the ill effects of drugs. We found that almost all the religious organisations and sects are aware and alive to the ill effects of intoxicants and drugs and, in their own way, advise people not to take intoxicants and drugs. Guru Nanak, the founder of the Sikh religion, said: "*Jhutha Madh Mool Na Peache, Jeh Ka Mool Visahe*" ("do not take worldly intoxicants as their impact is short-lived"); the Guru further said, "*Nam Khumari Nanka Chari rahe din rat*" ("get intoxicated by God's name, the intoxication of which lasts forever"). Gurbani says that after taking worldly intoxicants, the person cannot distinguish between good and bad: "*Aapna praya na pehchhaniae khasmhan dhake khae, Jit pitaye khasam visrae darghe milaye sjaaie.*" Similarly, all other religions and sects do preach against the ill effects of intoxicants and drugs. We, thus, sought the views and perceptions of people from various walks of life (through FGDs) and also through personal interactions with the respondents from 950 families of drug addicts and 616 non-drug addicts (control group). This section, thus, presents the perception of 1,566 respondents, both from the families of addicts and non-addicts. In addition to that input, we also obtained information through 77 FGDs (comprising 640 participants) and 40 case studies across the states under study.

Interestingly, all the 950 respondents from the addicts' households were of the perception that religious and spiritual organisations do play a positive role in addressing the problem of drug use and abuse in society. They are of the view that religious organisations motivate people not to indulge in the use of intoxicants and drugs as it has serious ill effects on the mind and body. However, respondents from the control group households have a different perception, which has been given in Tables 7.5 and 7.6. Nearly 60 percent of the 616 such respondents have a positive perception about the role of religious and spiritual organisations in curbing the use and abuse of drugs. But 41 percent of respondents disagreed with it and hold the perception that religious organisations do not play any meaningful and effective role in curbing the drug menace. The reasons for their perception have been given in Table 7.6. In all, there are 253 (Table 7.5) such respondents. Out of them, 30.4 percent are of the opinion that religious and spiritual organisations are indifferent to the problem of drugs in society, and, hence, lack commitment to curbing drugs.

Across states, the proportion of such respondents varies from 9.6 percent in Rajasthan to 44.4 percent in J&K. Thus, there is wide variation across

*Table 7.5* Role of religious organisations

| *State→* *Response↓* | *Punjab* | *Haryana* | *H.P.* | *J&K* | *Rajasthan* | *Total* |
|---|---|---|---|---|---|---|
| Yes | 240 (58.8) | 26 (50.0) | 37 (71.2) | 34 (65.4) | 26 (50.0) | 363 (58.91) |
| No | 168 (41.2) | 26 (50.0) | 15 (28.8) | 18 (34.6) | 26 (50.0) | 253 (41.1) |
| Total | 408 (100) | 52 (100) | 52 (100) | 52 (100) | 52 (100) | 616 (100) |

*Table 7.6* Reasons for ineffective role of religious organisations in tackling the drug menace

| *State→* *Response↓* | *Punjab* | *Haryana* | *H.P.* | *J&K* | *Rajasthan* | *Total* |
|---|---|---|---|---|---|---|
| Indifferent | 54 (32.1) | 4 (15.3) | 6 (40.0) | 8 (44.4) | 5 (9.6) | 77 (30.4) |
| Lack of role model | 38 (22.6) | 5 (19.2) | 3 (20.0) | 7 (38.9) | 10 (19.2) | 63 (24.9) |
| Lacking capability | 38 (22.62) | 7 (36.9) | 02 (13.3) | 01 (5.6) | 06 (11.5) | 54 (21.34) |
| Self-addicted | 38 (22.6) | 10 (38.4) | 4 (26.7) | 2 (11.1) | 5 (9.6) | 59 (23.3) |
| Total | 168 (100) | 26 (100) | 15 (100) | 18 (100) | 26 (100) | 253 (100) |

the states. Lack of role models in religious and spiritual organisations is another factor which has been put forward by 24.9 percent of the respondents. Across states, it varies from 19.2 percent in Haryana and Rajasthan and 38.9 percent in J&K. Approximately 23 percent of respondents said that even some people in the religious organisations consume one or more intoxicants or drugs. Hence, they lack moral authority to play an effective role against the prevalence of drugs in society. Across states, Haryana has the highest (38.4 percent) number of respondents with such a perception. It is followed by H.P. (26.7 percent), Punjab (22.6 percent), J&K (11.1 percent) and Rajasthan (9.6 percent). Another 21.34 percent of respondents said that religious and spiritual organisations lack the required capability and commitment to awaken the people against drugs. Across states, such a proportion varies from 5.6 percent in J&K to 22.62 percent in Punjab. Thus, there are multiple reasons for the ineffective role of religious and spiritual organisations in addressing the drug menace (Table 7.6).

In regards to the perception of those respondents (363, Table 6.5) who said that religious organisations play a good role in checking the drug menace, most of them revealed that these organisations do motivate the people against the use of drugs. They also have the perception that religious organisations, along with community participation, spread awareness against the ill effects of drug-addiction and abuse. During some of the FGDs, it was found that some of the drug de-addiction centres (DDCs) have involved religious and spiritual organisations for imparting spiritual lectures to addicts in their centres from time to time. Also, spiritual bodies such as Shiromani Gurdwara Parbandak Committee (SGPC), Art of Living, Brahm Kumaris, Dera Beas (Radha Soami) and other religious and motivational masters are making an impact on the people to keep away from drugs and other intoxicants. During an FGD in Rajasthan, participants informed us that they established "*Guru Nanak Krishna Mandir*" with the idea to maintain communal harmony in the city and also to awaken people against the use of intoxicants. The organisation is organising drug de-addiction camps with the help of police, health and education departments. During these camps, at village communities and among school children, awareness lectures and interactive sessions are organised on the ills of drug addiction. Some SGPC representatives associated with its *Dharm Prachar* Committee, created in four zones in the states of Punjab, Haryana and Rajasthan, implemented a general awareness programme about social evils, including drug abuse. Efforts are being made to dissuade youth from all types of intoxicants and drugs. Participants in one of the FGDs in Punjab revealed that the game of *kabaddi* in the recent past has accentuated the use of heroin and other drugs. Even some of the players are reported to have been involved in the smuggling of drugs. It was suggested that the *kabaddi* competitions should be closely monitored in Punjab to avoid the flow and transit of illicit drugs.

The participants in some of the FGDs with religious bodies also shared that *bhukki* and opium are still in use in some religious *deras*. The employees or volunteers, serving in such religious *deras* in Rajasthan, when visiting Punjab or Haryana often carry opium and *bhukki* for distributing/selling in the neighbouring states. Some of the followers and workers confessed that during their visit to Punjab in their *karsewa* vehicles they generally keep separate packets of *bhukki* to be offered at the inter-state police *nakas* (barriers) so that their vehicles are not searched on inter-state borders. This helps them to safely transit *bhukki* across the inter-state border. The participants also shared that some MPs and MLAs openly patronise illegal use of drugs like *bhukki*, opium and heroin.

The *chilmderas* are known where traditional drugs are used in *chilm* or *hookah*. Alcohol offering in some *deras* is common practice in Punjab as religious faith is linked to such offerings. It was also revealed that some selective *dera-sadhus* are in the habit of using intoxicants and even practice low-level drug peddling. Others make use of such places to carry out their illegal activities under the garb of religious *deras*.

It is clear from the foregoing discussion that the respondents have a mixed perception about the role of religious organisations in addressing the issue of the drug menace. However, a majority of the respondents believe that such organisations are playing a significant role in addressing the problem of drug abuse and addiction through motivational and awareness campaigns. Though the majority of the perceptions uphold the positive role of these organisations, yet a significant number of respondents find they lack in making all-out efforts to address the problem of intoxicants and drug addiction.

## 7.4 Role of Panchayati Raj Institutions (PRIs) and Urban Local Bodies (ULBs)

The Panchayati Raj Institutions (PRIs, village panchayats, Block Samitis and Zila Parisads) and Urban Local Bodies (ULBs) have been given enormous powers by the 73rd and 74th Amendments to the Indian Constitution. The states of India also adopted these amendments in their Legislative Assemblies. But most of the states have not effectively transferred functions, functionaries and funds. The government of Punjab adopted these constitutional amendments in 1994 but with a very low transfer of three Fs (finances, functions and functionaries). It is significant that these bodies represent the third tier of Indian democracy. In a democracy, elected representatives and democratic institutions are expected to play a proactively important role in the socio-cultural and politico-economic development of the region and the country. It is in this context that the third tier of democracy is also enshrined and expected to play an important role in local self-governance. The elected representatives are responsible for working in the social, economic and political interest of the people they represent. Awareness about the ill effects of drugs and curbing the use of illicit drugs in their jurisdiction is well within their purview and duties. In view of this, this section dwells on the stakeholders' perception of the role of panchayats and Urban Local Bodies in controlling the drug menace.

In response to a direct question about the role of PRIs and ULBs, 60 percent of respondents in the FGDs said that these bodies do not play any effective role in addressing the drug menace in their jurisdiction (Table 7.7). Across states, the proportion of such a response varies from 55.11 percent in Punjab to 75.66 percent in J&K. As compared to this, 39.66 percent of

*Table 7.7* Perception about PRIs and ULBs in tacking the drug menace

| *State→*<br>*Response↓* | *Punjab* | *Haryana* | *H.P.* | *J&K* | *Rajasthan* | *Total* |
|---|---|---|---|---|---|---|
| Yes | 430<br>(44.89) | 46<br>(30.26) | 66<br>(43.42) | 37<br>(24.34) | 42<br>(27.63) | 621<br>(39.66) |
| No | 528<br>(55.11) | 106<br>(69.74) | 86<br>(56.58) | 115<br>(75.66) | 110<br>(72.37) | 945<br>(60.34) |
| Total | 958<br>(100) | 152<br>(100) | 152<br>(100) | 152<br>(100) | 152<br>(100) | 1,566<br>(100) |

respondents answered in the affirmative, i.e., that these bodies do play positive roles in addressing drugs and drug-related problems. Across states, such a proportion varies from 24.34 percent in J&K to 44.89 percent in Punjab. Thus, the majority of the respondents are not satisfied with the role of PRIs and ULBs in tackling the issue of drug addiction and abuse. However, there have been some (though very few) examples where these bodies have taken this issue very seriously.

Table 7.1A (annexure) lists the reasons for which the respondents (621 out of 1,566) said that these bodies do play a positive role in addressing the drug problem in society. Nearly 49 percent of them hold the view that these bodies play an active role in controlling drugs. Across states, the proportion of such respondents ranges between 47 percent in Punjab and 57 percent in Rajasthan. About 31 percent of the respondents said that the panchayats have passed resolutions against the use and abuse of drugs, but not much beyond that. Across states, this proportion varies from 9.52 percent in Rajasthan to 37 percent in Haryana. 15.46 percent of respondents said that these bodies play a motivational role against the use of drugs, besides engaging the youth in sports, etc. Across states, such a proportion varies from 7.14 percent in Rajasthan to 25.76 percent in H.P.

945 (60.34 percent) of respondents said that the PRIs and ULBs do not play any meaningful role in curbing drug menace (Table 7.7). The reasons put forward by them are given in Table 7.2A (annexure). Approximately 51 percent of such respondents said that these bodies have an indifferent attitude towards the drug problem in society. Across states, between 45.28 percent (Haryana) and 69.57 percent (J&K) of respondents have the same perception. Vote politics, according to 22.33 percent of respondents is the reason behind the inactive role of PRIs and ULBs in curbing the drug menace. This proportion varies from 7.27 percent in Rajasthan to 34.88 percent in H.P. Another 9.52 percent of respondents are of the view that the elected representatives of these bodies are themselves addicted to intoxicants and drugs. Another 12.49 percent of respondents said that the PRIs and ULBs do not have any agenda to control drugs in society. Still, 2.12 percent of respondent revealed that some elected representatives are themselves engaged in drug supply. This has also been affirmed by an anonymous letter to us written by a person with societal concern residing at an important city (district headquarter) of Punjab. Non-cooperation by the civil and police administration, according to 2.96 percent of respondents, is also a reason behind such an attitude in these bodies. Thus, there are multi-pronged reasons for the indifferent and inactive role of PRIs and ULBs in addressing the drug menace in the states under study.

Government and governance are the key factors in formulating and implementing laws and policies and taking necessary measures to address the problem of the drug menace. Peoples' perception about the efficacy of government policies and measures is, thus, of great significance both for the government and society. Moreover, people's perception is an evaluation of the policies and measures and also provides a significant input to the government in reviewing, restructuring and reformulating laws and policies. In view of this, we have attained the perception of the families of drug addicts and non-addicts, besides discussing the views received in FGDs.

## 7.5 Government's role in addressing the issue of the drug menace

People, in general, have great faith in the government's capacity and capability to control the drug menace, as is evident from the responses of the respondents (Table 7.8). Nearly 88 percent of the respondents expressed confidence in the government's capability to address the issue. This proportion varies from 84.21 percent (Rajasthan) to 96.05 percent (H.P.) across states. Only 12.2 percent of respondents are skeptical about the governments' capability to deal with the problem.

Contrary to the overwhelming confidence in the government's capability, only 35.31 percent of respondents were, however, satisfied with the government's efforts and capability. Approximately 65 percent of respondents were not satisfied with the government's performance in dealing with the drug (Table 7.3A). Across states, this proportion varies from 43.42 percent in H.P. to 86.84 percent in Haryana. Thus, there is a very wide gap between people's confidence level and the government's performance. Table 7.4A enlists the reasons for the low level of satisfaction with the government's performance. Indifferent attitude, political patronage and corruption are three major reasons for the low level of satisfaction. At the aggregate level, 47.58 percent of respondents are of the opinion that the government's indifferent attitude towards the drug problem is behind their dissatisfaction. In other words, there is a low level of the government's sensitivity towards the problem. Across states, this proportion varies from 37.74 percent in J&K to 65.12 percent in Rajasthan. In the opinion of 25.86 percent of respondents, political patronage is the reason behind the indifference of the government. People are dissatisfied with the government's efforts because of political patronage to the business of drug smuggling. Corruption in government agencies is the reason for the government's indifference, according to 26.55 percent

*Table 7.8* Perceptions about the government dealing with the drug menace

| *State→ Response↓* | *Punjab* | *Haryana* | *H.P.* | *J&K* | *Rajasthan* | *Total* |
|---|---|---|---|---|---|---|
| Yes | 831 (86.74) | 138 (90.79) | 146 (96.05) | 132 (86.84) | 128 (84.21) | 1,375 (87.80) |
| No | 127 (13.26) | 14 (9.21) | 06 (3.95) | 20 (13.16) | 24 (15.79) | 191 (12.20) |
| Total | 158 (100) | 152 (100) | 152 (100) | 152 (100) | 152 (100) | 1,566 (100) |

of the respondents. Across states, this proportion varies from 14.39 percent in Haryana to 40.91 percent in H.P. J&K is an exceptional case where only 6.98 percent of respondents cited corruption as the cause for their low level of satisfaction with the government's efforts in dealing with the drug menace.

To fulfil the electoral promise, Congress, after assuming political power in Punjab, constituted an Anti-drug Special Task Force (STF) in March 2017 under the leadership of an Additional Director General of police (ADGP) to address the entire issue of the drug menace. The initial stints were promising but were also critiqued by certain sections that, being all powerful, the STF may have consequences for some innocent people where scores may be settled against people, or it may create barriers to the functioning of certain sectors, particularly the pharmaceutical sector and its allied fields. In consonance with this, a protest march was also held by medical practitioners alleging harassment by the officials under stricter new rules and the NDPS Act. In 2018, certain ambiguities were observed in the state government's approach towards this issue, which specifically focused on strict law enforcement against those involved in illegal trade with and rehabilitation of addicts. Its twin purpose was to check both supply and demand. The then-Chief Minister of Punjab expressed his inability to implicate a former minister, Bikram Singh Majithia, from Akali Dal in the drug case without concrete evidence, which was not appreciated by his own party members.

The STF also started losing its earlier enthusiasm, and the people started questioning the state government on its poll promise of eradicating drug abuse in a month. This was added onto by another controversy at the intra-department level between senior police officials, which had direct implications for the anti-drug campaign in the state, as the police officials were directly involved in the investigation of cases pertaining to drugs. Astonishingly, the STF report submitted to the Punjab and Haryana High Court was not made public for a very long period.

Punjab also initiated some new initiatives like Outpatient Opioid Assisted Treatment (OOAT) and Drug Abuse Prevention Officers (DAPO) in March 2018. The OOAT centres, unlike OST, would focus on all form of drug addiction including the intravenous drug users (IDUs) and DAPO would facilitate the bridging of drug addicts with official systems of rehabilitation through the voluntary work of people enrolled in this programme as officers. However, this programme faces obstacles owing to voluntary participation of people as officers without any remuneration for their work of locating addicts and peddlers and bringing them into the larger system. In 2018, the Punjab government, in collaboration with Punjabi University, Patiala (Punjab, India) also initiated a preventive programme titled "*Tu Mera Buddy*" (peer mentoring or peer support) programme which involved school children as volunteers to educate them and make them aware about the ill effects of drugs. It is primarily aimed at educating their peers, especially school and college students, to say no to drugs. The programme is also aimed at positive peer pressure by building barriers to drug use as senior buddies are trained to educate the junior buddies and peers to dissuade them from drug use. The "catch them young" phrase is best suited to characterise the Buddy programme, as prevention is far easier than cure for the affliction. The "*catch them young*" mantra can help society to be drug and addiction free (Sharma, 2021). The benefits and positive impacts of the Buddy system have been widely acknowledged by researchers (Sydow and Sandel, 1998; Kossinets and Watts, 2006; Anderson et al., 2015). Mamta (op cit) says that the Buddy programme is having a positive impact on the participants through reverse psychology, as students are not being taught what to do, rather, they are being empowered to decide whether to make or spoil their future.

In an effort to control the spread of drugs in the region, the Chief Ministers of the four Northwestern states, Punjab, Haryana, Uttarakhand and Himachal Pradesh, held a joint meeting in mid-2018. It was decided to hold six-month joint reviews by the Chief Ministers of the four states and monthly review meetings of the STF on this issue. On July 25, 2019, at the initiative of the then-Chief Minister of Punjab, Chief Ministers of eight North-Indian states held the second conference at Chandigarh on the drug menace in those states. On invitation from the Punjab government, we also shared the findings of our study. One important observation came up in that conclave: because of huge money in the drug trade, it is not an easy task to curb it, but the joint and determined efforts of all the North-Indian states can definitely make a big dent on the drug menace. It was a unanimous opinion that the states must share the real-time information among themselves if we are really serious about breaking the supply chain. However, catching the 'big-fish' was not an explicit agenda.

The governments in almost all the states are taking certain measures to address the problem of drug addiction and abuse. More recently, many state governments are showing their serious concern about the problem. The Union and state governments also observe 26th June as the International Day against drug abuse and illicit trafficking. The governments, on this day, highlight their efforts and achievements to curb the drug menace. The people are made aware about the ill effects of the drugs. The Government of Punjab gave an almost half-page advertisement in newspapers on June 26, 2019 in which the then-Chief Minister of Punjab stated that his government will not rest till Punjab is made free from drugs. The same advertisement enlists various steps taken by the Punjab government in its fight against drugs. These included enforcing the law (26,254 FIRs registered, 31,462 drug traffickers arrested, 725.1 kg heroin recovered, 388 absconders arrested) with effect from January 1, 2019. In an effort to de-addict the addicts, the Government of Punjab has set up 176 OOAT Clinics where 81,369 drug users are registered and 4.7 lakh drug users treated. To prevent the abuse, 5.25 lakh DAPOs have been registered and 40 lakh students have been made aware through the Buddy programme. A 24/7 helpline with phone number 181 has also been installed. In addition to that, several initiatives in the form of incentives and disincentive have been announced. Nonetheless, the efficacy of all the governments' initiatives is not pronouncedly visible on the ground. This is mainly because of the lack of motivation, commitment and dedication on the part of all the actors and agencies engaged in executing and implementing the initiatives and programmers. A lack of acknowledging the socio-cultural and politico-economic reasons behind drug addiction and abuse is also a reason for the low effectiveness of the government's programmes.

These perceptions have also been supplemented by the views expressed about Urban Local Bodies during FGDs, where, after the example of the Punjab government initiative was given, many participating executive officers of Municipal Committees (MCs) shared that the recently started Drug Abuse Prevention Officer (DAPO) programme of Punjab government is like a non-starter. The police approached the MC office only once to register the officials and voluntary DAPO without any follow-up. There was no training organised for them to teach them how to perform their duties in tackling the drug menace. It was suggested that every ward member should be assigned the responsibility of providing names of good volunteers as DAPO. The anti-drug laws should be strictly enforced and people's participation should be encouraged, increased and ensured. Also, teachers and students participating in FGDs mentioned that the DAPO scheme initiated to tackle the drug problem has not taken off. The DAPOs objectives could have been easily achieved by involving the ASHA Workers. In many cases, small-time drug peddlers had an opportunity to get registered under DAPO with the motive of promoting their illegal drug trade under its mask.

Of course, the government constituted a special task force (STF) to curb drug addiction and abuse. There was some initial success to the SIT, but both the supply and demand is going on nearly as usual. So much so, even the report of the SIT could not be made public. The only measure was the arrest of thousands of small-time drug smugglers, peddlers and addicts. No big fish was arrested. Significantly, the election manifesto of SAD/BJP (Srimoni Akali Dal and Bhartya Janta Party) and AAP also promised to curb the drug menace in Punjab. As a matter of fact, the drug menace has been one of the main election planks ever since the 2017 Assembly Elections in Punjab. Even in the 2022 Assembly elections, the drug menace was a major election plank, but not much success is visible on ground.

Much politicking is being done on the drug menace, but it is a far-cry from curbing the drug business and smuggling, according to respondents. In fact, people want strict action against the peddlers as well as big- and small-time smugglers of drugs. They are also of the view that, in order to decrease the use of illicit drugs, the government should allow controlled production of licit narcotics. Along with this, the government agencies must be more vigilant on the international and inter-state borders so that the drug supply chain is broken. Intensive and extensive awareness campaigns against the ill effects of drugs should also be conducted strictly. However, political patronage, corruption and a lack of commitment are the major hurdles in effectively denting the demand and supply chain. In fact, all the previously mentioned factors are interconnected and strongly indicate the nexus between police and politicians and big smugglers.

## 7.6 Perception of addicts' households about the role of police

Police are supposed to play an important role in implementing the anti-drug programme of the government. It is in this context that this section discusses respondents' perception about the role of police in implementing the anti-drug programme and curbing the drug menace. Table 7.9 highlights community perception about the role of police. Though it is a general expectation that police must play an important role in curbing the drug menace, and, hence, take strict action against the drug supplies and consumers of drugs, but community perception does not support this general expectation. Only 8.63 percent of respondents (82 out of 950) said that the police performs their duty strictly against the drug menace (Table 7.9). The rest of the respondents are at variance with this small proportion of respondents. Their perception is that, due to rampant corruption and political pressure, police lack seriousness in action and only take selective actions against the small-time drug suppliers, peddlers and drug consumers. The police often hesitate to catch the 'big fish.' The respondents openly said that, instead of catching the mother of thieves, the police generally catch the small-time thieves. In folk wisdom, it is often said, "*Chor nu na maro, chor di ma nu maro*" ("Instead of killing the thief, kill the mother of the thief") if you really want to wipe out the problem. This time-tested folk wisdom is completely applicable to the war against

*Table 7.9* Role of police in curbing the drug menace

| *State→* *Perception↓* | *Punjab* | *Haryana* | *H.P.* | *J&K* | *Rajasthan* | *Total* |
|---|---|---|---|---|---|---|
| Corruption in the department | 267 (48.55) | 44 (44.00) | 33 (33.00) | 29 (29.00) | 38 (38.00) | 411 (43.26) |
| Lack of seriousness | 68 (12.36) | 10 (10.00) | 13 (13.00) | 61 (61.00) | 37 (37.00) | 189 (19.89) |
| Selective action | 71 (12.91) | 20 (20.00) | 20 (20.00) | 03 (3.00) | 14 (14.00) | 128 (13.47) |
| Political pressure | 56 (10.18) | 15 (15.00) | 03 (3.00) | 02 (2.00) | 02 (2.00) | 78 (8.21) |
| Police as drug user and peddler | 47 (8.55) | 08 (8.00) | 01 (1.00) | 02 (2.00) | 04 (4.00) | 62 (6.53) |
| Police take strict action | 41 (7.45) | 03 (3.00) | 30 (30.00) | 03 (3.00) | 05 (5.00) | 82 (8.63) |
| Total | 550 (100.00) | 100 (100.00) | 100 (100.00) | 100 (100.00) | 100 (100.00) | 950 (100.00) |

the drug menace, but the police are found wanting in such a spirit. Also, the professional approach is missing.

Police personnel taking drugs also result in a lack of seriousness on the part of police. Table 7.9 reveals that 43.26 percent of the respondents said that, because of corruption in the department, the efficacy of police actions gets eroded. Across states, this proportion varies from 29 percent in J&K to 48.55 percent in Punjab. Another 20 percent of respondents are of the opinion that there is an utter lack of seriousness on the part of the police to curb the drug menace. Across states, this varies from 10 percent in Haryana to 61 percent in J&K. Thus, there is a huge inter-state variation in the perception of the respondents. Political pressure on the police is not very high, according to only 8.21 percent of respondents. However, corruption, lack of seriousness and selective action are intertwined, and without political patronage to the police and smugglers, the supply of drugs may not be possible at such a large scale. 6.53 percent of respondents said that some police personnel are also drug users and peddlers. Some of the respondents in the case studies also revealed that their parents gave big bribes to the police for not making a case against them when they were caught for drug peddling or drug consumption. All these factors mar the effectiveness of the police's war against the drug menace and, hence, the efficiency in implementing government programmes against drugs gets adversely affected.

## 7.7 Police's connivance and involvement as per media reports

It is a well-established fact that police personnel, especially some lower-level officers (station house officers [SHOs] and some other such officials), are directly or indirectly engaged in supporting/facilitating the drug business. According to the Union Minister of State for Home Affairs Kiren Rijiju's statement in the Rajya Sabha in June 2016, out of the 68 arrested policemen since 2014, 53 were from the Punjab police (Hindustan Times, June 13, 2016). Very recently, a media report revealed that a DSP (Deputy Superintendent of Police) was arrested under the NDPA Act for taking a Rs. 10 lakh bribe from a drug supplier in Tarn Taran District, Punjab (The Tribune, July 7, 2022). Another official (Assistant Sub-Inspector) was also named in this case. Another report (The Tribune, May 24, 2022) stated that five lower-level police officials were arrested because of their involvement in a drug racket. Missing contraband in about 65 criminal cases also points towards the involvement of the police in protecting the drug suppliers (The Tribune, November 20, 2021). The involvement of some officials from Central Jail, Patiala in facilitating the supply of drugs to the kingpin lodged in the jail also confirms the perceived connivance between police and drug peddlers. According to the report, "The kingpin. . . in jail for the last several years, had reportedly been earning from Rs. 5–10 lakh per month by selling drugs to fellow inmates" (The Tribune, April 12, 2019). This was revealed by Ludhiana Police to the Punjab and Haryana High Court. The High Court took serious note of it (Malik, 2022). The over-utilisation of capacity (when a much large number of addicts than capacity are admitted) by the private drug de-addiction centres (DDCs) also indicates the implicit support of police (Hindustan Times, July 31, 2018).

The appointment of a 'tainted' Senior Superintendent of Police (SSP) of district Moga (infamous for drug business), Punjab, in place of his predecessor (who was transferred because of his alleged involvement in the drug business) in 2018 is a classic case of high police officials' and politicians' support for the drug business (Hindustan Times, July 4, 2018a). According to a media report, the said SSP allegedly received Rs. 40 lakh to let off three junior cops in a 2013 drug case. Ironically, despite this, the officer still managed to get plum post. The report further says that a powerful Minister from Majha region (who later became a relative of the said SSP) had recommended his posting. Some of the senior functionaries of state Congress and some Ministers in Punjab expressed shock at the appointment of the tainted SSP (Hindustan Times, July 4, 2018b).

In another significant case, an ex-IPS officer, Saji Mohan (former Zonal Director with the Narcotic Control Bureau [NCB], Chandigarh and Joint Director, Enforcement Directorate) was sentenced to 15 years in jail for smuggling drugs. His then-driver, Constable Rajesh Kumar Kataria, the co-accused, was awarded ten years imprisonment. Mohan was caught with 10 kg of heroin smuggled from across the border via J&K. He would allegedly steal over 50 percent of contraband seized by NCB and sell it to peddlers in various cities (The Tribune, August 20, 2019). A Border Security Force (BSF) constable was dismissed for his involvement in cross-border smuggling of drugs and weapons (The Tribune, August 8, 2020).

The prevalence of drugs in prisons as well as the disposal of contraband (without the knowledge and permission of the high ups) caught in the prisons is also a serious problem. The media's (The Tribune, May 4, 2022) report regarding two ex-DIGs (Deputy Inspector Generals) of police for disposing of drugs without the knowledge of senior police officers is an indication towards that. The inordinate delay in registering the case against the two accused also speaks about the questionable role of police. As per the media report, the matter pertained to the period between 2005 and 2011, during which period the accused were posted as jail superintendents at Ferozpur Jail. It is alleged that, against 241 seizures of intoxicants and mobile phones from the jail inmates, the accused officials allegedly reported only one incident to police. The case has been registered under the NDPS Act and also the Prevention of Corruption Act.

Similar views were also raised during FGDs with ULBs, religious and spiritual bodies and medical experts. Most of the participants expressed their concerns about the dishonest and insincere functioning of the police department in controlling the drug menace. It was a common perception that police are the only law-enforcing agency that can play a formidable role in curbing the drug menace. In their perception, the police generally have information about notorious people involved in drug smuggling and peddling. All the hot points in the village and *mohallas* of any city are in the knowledge of the police, especially in the knowledge of the station house officers (SHOs). On condition of anonymity, many respondents also revealed that most of the plum police stations (thanas) 'famous' for drug smuggling are even 'auctioned' by the powers that be and the SHOs pay 'monthly' (monthly payment) to the higher police officials and the politicians. They further said that the inordinate long posting of some SHOs at some particulars police stations is a testimony of their claim. They even said that the police, especially the lower ranked officials and staff, are often hand-in-glove with the drug smugglers and peddlers for petty gains. Many of them are also even habitual takers of drugs. These officials protect the drug peddlers and their illegal activities. Such corrupt practices dilute the efforts made by other sincere officers in the department. Similar views were also raised during FGDs with teachers and students and with members of various religious and spiritual bodies.

Participants also disclosed that if well-meaning police officers try to take effective measures, they fail to sustain them, as they do not often get the required support from the high-ups and elected representatives. Many times, political interference does not allow such officers to work in the desired direction. Often, such officers are transferred from such assignments. Some police officials from Himachal Pradesh (H.P.), during FGD, revealed that, in spite of hard efforts of the police, the trade is going on unabated. The police have very limited force to act and the terrain is difficult. Some officers were of the view that section 50 of the NDPS Act does not allow police personnel to search the accused in case of any suspicious circumstances. Further, the witnesses often turn hostile and the efforts made by the investigating officer (IO) go to waste. The criminals get the benefit of the doubt and often get relief from the court. The court proceedings have serious gaps, which is a big challenge for the IOs. They suggested that the legal process needs to be expedited as a priority. Action should be taken against hostile witnesses and not against the IOs. On many occasions, intoxicants like *charas* were recovered, but under the undue pressure exerted by the villagers, the culprits were released.

It is clear from the foregoing discussion that the role of police in tackling drug addiction and abuse is not above board and, hence, there is a need to address the perception of the people. Off the record, many of the respondents said drug peddling and smuggling is just not possible without the explicit and implicit support and convenience of police and political patronage to the drug suppliers (read 'big fish'). According to experts, the confiscation of such a big consignment (532 kg heroine) on June 26, 2019 at Attari (the international border between India and Pakistan) could not cross the border without the connivance of powerful persons in the bureaucracy and the police (Ranjan, 2019) and maybe of some bureaucrats. It is beyond comprehension that for a long period, India did not install the full-body truck scanners at the Indo-Pakistan border at the Attari Integrated check post (ICP), whereas on the Pakistan side there is a full-body truck scanner. Another moot question is how did the authorities on the Pakistan side allow the truck to cross over to the Indian side despite the scanner? One can understand that it may be a part of Pakistan's 'proxy war' against India, but what about India's safety measures? Despite the fact that the Indo-Pakistan border has always been an 'alive' border, and frequent drug smuggling from the 'Golden Crescent' is prevalent, why did not the government of India install the full-body truck scanner when the ICP at Attari came into operation in 2012? Besides, it also puts a question mark on the performance of India's intelligent agencies and the para-military forces deployed at the international borders, especially the one between India and Pakistan.

## 7.8 Role of political leadership in the eyes of households and civil society

Though one would like to believe that political parties and leaders are not involved in patronizing the drug smugglers and peddlers, yet the perception of the people does not support such a belief. During our interaction with people from various walks of life (through FGDs), it has come out that some political leaders from across the political parties have been patronizing the drug business and there is a well-structured network down the line. Such a phenomenon has always been there in history, especially during the colonial period. The opium war fought between Britain and China is the most notorious example of political patronage and the nexus between opium-supplying companies and political leaders.

> In the first half of the nineteenth century, the British east India Company and sundry British business people made fortunes by exporting drugs, particularly opium, to China. Millions of Chinese became addicts, debilitating the country both economically and socially. In the late 1830s the Chinese government issued a ban on drug trafficking, but British merchants simply ignored the law. Chinese authorities began to confiscate and destroy drug cargos. The drug cartels had close connections in Westminster and Downing Street – many MPs and Cabinet Ministers in fact held stock in the drug companies – so they pressured the government to take action. In 1840 Britain duly declared war on China in the name of 'free trade. . . . In the late nineteenth century, about 40 million Chinese, a tenth of the country's population, were opium addicts.
>
> (Harari, 2011, p. 364)

The panchayats that are raising their voices and mobilising support against drug abuse are facing resistance from anti-social elements who are getting the political and police patronage implicitly as well as explicitly. Panchayat members and community members attending the FGDs openly revealed that most the political parties openly distribute alcohol and *bhukki* in lieu of Votes during elections.

Some of the respondents (on the condition of anonymity) confided that there is a deep-rooted nexus between some political leaders, police officials and big drug suppliers/smugglers. In their considered opinion, this unholy tripartite nexus (police, smugglers and politicians: PSP) is ruining the youth for future generations. In their perception, the drug business at this scale is just not possible without the connivance of political leaders and police with the drug smugglers and peddlers. The quick, high and huge return is the reason behind such a nexus. Such views were also aired at the Chief Ministers' conference of eight North-Indian states held at Chandigarh in July 2019. One of the CMs even said that it is mainly because of the mind-boggling return that the drug business is flourishing and, hence, it is not so easy to curb it. Unfortunately, the well-connected and well-organised people behind this PSP nexus are doing it for their own narrow-vested interest, which is proving counterproductive. They further said that, actually, it is mainly because of this nexus that 'big fish' are not being caught. They even revealed that almost all the political parties take huge election funds from the big drug-smugglers. And in the process, they even ignore the larger enlightened interests of the region and the basic issues of the people. Almost all the respondents were of the view that Punjabi youth are emigrating mainly because of three reasons: unemployment, the drug menace and the large-scale prevalence of organised gangs. Such a situation has developed mainly due to the previously said unholy nexus. In their opinion, it is just not possible to attain positive results in curbing the drug menace and reversing the trend without breaking the PSP nexus. Many of the respondents were really at pain because of such a pathetic scenario.

The previously stated perception of the people has also been supported by Sahni (2019), who said that there is a need to recognise the insidious way of war by narco-terrorism. The networks of collaborators within Punjab, according to him, are no less dangerous than terrorists with bombs and bullets. He writes,

> Unfortunately, their impact and role in devastating the State remains largely unacknowledged. Tens of thousands of petty smugglers have, no doubt, been arrested over the past years. But the "big fish", the masters of the game, remain beyond the reach of the enforcement agencies.

Many people in Punjab revealed the names of some political leaders (for the sake of ethics and anonymity we are not mentioning their names), who, in their perception and according to their knowledge, are behind the drug menace. The involvement of one such big leader of a political party, who remained in the prison, was revealed by an alleged drug smuggler, Jagdish Bhola. It is mainly because of political patronage and the PSP nexus that the drug menace has assumed such an alarming scenario and the situation has gone from bad to worse, particularly in Punjab. The following section dwells on people's perceptions about the role of political leaders in the drug use and abuse across the states.

### *7.8.1 Distribution of intoxicants and drugs during elections*

It is a well-known fact that the political parties and their candidates distribute intoxicants and drugs in order to woo voters in their favour, besides doing irrational competitive political populism. It is equally true that all the voters do not cast their vote by taking intoxicants and drugs, but a good number of them do vote for such considerations. Even elections to religious bodies are not totally free from the distribution of intoxicants and drugs. This has been witnessed during so many elections in the past. The Election Commission of India, too, has revealed these facts from time to time.

Table 7.10 clearly highlights that the distribution of intoxicants and drugs (mainly alcohol, poppy husk and opium) by every political party during the elections have been taking place at a very large scale. Approximately 94 percent of respondents at the aggregate level have supported this viewpoint. Across states, their proportion varies from 79 percent in J&K to 99.34 percent in Rajasthan. Just 5.68 percent of respondents said distribution of intoxicants and drugs to voters is not there. This proportion in Punjab is 98 percent. Between 2 to 3 percent of the respondents said certain illicit drugs are also distributed during the elections. With such nefarious activities the political parties lose the moral authority to curb the drug business, besides de-motivating well-meaning and dedicated police officials and thereby puncturing government programmes.

### *7.8.2 Political patronage to drug suppliers*

It has come out from the households' responses that political leaders patronise and often have a personal interest in promoting the drug business, though they have a different public face. Out of all the 1,566 respondents, 53 percent are of the perception that political leaders are involved in patronizing the drug business. Across states, their proportion varies from 40.13 percent in Rajasthan to 57.41 percent in Punjab. Thus, political patronage is very high in all the states under study. About 17 percent of the total respondents hold the opinion that political leaders are personally involved in the drug business. The response is highest (22.37 percent) in Haryana, followed by

*Table 7.10* Distribution of intoxicants and drugs by political parties to woo voters

| *State→*<br>*Response↓* | *Punjab* | *Haryana* | *H.P.* | *J&K* | *Rajasthan* | *Total* |
|---|---|---|---|---|---|---|
| Yes | 939<br>(98.02) | 144<br>(94.74) | 123<br>(80.92) | 120<br>(78.95) | 151<br>(99.34) | 1477<br>(94.32) |
| No | 19<br>(1.98) | 08<br>(5.26) | 29<br>(19.08) | 32<br>(21.05) | 01<br>(0.66) | 89<br>(5.68) |
| Total | 958<br>(100.00) | 152<br>(100.00) | 152<br>(100.00) | 152<br>(100.00) | 152<br>(100.00) | 1566<br>(100.00) |

J&K (18.43 percent) and Punjab (17.95 percent). Thus, about 70 percent of respondents hold the view that political patronage and political leaders' personal stake in the drug business is quite high. This, in turn, adversely impacts government programmes to break the supply chain and other measures to curb the drug menace. At the aggregate level, 25.13 percent of respondents hold such views. Across states, their proportion varies from 24.63 percent in Punjab to 48.68 percent in Rajasthan (Table 7.11).

Almost similar views have been expressed by drug addicts. At the aggregate level, 38.84 percent of drug addicts said that the drug business is being patronised by political leaders. Among the states, this proportion ranges between 33 percent in J&K and 44 percent in Haryana. Regarding personal interest in the supply of drugs, 27.47 percent of respondents hold the view that political leaders do have a personal interest in expanding the drug business (Table 7.12). Across states, it varies from 21 percent in Haryana to 29.27 percent in Punjab. These two factors led to the third one, and that is

*Table 7.11* Political patronage to drug suppliers: Household's perception

| *State→ Response↓* | *Punjab* | *Haryana* | *H.P.* | *J&K* | *Rajasthan* | *Total* |
|---|---|---|---|---|---|---|
| Political patronage | 550 (57.41) | 73 (48.03) | 80 (52.63) | 66 (43.42) | 61 (40.13) | 830 (53.00) |
| Personal interest in supply* | 172 (17.95) | 16 (10.53) | 34 (2.37) | 28 (18.43) | 17 (11.18) | 267 (17.05) |
| Adverse impact on curbing drugs | 236 (24.63) | 63 (41.45) | 38 (25.00) | 58 (38.16) | 74 (48.68) | 469 (25.13) |
| Total | 958 (100.00) | 152 (100.00) | 152 (100.00) | 152 (100.00) | 152 (100.00) | 1,566 (100.00) |

* Mainly includes those who are drug users and peddlers

*Table 7.12* Drug addicts' views about political patronage to drug suppliers

| *State→ Response↓* | *Punjab* | *Haryana* | *H.P.* | *J&K* | *Rajasthan* | *Total* |
|---|---|---|---|---|---|---|
| Vested patronage | 223 (40.55) | 44 (44.00) | 34 (34.00) | 33 (33.00) | 35 (35.00) | 369 (38.84) |
| Create hindrances in supply* | 161 (29.27) | 21 (21.00) | 27 (27.00) | 24 (24.00) | 28 (28.00) | 261 (27.47) |
| Adverse impact on curbing drugs | 166 (30.18) | 35 (35.00) | 39 (39.00) | 43 (43.00) | 37 (37.00) | 320 (33.58) |
| Total | 550 (100.00) | 100 (100.00) | 100 (100.00) | 100 (100.00) | 100 (100.00) | 950 (100.00) |

* Mainly includes those who are drug users and peddlers

the adverse impact on drug curbing efforts of the government. At the aggregate level, 33.68 percent of drug addicts shared that political patronage and intervention puts a great deal of hurdles in the effective implementation of government policies and strategies to curb the drug business. Across states, the proportion varies from 30 percent in Punjab to 43 percent in J&K. It is clear from the responses of households and drug addicts that the drug business and trade may not be possible without the tacit and active support of politicians and the police. In fact, there is a strong and deep-rooted nexus between smugglers, police and politicians (PSP).

Arora and Kaura (2017), in their study, also highlighted that the prevalence of drug-cartels and powerful drug-traffickers has weakened the law enforcement agencies and local political organisations. Further, the study (with reference to a retired IPS officer in Punjab, Shashi Kant) said that the major political parties are hand-in-glove with big drug smugglers in Punjab. Kant, a former DGP of Punjab, claims that he handed over a list of 90 people involved in drug smuggling to the then-SAD-BJP government (2012 to 2017). That list included the names of politicians across the spectrum (some sitting ministers, a number of former ministers and sitting and former MLAs), certain very senior police officers, some administrative services officers (IAS) and a large number of Station House Officers (SHOs), besides a few NGOs (Indian Express, June 11, 2016). The study further says that in January 2014, Jagdish Singh Bhola had claimed that Bikram Singh Majithia, was involved in the multi-crore drug trafficking racket (Sehgal, 2014).

## 7.9. Some media reports highlighting the Police-Smugglers-Politicians (PSP) nexus

The media reports also indicate the unholy nexus between police, smugglers and politicians (PSP). The police-smugglers-politician nexus has been amply highlighted by Ramachandaran (2023). The replacement of one tainted senior superintendent of Police (SSP) with another tainted SSP of district Moga at the behest of some heavy-weight political leaders of the ruling party (then Congress) is in itself a proof of political-police patronage to the drug smugglers. According to the then Inspector General Police (IGP) Bathinda, the dubious manner in which the accused SSP let off the accused in a drug smuggling case in itself is an evidence of the police's connivance with smugglers (Hindustan Times, July 4, 2018).

The Times of India (February 14, 2017) also reported the dubious role of SP (Superintendent of Police) level officer Satwinder Singh's connection to the Pathankot Attack by Pakistan militants. The arrest is a slap on the face of all powerful leaders who slept for years on issues at the heart of Punjab's soul (The Tribune, December 22, 2021). Niranjan Singh (an ex-senior official of the Enforcement Directorate [ED] of the government of India), who was investigating the Jagdish Bhola's case, said that the action is too late. It was also reported in the media that Niranjan Singh was transferred while the investigation was still in progress and at a very crucial stage. This also raises suspicion that someone in the government of India was also shielding a very important Minister (who was later caught under the NSDP Act and was put into prison) of the SAD-BJP government. Paradoxically, the said minister, Bikram Singh Majithia (whose name figured in the Jagdish Bhola case), was exonerated of his involvement in drug racket by the then Chief Minister of Punjab (*Hindustan Times* 18 March 2015). In another media report (Punjabi Tribune, May 14, 2022) Navjot Singh Sidhu (former President Punjab Pradesh Congress) said that breaking the nexus between drug smugglers and politicians is a pre-condition to curb the drug menace in Punjab. The Punjab's STF report on drugs has allegedly faced many administrative and legal odds despite its submission (between February and May 2018) to the Punjab and Haryana High Court. The report remained pending before the High Court for a long period and, hence, the legal course got delayed for reasons best known to the Court and the government of Punjab. The delay in taking action on the three reports also points out to some tacit PSP nexus. The Punjab and Haryana High Court ordered the Punjab government to give a status report on it (The Tribune, March 30, 2022). The High Court also took serious note of a 'shoddy probe' in a drug case (The Tribune, May 25, 2022). Nonetheless, the respondents were of the view that the judiciary should be more proactive in drug-related cases and suggested fast-track designated courts because it is very serious threat to society.

The very fact that the Shrimani-Akali Dal and Bhartiya Janta Party (SAD-BJP) government (2007 to 2017) did not take any serious cognizance of the widespread drug menace in Punjab (despite the fact that the drug menace was an important pole plank in the 2007 and 2012 Assembly elections and despite the fact that, in Jagdish Bhola's case, there was a pointer towards the involvement of a powerful minister of SAD) also speaks volumes about the unholy PSP nexus. Congress, after assuming the reins in Punjab in 2017, constituted an anti-drug STF (Special Task Force), but did not take the STF inquiry to a logical conclusion (even changing the top most officer of STF mid-way), which also indicates weak political will and an uninspiring approach to dealing with the drug menace. In the opinion of civil society, such conduct may be because of some tacit understanding between the then-Chief Minister and the SAD President, who is a close relative of the allegedly involved Minister. The powerful Minister was, however, arrested in December 2021, and that, too, when there was much hue and cry from the top political leaders of the Punjab Congress visualizing apparent defeat in the forthcoming state assembly elections.

The central leadership of Congress also took a serious note of such developments and eventually the CM, Captain Amarinder Singh, had to lose the CM's position before the 2022 Assembly elections. It is significant to mention that, when our empirical work was in progress, we got an anonymous handwritten letter (in English) indicating the involvement of a number of local people in drug peddling and the supply of drugs. The letter, from one of the district headquarters of Punjab, listed the names of 52 persons (with their mobile numbers) who, according to the letter, were directly involved in the drug business. Many of them were directly or indirectly being shielded by political leaders and police personnel. Incidentally, this letter was addressed to the Deputy Commissioner and SSP of the concerned district besides 18 other dignitaries including the Prime Minister, Chief Minister and DGP, Punjab.

In fact, such instances are not isolated; often, we came across such information during our interaction with people from various walks of life at the time of field visits. Unfortunately, the unholy nexus between police, big smugglers (mother of the thief) and the politicians, according to respondents, is mainly responsible for not catching the 'big fish.' The bureaucrats' tacit support of the drug menace often does not come to the fore, but their tacit connivance cannot be ruled out, according to the respondents. The legal lacuna in case preparation and presentation of the case by the police and the very low rate of conviction also discourages and disappoints the well-meaning police officials in upholding their 'war on drugs.' The participants in the FGDs said, very emphatically, that without catching and punishing the 'mother of the thief,' it is virtually impossible to break the supply chain of drugs.

The role of political leaders both at the local and state level is not above board, according to respondents, as far as the drug problem is concerned. Almost similar is the view of respondents for the police. In fact, the true perception of the people is that there is a strong and deep-rooted nexus between some political leaders, police officials and drug-smugglers. Corruption in the police has come up as one of the significant reasons behind the spread of drug abuse and addiction. Nonetheless, a very high proportion of the respondents has faith in the government's capability to address the drug menace, provided there is political and bureaucratic will and sincere and determined efforts are made. All the stakeholders will have to join hands and work in the missionary mode to curb the drug menace.

In a nutshell, people and civil society are not satisfied with the efforts of the religious organisations, political leadership, police and government and, hence, they do not hold much of a positive perspective about the role of these agencies. They also are of the view that even the judiciary is very slow to deal with legal issues related to the drug menace. As such, people and members of civil society are not very hopeful of getting rid of the drug menace. Nonetheless, they are of the view that breaking the supply and demand chain is sine qua non for curbing the drug menace, and this needs a strong politico-bureaucratic-will.

# 8 Conclusion

According to the World Health Organisation (WHO), drug or alcohol addiction is the repeated use of a psychoactive substance or substances to the extent that the user (referred to as an addict) is periodically or chronically intoxicated, shows a compulsion to take the preferred substance (or substances), has great difficulty in voluntarily ceasing or modifying substance use, and exhibits determination to obtain psychoactive substances by almost any means. The prevalence and spread of the drug menace is a global phenomenon and is embedded into the socio-cultural and politico-economic systems, hence, a systemic problem. There is a triangular relationship between the supply of and demand for drugs. The three ends of the triangle are countries of production, countries of trans-shipment, and countries of targeted consumption. Paradoxically, all three sets of countries have convergence and divergence of 'interests.' The producer countries have a 'great economic interest' and the targeted countries generate 'demand' for drugs, while the third set of countries provide the 'safe' transit route for drugs. There are three major global centres (and hence a triangle) of heroin and cocaine production and processing in the world. These are the Golden Triangle (Myanmar, Thailand and Laos), the Golden Crescent (Afghanistan, Iran and Pakistan) and South America. The rich and developed countries such as the USA, Canada and the EU are the targeted countries because of their higher purchasing power. Countries sharing the border with the producer countries become transit routes and, hence, are vulnerable to the drug menace (UNODC, 2004). The changing pattern has been a transition from natural drugs to derivative and synthetic drugs, which has further accentuated the global challenge. The change in drug use pattern is also observable in the context of age category, where people as young as 16 become victims of drug abuse (Charles, Bewley-Tylor, and Neidpath, 2005) and the previously sanctified norms and sanctions on the use of drugs stands breached or broken. Increased communication and connectivity has also become very handy to the drug producers as they supply drugs across international borders. It has also led to financing and promoting narco-terrorism, which is posing a serious threat to global peace and development.

DOI: 10.4324/9781003318019-8

The global community and countries are trying to address the drug menace individually as well as jointly. The UN Convention on Narcotic Drugs in 1961 is an important landmark in addressing drug trafficking across borders. The UN General Assembly passed a resolution (resolution 42/112 of December 7, 1987) to observe June 26 as the International Day Against Drug Abuse and Illicit Trafficking and, since 1988, it has been observed on the 26th of June every year. A number of international agencies, such as the United Nations Office of Drugs and Crime (UNODC), the United Nations Drug Control Programme (UNDP) and the International Narcotic Control Board (INCB), are making conscious efforts to curb the menace by highlighting the issue and spreading awareness about the ill effects of the drug menace. The reports of these agencies and other scholarly studies have amply highlighted the health and developmental challenges posed by the ever-increasing drug menace to the global community.

The debate and discourse concerning factors that have led to an increasing use and abuse of drugs vary between holding the individual drug addict responsible for addiction or holding responsible the socio-cultural, economic and political system that is pushing an individual into drug addiction and abuse. Different disciplines have vacillated between various permutations and combinations within these two larger constructs of the debate. Most of the studies reviewed indicated that mainly teens and youth are succumbing to drug addiction and abuse. Its implications have been variedly understood with each implication intertwined with the other, impacting all the social, economic and political institutions the world over.

The visible change in drug use patterns commenced in the Indian context during the 1980s, when India inadvertently became a part of the drug trafficking route between the Golden Crescent (West-Asian production centre) and the Golden Triangle (East-Asian production centre). Within the country, the locations sharing an international border became more vulnerable since they fell directly on the trans-shipment routes. Punjab (along with some other Northwestern states of India) happened to be one such state, sharing a long border (553 kms) with Pakistan and, hence, became a transit route for drug trafficking. The trend has witnessed an increase since the 1980s, when heroin entered into trafficking and became part of the underground economy of the drug business in the country.

The initial response of successive Indian governments, both at the centre and state level, was of denial, which continued for a long period of time. The issue acquired prominence after the enactment of the Narcotic Drugs and Psychotropic Substance (NDPS) Act, 1985. However, the denial attitude and approach of the successive governments of Punjab cost the state very dearly as there has been a multi-fold increase in the usage of drugs, even that of heroin over the same period of time. In spite of its own acceptance in the court of law in Punjab and Haryana High Court in 2009, the then-government of Punjab and its successive governments failed to deal with this issue both at a moral and policy level. The drug addiction and abuse continued to increase and spread its tentacles across the state. The geo-political location of Punjab and the already prevalent culture of using traditional drugs and alcohol augmented the problem further.

Misinterpretation of the findings of a drug addiction study (Sandhu, 2009), highlighted the issue out of proportion. The entire sample of Sandhu's study was of drug addicts (who were addicted to alcohol, tobacco and hard drugs) and, among them, 73 percent were youth in the age group of 16 to 35 years. By any stretch of imagination, this does not mean that '73 percent' of Punjabi youth are drug addicted. Sandhu's findings were grossly misinterpreted and misrepresented by the government of Punjab. In its affidavit submitted to the Punjab and Haryana High Court in 2009, it made the submission that about 70 percent of youth in Punjab are addicted to drugs. Paradoxically, the state government neither corrected its position nor took any corresponding remedial measures despite its confession of the drug menace in Punjab. The arrest of some prominent public figures in 2012 started awakening the government from slumber.

To add fuel to it, the Bollywood movie, *Udta Punjab* (released in 2016) created an image of the state as afflicted by drug addiction to the extent that the youth of Punjab are in a rut and drugs a common visual on the roads in the state. The reporting and misreporting of facts about drug addiction and abuse in Punjab provided the impetus and motivation to undertake the present study. The main objective was, thus, to understand the ground reality and our quest for it guided us to also study Punjab's neighbouring states. Our research programme was commissioned and funded by the Indian Council of Social Science Research (ICSSR), the Government of India's HRD Ministry.

In the wake of ensuing Punjab's Legislative Assembly election of 2017, the drug menace in Punjab became a prominent issue with all the political parties of the state and they were compelled to include it in their election manifestos. There was high anti-incumbency for the previous SAD-BJP government and the drug menace was one of the prominent election issues. There has been high skepticism among the populace of the state over the years regarding connivance between political leaders, police and drug smugglers, without which the spread of drugs, especially to such a huge extent, was not possible. The drug menace was also a prominent poll plank in the 2022 Assembly Elections of Punjab.

The present study was envisaged to understand the ongoing discourse on various parameters of drug addiction and abuse and then contribute to the existing understanding and literature. The study pertains to five states of Northwest India, with a central focus on Punjab. The other four states are Haryana, Himachal Pradesh, Rajasthan and the Jammu division of Jammu and Kashmir. These are all neighbouring states of Punjab. The districts from these states were selected based upon the National Crime Record Bureau (NCRB) data on seizures of drugs and presence of private and government de-addiction and rehabilitation centres. The districts selected from the state of Punjab were Amritsar (which included both Amritsar and Tarn Taran districts, as Tarn Taran was earlier part of Amritsar), Bathinda (which included both Mansa and Bathinda, as Mansa was earlier part of Bathinda), Sangrur, Moga, Ludhiana, and Jalandhar. From Haryana, districts of Sirsa and Ambala were selected, from Jammu and Kashmir (J&K) it was Kathua and Jammu, from Himachal Pradesh (H.P.) it was Kullu and Kangra and from Rajasthan it was Sriganganagar and Hanumangarh.

Our study is based on a review of literature and secondary as well primary data. The empirical part of the study dwells on the quantitative and qualitative data and information collected from 3,386 respondents. Primary data was collected from 950 addicts and their household members (950), 190 hidden addicts, 616 control group households (households with no addict), 640 participants in 77 focus group discussions (FGDs) and 40 case studies across the states. Given the size of the sample and spatial spread of the respondents, we can safely claim that ours is a representative study and is the first of its kind focusing on the Northwestern states of India. It is pertinent to mention that, in compliance with ethical requirements, we got prior consent of all the respondents and, in view of their privacy, we have not disclosed their identities. Though the research programme was commissioned by the ICSSR and permitted by the Centre for Research in Rural and Industrial Development (CRRID), yet we also got the permission to collect the primary data from the concerned authorities of all the five states. It needs to be mentioned that getting necessary permissions from the concerned ministries and government departments of the selected states was a very time consuming task; so much so that Punjab took almost eight months to give permission. Similarly, persuading the respondents to come forward and identifying the hidden drug addicts was also an uphill task. All this caused unnecessary delays in starting our primary survey and field visits.

Unlike many previous studies, our study included only those illicit drugs which are under the purview of the Narcotic Drugs and Psychotropic Substances (NDPS) Act, 1985 and does not include liquor and tobacco. The main objective of our study was to understand the socio-cultural and politico-economic dynamics of drug addiction and abuse and not to estimate its extent. As such, we have studied only the addicts who were either taking treatment (as in-patients) in the drug de-addiction centres (DDCs) or were undergoing follow-up treatment and, through them, we reached their households. We also studied the hidden drug addicts (those who did not fall in the two mentioned categories but were addicted to drugs without the knowledge of their household members) by indentifying them through the snowball sampling method.

## Main findings

The main issues that were intended to be understood and analysed included changing trends and patterns of drugs associated with drug addiction and abuse in Punjab, Haryana, Himachal Pradesh, J&K and Rajasthan. The secondary data revealed that there is quite a high incidence of drug usage in these five states. The study discussed the socio-economic profile of the addicts and their households, the process of drug addicts' initiation into addiction, patterns of drug addiction and the socio-economic cost of drug addiction. The study also gathered the community perception about the role of civil society, religious organisations and government institutions including police, elected representatives and political leaders.

As regards gender-composition of addicts, it was found that almost all the drug addicts were males in the drug de-addiction (DDCs) centres, rehabilitation centres and such other centres dealing with drug treatment. The proportion of female drug addicts in our sample is negligible. This is mainly for two reasons. One, the consumption of drugs among females in general is not very common; mainly because of socio-cultural reasons and social taboos. Two, even from amongst those females who are consuming intoxicants, they may not be subject to serious addiction and hence not coming to DDCs. However, some of the respondents during our interactions with various social groups and other knowledgeable persons were of the view that there are some females, even young girls, taking intoxicants, but they refused to reveal their identities, mainly because of a bad reflection on the parents' image, which may even have reflections on the matrimonial prospects of the unmarried girls. So, in the case of females, the first attempt is to conceal their identity.

In regards to the gender composition of household heads (HHs), nearly 21 percent of households are being headed by females, mainly housewives and widows. Most of the addicts are from households whose heads are in the age group of 35 to 65 years. This seems to be because this is the age group when HHs are heavily busy with their commitment to economic and social responsibilities while their children are in the adolescent age and could be easily enticed towards intoxicants. It was also found that a significant number of drug addicts belong to households whose heads are illiterate or just literate. The majority of addicts come from nuclear families.

In regards to the location of the households, the majority of the addicts are from rural households, but the difference between rural and urban households is not significant after normalising the number with rural-urban population. Among the rural households, the majority were agricultural households. Among social characteristics, the prevalence of drug addiction is nearly religion neutral, but across the states a higher proportion of addicts belong to the religion being practised by the majority of the population. Though the spread of drugs occurs among all the social castes, yet the drug incidence is higher in the general category in comparison to their proportion in the total population of the particular state. Nonetheless, drug addiction may not be attributed to any specific social and economic class of households. There may be multiple socio-economic reasons for youth falling prey to intoxicants and drugs. There is need for further research to identify those reasons in depth and detail.

Age of drug addicts is a serious and worrisome concern since a very high proportion (73 percent) of the addicts were in the age group of 17 to 35 years, which is termed as youth-age. This finding corroborates with the finding of an earlier study (Sandhu, 2009), but that was only confined to Punjab with a very small sample. If we add the age group 35 to 45 years, then 88.47 percent of the addicts fall in the age group of 17 to 45 years. Being a highly productive phase of one's life, this is a heavy loss to society and the economy. Significantly, a sizeable majority of the addicts are educated up to senior secondary (12th standard) level.

The occupational data of the addicts reveals that, on the face of it, unemployment is not the main reason behind drug addiction, but being underemployed and low-paid (working poor) seem to be among the main reasons for drug addiction. The majority of the drug addicts are from agricultural households and households with low-paid miscellaneous economic activities. Most private jobs can also be clubbed with such activities. Significantly, a good number of workers in such activities are working poor. Their low income, along with poverty (leading to frustration and economic distress), seems to be the defining factor behind youth becoming addicts and peddlers. But this needs further research. Perhaps, poverty and low-income of the households are behind the higher proportion (58 percent) of addicts starting work in the age group of 14 to 20 years, when most of them should be in schools and colleges. Poverty and low-income may be significant reasons behind the entry of children and teenagers into the labour market and, in turn, the main cause of the high drop-out rate in schools. Significantly, 3.6 percent of the addicts started economic activity even before attaining the age of 14.

## Factors behind drug addiction

The consumption of intoxicants by elders in the household, especially fathers, exerts a significant influence in enticing youth towards intoxicants and other drugs. Medical experts and councillors also support such a view. At the aggregate level, about 77 percent of households have at least one member (mainly male) consuming one or more intoxicants. Generally, the father of the addict is in the habit of consuming intoxicants. Alcohol is the single most dominant intoxicant being consumed by elders in the family.

The majority (65 percent) of the addicts got initiated into the consumption of intoxicants between the age group of 14 to 20. A little more than 10 percent of addicts got hooked on intoxicants between 7 to 14 years of age. The majority of them were school-going children or school drop-outs. Thus, up to 20 years of age, 75 percent of addicts started consuming intoxicants. The proportion goes up to 93 percent by the age of 25. Alcohol and tobacco were the main intoxicants consumed by addicts for the first time. Approximately, 48 percent of the respondents started taking hard drugs (illicit, as well) between the age group of 14 to 20 years.

The empirical data shows that approximately 83 percent of the addicts got hooked on intoxicants and drugs under the peer pressure of classmates and friends. The addicts further revealed that, in the beginning, they started taking intoxicants and drugs mainly for fun and pleasure (in pursuit of bio-chemical pleasure), but with the passage of time they developed liking and lust for intoxicants and drugs. They never knew when their hobby led them to habit formation and, in turn, to drug addiction. There were hosts of other socio-cultural reasons in the background which created circumstances that pushed them to the consumption of intoxicants and drugs.

Disharmonious relations among family members (especially disrupted relations between parents) were among the most important reasons for children getting into drugs. Failure in love relations (including non-acceptance of marriage proposals by parents) was also an important reason for their initiation into drugs. A feeling of neglect and nagging during childhood, parents' son preference, loneliness, stigma and curiosity were some other important reasons for children's initiation into intoxicants. Unfulfilled aspirations and failure in life were also responsible for enticing them towards drugs. Increasing disconnects between parents and children are making the latter more inclined towards their peer group. The ever-increasing trend of the nuclear family, shrinking community interaction and a growing sense of individualism is leading to a perceived sense of loneliness and, in turn, leading to refuge in the company of peers and intoxicants. Under such an 'enabling' social environment, substance use becomes attractive to teenagers and young adults.

Besides the previously mentioned social factors, there are certain important economic factors which are responsible for drug addiction. Unemployment and easy money (quick and ill-gotten money from illegal dealing in drugs) are two prominent factors. In the case of control group respondents (616 respondents from households with no addict), 60 percent have the perception that youth are getting into drugs because of unemployment, under-employment and low-paid economic activities. Similar reasons also emerged during FGDs with village panchayat members and teachers and students from various educational institutions. Besides the previously mentioned social and economic factors, easy availability and supply of drugs is also one of the important causes for initiation into drugs. Punjab, being the transit route of drug trafficking, is more vulnerable to the drugs menace.

## Main drugs, source, methods of consumption and relapsing

The ten major drugs being commonly consumed in the states under study are: heroin (*chitta*/brown sugar), opium, tramadol, poppy husk (*bhukki*), cannabis (*bhang*/*sukha*), marijuana (ganja/smack), buprenorphine, codeine, hashish (*charas*), and cocaine. Some of the drugs are more popular and some are less popular across the states. Heroin is more popular in Punjab and Jammu and Kashmir (J&K) than the other three states. The use of opium is higher in Punjab and Haryana. Poppy husk is a preferred drug in the *Malwa* region of Punjab, Haryana and Rajasthan. Tramadol is more popular in Punjab and the use of cannabis is higher in Himachal Pradesh (H.P.) and J&K. As compared to other states, the use of marijuana is higher in Haryana, Punjab and J&K. Buprenorphine is more popular in Punjab and Haryana. The use of codeine is higher in J&K. Cocaine is also used, though by a small number of addicts, in almost all of the states.

On average, an addict uses more than three drugs. This is mainly because of the availability/non-availability factor and the relative cost of the drugs. In the event of non-availability of a particular drug, the addicts do substitute other available (also cheap) drugs in order to satisfy their need. Thus, addicts' access to a particular drug and affordability are important factors for the use of a particular drug(s). At the aggregate level, the majority of the addicts have a preference for heroin (54 percent) and poppy husk (49 percent), followed by opium (49 percent), cannabis (41 percent), tramadol, marijuana, buprenorphine, hashish/*charas*, codeine and cocaine.

The biggest source of drug supply are the drug peddlers, the most important link in the supply chain between the suppliers and the end consumers. The motive force, inter alia, behind this chain is huge and quick money. This, along with allurement for drug consumption, is a strong motivator for the drug peddlers. Currently, women have also entered into drug peddling and trade, which must be a cause of serious concern for society, security forces and the government. The cross-border as well as internal drug suppliers are deliberately luring women (mainly unemployed) to evade suspicion of the security agencies. Besides peddlers, friends and chemists are the other sources of drugs. However, drug addicts are not confined to one source; instead they use multiple sources of supply.

Mainly three methods of taking drugs are popular among the addicts. These are oral consumption, injecting and inhaling. On average, each addict uses 1.29 methods of consuming drugs. Oral consumption of drugs is the most popular method, followed by inhaling and injecting. Sharing the same syringe by two or more addicts is quite normal across states, and this leads to certain serious ailments such as HIV and AIDS among the addicts. Pleasure, relaxing and energy (biochemical pleasure) are the post-consumption experiences as revealed by the addicts. At the aggregate level, 53 percent of respondents revealed that they draw pleasure after consuming the drug(s), followed by relaxation and energy.

Relapsing is a serious problem, as the majority of addicts are plunging into relapsing after de-addiction treatment. About 66 percent of the addicts who underwent treatment in the de-addiction centres again got into drug consumption mainly due to peer-pressure, curiosity and withdrawal symptoms.

## Social and economic cost

Addiction is a potential social disease which adversely affects an addict's life as well as that of their family and society. There is an immense social cost of drug addiction and abuse in terms of the adverse impact on the health of the drug addicts, which in turn impacts an addict's capacity to lead a healthy life and reap the full potential of the productive years of their life. Serious ailments such as HIV and hepatitis A and hepatitis C are other adverse impacts on the addict's health. Depression, anxiety, panic disorders, aggression, hallucinations and paranoia are other ill effects of drug addiction and abuse. More than 35 percent of the respondents said that their addict family members, mainly son(s), are suffering from multiple serious ailments. About 50 percent of addicts admitted that they are suffering from multiple health issues because of their habit of drug addiction and abuse. The premature deaths caused by such ailments has both social and economic ramifications. The age group of the premature deaths is another major economic cost for the family, society and the economy.

The social cost has implications for economic costs and vice-versa. In fact, drug addiction and abuse is a serious drag on socio-cultural and economic development. As a matter of fact, the drug menace anywhere is a threat to socio-cultural and politico-economic stability everywhere, just as poverty anywhere is a threat to prosperity everywhere. Parents, siblings and relatives of the addicts have to bear an uncalculated social cost in terms of family status and self-esteem, and in lending social and emotional support to their addict family member(s). The adverse impact of drug addiction on the family's image is the most serious effect as nearly 73 percent of households revealed that they are suffering from a deterioration in their image in society due to the drug addiction habit of the family member. In fact, the families are suffering from a double-whammy: economic loss due to the diversion of time and energy, and additional financial burden. They are losing the earnings/productivity of the addicted members, besides spending on their health issues. Even the productivity of the family members is negatively impacted because of disturbed peace of mind, besides attending to the addict at the cost of their health and productivity.

The adverse impact of addiction is not confined to social image and health issues; it has multiple social manifestations for intra-family relations, especially within the nuclear family. Mistrust and trust deficiency among the family members, quarrels, violence, emotional distress and divorce are some of the major ramifications for intra-family relations. More than 83 percent of the respondents revealed that there is a serious trust deficit for the addict. Besides health and relationship issues, the addicts get entangled in a number of anti-social activities, such as theft and peddling, which often results in arrest by the police and even conviction.

The habit of drug addiction and abuse causes a series personal loss to the addicts in terms of self image, work, family life and studies. Out of all the 1,140 respondents, 78 percent admitted the adverse impact of drug addiction on their personal image in society. Nearly 31 percent of respondents admitted that they are suffering from image loss (also in terms of relations) in the neighbourhood and in their friends' circles. Disturbance in family life (many times leading to serious consequences, even leading to constrained matrimonial relations and emotional disturbance to children) has been reported by 66 percent of the respondents.

### Economic cost of drug addiction and abuse

Widespread drug use and abuse puts a huge financial burden on the addict and his/her family, health services, law and order, governance and prisons, yet the calculation and estimation of the economic cost of drug addiction and abuse is a complex phenomenon. So, we mainly collected data of daily expenses on drugs by the addicts, such as their expenditure on treatment, premature deaths and sources of money for the purchase of drugs and treatment. It was found during the survey that more than 97 percent of the addicts experienced financial loss due to their habit of drug addiction and abuse. About 67 percent of addicts were incurring between Rs. 200–1,000 on their daily dose of drug, while the proportion of addicts spending between Rs. 1,000–2,000 is 15 percent and the remaining were spending above Rs. 2,000 daily. More than 60 percent of the addicts, on average, have spent up to Rs. 20,000 on treatment while 35 percent spent between Rs. 20,000 and 100,000. Only 5 percent of addicts spent between Rs. 100,000–200,000, on average, on treatment. The higher expenditure incurred on treatment is mainly in the private de-addiction and so-called rehabilitation centres.

There are multiple sources of money for purchasing drugs, ranging from self-financing to drug peddling. The most important source of money, as revealed by 71.84 percent of addicts, is self-earnings. About 63 percent of addicts used pocket money for purchasing drugs; stealing and selling family goods and drug peddling were their other sources for purchasing drugs. Significantly, the addicts, on average, have 1.6 sources of money with which to purchase drugs. However, family is the most important source of financing treatment. About 74 percent of the addicts revealed that their treatment expenses are being borne by their family, mainly parents. Most of the families revealed that they exhausted their past savings on the treatment. Significantly, a good number of households revealed that they had to raise a loan for the treatment of their addicted family member and also had to sell some land or other economic assets belonging to the family. Our case studies have amply revealed such incidences.

There are numerous hapless old parents whose young sons are either hooked on drugs or have even died due to an overdose of drugs. The addicts in our sample revealed that they know 1,059 addicts who died prematurely due to drug addiction and abuse. Similarly, there are a very large number of young widows who lost their husbands due to their drug addiction and are now passing through numerous socio-economic sufferings. In addition to social loss, there is also an immense economic loss to the households, society and the country. Due to the non-availability of data, we could not generate the exact number of such deaths.

The economic cost of married drug addicts (more so that of the married and prematurely deceased) impacts both the wife and the parents, but the calculation of socio-economic costs for the wife and children is beyond comprehension and computation, as the children's career prospects are worst affected by the premature death of their father. The growth of children can rarely reach full potential in the absence of a father. The data revealed that about 38 percent of the prematurely deceased persons were married. The calculation of economic cost for the parents, society and the country is not an easy task, as who knows what could have been their socio-economic contributions to their family, society and the country?

### Role of religious organisations, government, elected bodies, police and political parties

The government, elected bodies, police, political parties, NGOs and religious organisations often claim that they are doing a lot to curb the drug menace and spread awareness about the ill effects of drugs. Some of them, often backed by the law, also take preventive measures to dissuade people from taking drugs, and rightly so, as it is what society expects from them. However, often there are gaps between their claims and ground reality. It is in this context that we tried to gather community perceptions/views/opinions about the claims and role of the institutions, as community is considered the mirror through which we can see the ground realities. Significantly, 59 percent of the respondents from the drug addicts' households are of the opinion that no awareness activities are being carried out. Contrary to this, 44 percent of respondents from the control group were of the view that awareness activities are being carried out whereas approximately 49 percent of the respondents did not agree. Most of the respondents (82 percent) said that promotion of gun culture, drugs and vulgarities through songs, social media, movies, and even on some T.V. channels is a powerful tool to entice youth towards many social ills, including drug addiction and abuse.

Significantly, all the respondents from the addicts' households and the majority from the control group households were of the opinion that religious and spiritual organisations do play a positive role in addressing the problem of drug use and abuse in society. However, 41 percent of respondents from the control group did not agree to this, as they found them lacking in all-out efforts to address the problem of intoxicants and drug addiction. In response to a direct question about the role of the third tier of Indian Democracy, viz., Panchayati Raj Institutions (PRIs) and Urban Local Bodies (ULBs), 40 percent of respondents said that these bodies play an effective role in addressing the drug menace in their jurisdiction, while 60 percent did not agree, mainly because of an indifferent attitude towards the drug problem in the society and vote politics.

In regards to the government's role in controlling the drug menace, nearly 88 percent of the respondents expressed confidence in the government's capability to address the issue. However, contrary to the overwhelming confidence in the government's capability, 65 percent of respondents were not satisfied with the government's performance in dealing with the drug menace.

However, more recently, many state governments are showing their serious concern about the problem. The Union and State governments also observe 26th June as the International Day Against Drug Abuse and Illicit Trafficking. Nonetheless, the efficacy of all the initiatives of the governments is not pronouncedly visible on the ground. This is mainly because of the lack of motivation, commitment and dedication on the part of all the actors and agencies engaged in executing and implementing the initiatives and programmers. This, in turn, is due to indifferent attitudes, political patronage and corruption. Lack of acknowledging the socio-cultural and politico-economic reasons behind drug addiction and abuse is also an important reason for the low effectiveness of the government's programmes. These perceptions have also been supported by the views expressed about Urban Local Bodies during FGDs. In fact, people want strict action against the peddlers as well as big- and small-time smugglers of drugs. The fact of the matter is that much politicking is being done on the drug menace but curbing the drug business is a far cry from expectations, according to respondents.

In regards to the role of police, only 9 percent of household respondents said that the police are effectively discharging their duties to curb the drug menace, while 91 percent of respondents are at variance with this. Their perception is that, due to rampant corruption and political pressure, the police lack seriousness in action and only take selective actions against the small-time drug suppliers, peddlers and drug consumers. The legal lacuna in case preparation and the presentation of cases by the police and the lower rate of conviction also discourages and disappoints well-meaning police officials in upholding their 'war on drugs.' The police often hesitate to catch the 'big fish.' Some of the respondents in the case studies also revealed that their parents bribed the police to not make a case against them when they were caught for peddling or possession of drugs.

In regards to the role of political leaders and parties, though one would like to believe that they are not involved in patronizing the drug smugglers and peddlers, yet the perception of the people does not support such a belief. In view of more than 95 percent of all the respondents, the political parties and their candidates distribute intoxicants and drugs in order to woo voters in their favour. During our interaction with people from various walks of life (through FGDs), it has come out that some political leaders from across political parties have been patronising the drug business and there is a well-structured network down the line. Some of the respondents (on the condition of anonymity) confided that there is a deep nexus between some political leaders, police officials and big drug suppliers/smugglers. The quick and high return, in the people's perception, is the reason behind such a nexus. Unfortunately, the well-connected and well organised people behind this nexus are doing it for their narrow vested interest which is proving counterproductive. They further said that, actually, it is mainly because of this nexus that 'big fish' are not being caught. The participants in the FGDs said, very emphatically, that without catching and punishing the 'mother of the thief,' it is virtually impossible to break the supply chain of drugs.

Apart from this, the majority of the respondents have the perception that political leaders are involved in patronising the drug business and even hold the opinion that some political leaders are personally involved in the drug business. Almost similar views have been expressed by the drug addicts. At the aggregate level, 34 percent of drug addicts shared that political patronage and intervention puts a great deal of hurdles in the way of effective implementation of government polices, and strategies to break the supply chain which is sine qua non to curb the drug business. The media reports have also highlighted the unholy nexus between police, smugglers and politicians (PSP). The bureaucrats' tacit support of the drug menace often does not come to the fore, but tacit connivance of some of them cannot be ruled out, according to the respondents.

## Recommendations

It may be safely concluded from the existing literature and the findings of this study that the problem of drug addiction and abuse is the manifestation of deep-rooted and widespread distortions in the socio-cultural and politico-economic system. Since the drug menace is systemic and multi-dimensional, the solution shall have to be systemic and multi-pronged. In fact, drug addiction and abuse is the symptom of a socio-cultural, economic and political illness. In view of this, there is need of a holistic approach to address the issue, rather than a piece-meal and symptomatic solution. There is a need to break the supply chain and curb the demand. Both preventive and curative measures shall have to be devised and implemented with a missionary zeal and in a missionary mode. Since the drug menace is an evolving phenomenon, there is a need to adopt evolving compatible policies, strategies and measures to address the issue. In view of this, there are three fundamental challenges: to curb supply of and demand for drugs, to de-addict and rehabilitate the addicts, and to prevent new entry, especially that of teens, into drug consumption. However, during the course of this study and from the earlier studies, it is our understanding that a complete root-out of drug addiction and abuse may not be possible in the near future, but we can certainly reduce its supply and demand and thereby the ill effects of the drug menace.

Curbing the supply of drugs involves both the external and internal sources of supply as drugs are being supplied from both these sources. This means regional and global cooperation and sharing real-time data and information at the regional and global levels. In view of the inter-state spread of the problem, there is an urgent need to have inter-state deliberations at the highest level, and comprehensive collaborations among all departments and agencies dealing with the drug menace must be in place. Meticulous implementation of policies is the hallmark for drug control. The state governments and concerned agencies will have to be above board and effectively implement these policies. Political parties would have to shun their vested interests and narrow politics on the issue of drugs and come forward for cooperation on this national issue. The unholy nexus between police, smugglers and politicians (PSP) needs to be acknowledged since it has openly been reported in our study and numerous media reports have also highlighted it from time to time. The PSP-nexus must be broken in a dispassionate mode and it must be ensured that it does not evolve again. It would require very high level socio-cultural and politico-economic consciousness among political leadership, the police, bureaucracy and all other stakeholders. Vigilance at the international borders needs to be fortified to keep a hawk's eye on any infiltration of drugs from across the border, especially in view of the drug supply from the Golden Crescent and the Golden Triangle. This would require the unimpeachable integrity of the forces on the borders. In this context, cooperation of the central government and central agencies is of utmost importance.

In view of the long term socio-cultural and politico-economic ramifications of the drug menace, the judiciary, too, shall have to be more sensitive and pro-active in delivering justice in a reasonable timeframe. Legal action against main drug suppliers and peddlers, rather than only small-time peddlers and drug addicts, must be dealt with as a priority, maybe through fast track route. In view of some significant media reports indicating the prevalence of drugs in jails, it is suggested a thorough study of jails be undertaken to gauge the penetration of this phenomenon within punitive state institutions. The jail administration will also have to be more sensitive to the issue as there is quite a high prevalence of drugs in the jails.

It is in this context that there is a felt need, amongst all sections of people across India as well as across countries, for formulating comprehensive and effective anti-drug policies. Governments, policy makers and all other stakeholders must join hands to draw a short, medium and long term policy and strategy to curb the drug menace and effectively implement those policies. The state and central governments will have to be the vanguard for this crusade. Depending on the spread and intensity of the problem, anti-drug regional councils must be in place. Any laxity and indifferent attitudes would have very serious implications for national security and the socio-cultural, politico-economic stability of India. It is, thus, sine qua non that not only India but the entire global community and international agencies must join hands to curb the drug menace since it is a global phenomenon. The fundamental challenge, however, is how to bring the producers, consumers and transit countries on board as there is clash of interest. In the solution to this challenge, there is an urgent need to focus on demand and supply management. The recent confiscation of a huge quantity of heroin at various locations in India and elsewhere in the world needs to be examined and viewed in this context.

There is a need to identify and address the fundamental socio-cultural and politico-economic reasons behind drug addiction and abuse and address those issues in a time-bound and evolving mode if we really want a sustainable solution. Curbing the drug menace and relapsing is next to impossible without eradicating the root-cause behind drug demand and supply. On the socio-cultural front, there are several issues related to the individual, family and community which are responsible for pushing millions of adolescents and youth towards intoxicants and drugs. This study has tried to identify certain socio-cultural and politico-economic dynamics of drug abuse and addiction in this context. Consumption of intoxicants by elders in the household, disharmonious intra-family relations, peer pressure, unemployment, underemployment and the prevalence of a large number of working-poor are some of the important factors responsible for initiating teens and youth into drugs.

More specifically, there is a need to create a nuanced understanding of the difference between de-addiction and rehabilitation in the case of drug addiction. De-criminalising drug addicts must be made a priority in order to make addicts come forward without fear of incarceration and stigmatisation. They should be treated as patients and not culprits. In fact, there is an urgent need to change the attitude towards addicts, as they are victims of the distortions in the socio-cultural and politico-economic system. As such, counselling must be an important component of the de-addiction and rehabilitation process. Given the existing inadequacy of councillors and supporting staff, a qualified cadre of clinical psychologists must be ensured to deal with this. Counselling of family members is central to prevent drug addiction and relapsing of addicts. Social and community counselling is also important to change the socio-cultural attitude towards the addicts. This component needs to be developed and integrated in the policy for drug addiction prevention, de-addiction and rehabilitation. The councillors must deal with the addicts at the emotional and psychological level and that, too, with dedication and missionary zeal. Rehabilitation must not be restricted to counselling of the addict or his/her family. The rehabilitation of the de-addicted persons in society is possible only when he/she is accepted in society and his/her concerns are addressed. The addict, too, would have to muster the willpower to come out of the vicious circle. In view of the fact that childhood experiences do impact adults, young parents and extended families should be counselled from time to time, for which school teachers, NGOs, religious organisations and members of civil society could be roped into doing. The interaction of parents and teachers with the child must become a regular feature in order to know about his/her peers and any undue change in his/her behaviour. It is also necessary to identify unregistered and hidden drug users, including females.

Since the problem of drug use starts at an early age, the awareness system among school-going children, especially from elementary schools onwards, must be a continuous programme. There must also be a constant vigil around the schools and colleges. There is also a need to spread awareness among the school drop-outs and out-of-school children. This may prove to be the most potent strategy to combat drug addiction and abuse liable to spread in the future. Awareness activities in terms of the visits of specialist psychologists to schools and colleges for interaction with students must be considered. There is a need to enhance vigilance around the schools and colleges and at other sensitive locations. The proactive role of parents, teachers, students, elected representatives, police, political parties, religious organisations and NGOs is sine qua non in such social movements. It would not be out of context if we suggest that there is a need to evolve a counselling process to sensitise all the mentioned agencies and stakeholders so that they could approach the issue with commitment and a professional approach. Interaction between various stakeholders, like psychiatrists, psychologists, de-addiction and rehabilitation centre owners, NGOs working in the field and pharmacists, needs to be enhanced to play a proactive role in addressing the problem. The officials in the government de-addiction centres must be tuned to go beyond their impersonal approach to deal with the addicts. Similarly, the private de-addiction centres must rise above only the monetary consideration. There is an utmost necessity to establish rehabilitation centres for the de-addicted persons as we have not come across the presence of rehabilitation centres.

Religious institutions and organisations, especially at the local level, can play a proactive role in dealing with drug addiction by involving youth in spiritual activities like meditation, yoga, community work, etc. The initiative being taken by youth clubs and civil societies in and around their local areas must get support from civil society, religious organisations, local leadership, police and the government. Theatre groups could be involved in creating plays with theme-based message against drug addiction performed in local public areas to spread the message and information. The theatre and television departments of universities can play a formidable role in this. Students and teachers of colleges, too, must be mobilised to lead awareness campaigns. Local neighbourhoods and communities need to be sensitised for increased cooperation with addicts and their families. The Panchayti Raj Institutions (PRIs) and Urban Local Bodies (ULBs) must play proactive and accountable roles in matters of complaints or reporting on drugs. These local bodies should also facilitate and promote sports activities and libraries at the local level to engage the youth constructively, in addition to launching awareness campaigns. A social movement against the prevailing drug menace, with a missionary zeal, is required if we really want to eradicate this evil.

The government programmes against drug addiction, such as the Buddy programme, OOAT and DAPO (initiated by the government of Punjab), must be strengthened and implemented more effectively. A third party evaluation of such programmes must be conducted to know the outcome of these programmes. Third party evaluation of the various de-addiction and rehabilitation centres should also be carried out.

Media must be used to spread information and awareness about the ill effects of drug addiction throughout the year and not limited to timeframes near international drug de-addiction day. Protection of whistle blowers in such cases must be ensured.

Last, but not least, the possibilities and potential benefits of the controlled production of licit drugs (and restricted use thereof) and of some traditional intoxicants may also be explored to dissuade addicts and potential addicts from the use of more harmful and illicit drugs. This may, however, be done after a wider consultation and acceptance, as this is a double-edged weapon. It also needs a careful, frequent review to identify its pros and cons.

These recommendations are primarily based on our study, field observations and existing literature. It is hoped that our recommendations would help in formulating policies at state and national levels to deal with the drug menace.

# References


Advani, R. (2013). *Factors driving drug abuse in India's Punjab* (Working paper No-117). National University of Singapore. https://www.files.ethz.ch/isn/170331/ISAS_Working_Paper_No__177_-_Factors_Driving_Drug_Abuse_in_India%27s_punjab_24092013171919.pdf

Ambekar, A. (2012). *HIV prevention among injecting drug users and their female sex partners: Implementation gaps and barriers (a study in Punjab, Haryana and Chandigarh)*. United Nations Office on Drugs and Crime, Regional Office for South Asia, Regional Office for South Asia. https://www.unodc.org/documents/southasia/publications/research-studies/PunjabHaryana_Study_Gaps–Barriers-Book_03-08-12.pdf

Ambekar, A., & Tripathi, M. B. (2008). *Size estimation of injecting drug use in Punjab, Haryana and Chandigarh*. United Nations Programme on HIV and AIDS.

Anderson, M. K., Tenenbaum, L. S., Ramadorai, S. B., & Yourick, D. L. (2015). Near-peer mentor model: Synergy within mentoring. *Mentoring and Tutoring: Partnership in Learning*, 23(2), 116–132. https://doi.org/10.1080/13611267.2015.1049017

Arora, R. K., & Kaura, V. (2017). *War on drugs: Challenges for the Punjab Government*. ORF Issue Brief No-176. https://www.orfonline.org/wp-content/uploads/2017/05/ORF_IssueBrief_176_DrugsPunjab.pdf

Atici, S. G. (2022). The spaces between fault/lines: Collaborative politics of addiction in Japan. *Contemporary Drug Problems*, 49(3), 299–318. https://doi.org/10.1177/00914509221084383

Avasthi, A., Basu, D., Subodh, B. N., Gupta, P. K., Goyal, B. L., Sidhu, B. S., Gargi, P. D., Sharma, A., & Ghosh, A. (2019). Epidemiology of dependence on illicit substances, with a special focus on opioid dependence, in the State of Punjab, India: Results from two different yet complementary survey methods. *Asian Journal of Psychiatry*, 39, 70–79. https://doi.org/10.1016/j.ajp.2018.12.008

Avasthi, A., Basu, D., Subodh, B. N., Gupta, P. K., Sidhu, B. S., Gargi, P. D., Sharma, A., Ghosh, A., & Rani, P. (2018). Epidemiology of substance use and dependence in the state of Punjab, India: Results of a household survey on a state-wide representative sample. *Asian Journal of Psychiatry*, 33, 18–29. https://doi.org/10.1016/j.ajp.2018.02.017

Balze-Temple D., & Lo, S. K. (1992). Stages of drug use: A community survey of Perth teenager. *British Journal of Addiction*, 87(2), 215–225. https://doi.org/10.1111/j.1360–0443.1992.tb02695.x

Basu, D., Aggarwal, M., Das, P. P., Mattoo, S. K., Kulhara, P., & Varma, V. K. (2012). Changing pattern of substance abuse in patients attending a de-addiction centre in north India (1978–2008). *Indian Journal of Medical Research*, 135(6), 830–836.

Beck, J. (1998). 100 years of "just to say no" versus "just say no". *Evaluation Review*, 22, 15–45.

Bhattacharji, R. (2019). Attari exposes scale of Punjab drug market. *The Tribune*, July 3. https://www.tribuneindia.com/news/archive/comment/news-detail-796293

Bourgois, P. (2012). Bringing HIV, substance abuse and homelessness into the university of Pennsylvania anthropology museum through photo-ethnography. *Social Innovation Journal*, 10, 433–444.

Bourgois, P., & Schonberg, J. (2009). *Righteous dopefiend*. University of California Press.

Carlson, R. G. (1996). The political economy of AIDS among drug users in the United States: Beyond blaming the victim or powerful others. *American Anthropologist*, 98(2), 266–278. http://www.jstor.org/stable/682886

Chandrasekhar, C. P., Ghosh, J., & Roychowdhury, A. (2006). The "demographic dividend" and young India's economic future. *Economic and Political Weekly*, 41(49), 5055–5064.

Charles, M. (2001). Drug trade in Himachal Pradesh: Role of socio-economic changes. *Economic and Political Weekly*, 36(26), 2433–2439.

Charles, M., & Britto, G. (2001). The socio-cultural context of drug use and implications for drug policy. *International Social Science Journal*, 53(169), 467–474.

Charles, M., Bewley-Tylor, D., & Neidpath, A. (2005). *Drug policy in India*. Briefing Paper, International Drug Policy Consortium, The Berkley Foundation Drug Policy Programme. https://www.aidsdatahub.org/sites/default/files/resource/drug-policy-india-2005.pdf

Chauhan, P. (2015). Chemicals from pharma units being misused. *The Tribune*, September 13. https://www.tribuneindia.com/news/archive/features/chemicals-from-pharma-units-being-misused-131829

Cohen, A. (2014). Crazy for Ya Ba: Methamphetamine use among northern Thai youth. *International Journal of Drug Policy*, 24(4), 776–782. https://doi.org/10.1016/j.drugpo.2014.06.005

Dainik Bhaskar. (2017). *Nasho par survey ki chithi 5 mahino se sehat vibhag mein attki, mantri ko pata hi nahi* (Letter on survey pending in the health department for 5 months, Minister does not know it). *Dainik Bhaskar*, November 5.

Das, V. (2015). *Affliction: Health, disease, poverty*. Orient Blackswan Private Limited.

Dikshit, S. (2019). Fallout: A nation compromised. *The Tribune*, July 7. https://www.tribuneindia.com/news/archive/features/fallout-of-drugs-a-nation-compromised-798282

DNA. (2014). Drug menace reaches alarming proportions in Punjab. *DNA India*, December 31. http://www.dnaindia.com/india/report-2014-d rug-menace-reaches-alarming-proportions-in-punjab-2048382

DNA. (2015). Maximum drug patients in Punjab users of opium, poppy husk, smack. *DNA India*, January 4. http://www.dnaindia.com/india/report-maximum-drug-patients-in-punjab-users-of-opium-poppy-husk-smack-2049594

Dube, S., Chaudhary, A., Mahajan, R., Purohit, R., Singh, G., Soni, R., Girdhar, S., Sharma, S., Satija, M., & Gill, P. (2014). Prevalence of opiate abuse in rural area of Punjab. *The Internet Journal of Health*, 14(1), 1–6.

Embleton, L., Atwoli, L., Ayuku, D., & Braitstein, P. (2013). The journey of addiction: Barriers to and facilitators of drug use cessation among street children and youths in Western Kenya. *PLoS One*, 8(1), e53435. https://doi.org/10.1371/journal.pone.0053435

Fox, T. P., Oliver, G., & Ellis, M. S. (2013). The destructive capacity of drug abuse: An overview exploring the harmful potential of drug abuse both to the individual and to society. *ISRN Addiction*, 1–6. https://doi.org/10.1155/2013/450348

Ganguly, K. K. (2008). Pattern and process of drug and alcohol use in India. *ICMR Bulletin*, 38(1–3), 1–8.

Ganguly, K. K., Sharma, H. K., & Krishnamachari, K. A. V. R. (1995). An ethnographic account of opium consumers of Rajasthan (India): Socio-medical perspective. *Addiction*, 90(1), 9–12.

Ghuman, R. S. (2012). Development paradigm, nature of employment and need for social protection for workers: Global and Indian scenario. *Indian Journal of Labour Economics*, 55(1), 77–110.

Ghuman, R. S., & Sharma, R. (2018). *Emerging water insecurity in India: Lessons from an agriculturally advanced state*. Cambridge Scholars Publishing.

Ghuman, R. S., & Sharma, R. (2021). Global unemployment and inequality during 1991–2019: Reflections from secondary data. *Economic & Political Weekly*, 56(42), 39–46.

Gill, S. S. (2013). Gun culture in Punjab. *Economic and Political Weekly*, 48(8), 16–18.

Global Burden of Disease Study. (2015). Global, regional, and national incidence, prevalence, and years lived with disability for 301 acute and chronic diseases and injuries in 188 countries, 1990–2013: A systematic analysis for the Global Burden of Disease Study 2013. *The Lancet*, 386(9995), 743–800.

Gorsuch, R. L., & Butler, M. C. (1976). Initial drug abuse: A review of predisposing social psychological factors. *Psychological Bulletin*, 83(1), 120–137.

Gupta, V. K., Kaur, P., Singh, G., Bansal, P., & Sidhu, B. S. (2014). Comprehensive evaluation of drug de-addiction centres (DDCs) in Punjab (Northern India). *Journal of Clinical Diagnostic Research*, 8(3), 52–55.

Harari, Y. N. (2011). *Sapiens: A brief history of mankind* (p. 364). Vintage.

Harari, Y. N. (2015). *Homo Deus: A brief history of tomorrow* (p. 46). Vintage.

Hardon, A., & Hyman, T. D. (2014). Ethnographies of youth drug use in Asia. *International Journal of Drug Policy*, 25(4), 749–754.

Hindustan Times. (2015). 'Badal exonerates Majithia of drug racket involvement', *Hindustan Times*, March 18.

Hindustan Times. (2016). 53 Punjab cops arrested in drug cases since 2014. *Hindustan Times*, June 13. https://www.hindustantimes.com/punjab/53-punjab-cops-arrested-in-drug-cases-since-2014/story-LE2f2pwvAmsFStjrCEV0tO.html

Hindustan Times. (2018). Private drug de-addiction centre filled three times its capacity. *Hindustan Times*, July 31. https://www.hindustantimes.com/punjab/private-drug-de-addiction-centre-in-patiala-filled-three-times-its-capacity/story-Y6e0BP262fgBxtQUvSGRLM.html

Hindustan Times. (2018a). Dose of death in Punjab's veins. *Hindustan Times*, July 4. https://www.hindustantimes.com/punjab/ht-spotlight-dose-of-death-in-punjab-s-veins/story-Kk8AySISWUNojAORDqxH1K.html.

Hindustan Times. (2018b). One tainted SSP out, another in; Captain Govt's damage Control move baffles Congress leaders. *Hindustan Times*, July 4.

Indian Express. (2014). Modi warns against narco-terrorism route to destroy India. *The Indian Express*, April 25. https://indianexpress.com/article/political-pulse/modi-warns-against-narco-terrorism-route-to-destroy-india/

Indian Express. (2016). Punjab's war on drugs: Such a short, toxic journey. *Indian Express*, June 11. https://indianexpress.com/article/india/india-news-india/punjab-drugs-influx-pakistan-border-trade-canada-2846275/
Indian Hemp Drugs Commission. (1884). *Report of the Indian hemp drugs commission 1893–94*. Government Central Printing Office.
Institute for Social Development Studies. (n.d.). *Factsheet on drug addiction and HIV*. Institute for Social Development Studies. https://www.icrw.org/wp-content/uploads/2016/10/Fact-Sheet-on-Drug-Addiction-and-HIV.pdf
International Narcotics Control Board (INCB). (2013). *Economic consequences of drug abuse*. Annual Report, Chapter 1. https://www.incb.org/documents/Publications/AnnualReports/Thematic_chapters/English/AR_2013_E_Chapter_I.pdf
International Narcotics Control Board (INCB). (2021). *Report of the International Narcotics Control Board*. https://www.incb.org/incb/en/publications/annual-reports/annual-report-2021.html
Jiloha, R. C. (2009). Social and cultural aspects of drug abuse in adolescents. *Delhi Psychiatry Journal*, 12(2), 167–175.
Kalra, I., & Bansal, P. D. (2012). Socio demographic profile and pattern of drug abuse among patients presenting to a de-addiction centre in rural area of Punjab. *Delhi Journal of Psychiatry*, 15(2), 327–331.
Kanwar, K. (2012). Losing Punjab to drugs. *The Indian Express*, July 3. http://www.newindianexpress.com/opinion/columns/kamlendra_kanwar/Losing-Punjab-to-drugs/2012/07/03/article556841.ece
Kossinets, G., & Watts, D. J. (2006). Empirical analysis of an evolving social network. *Science*, 311(5757), 88–90.
Lakshminarayana, J., & Singh, M. B. (2009). Opium addiction among rural population in desert districts of Western Rajasthan: Some observations from the study. *Journal of Human Ecology*, 25(1), 1–4. https://doi.org/10.1080/09709274.2009.11906125
Lal, B., & Singh, G. (1979). Drug abuse in Punjab. *British Journal of Drug Addiction*, 74, 411–427. https://doi.org/10.1111/j.1360-0443.1979.tb01370.x
Lasco, G. (2014). Pampagilas: Methamphetamine in the everyday economic lives of underclass male youths in a Philippine port. *International Journal of Drug Policy*, 25(4), 783–788. https://doi.org/10.1016/j.drugpo.2014.06.011
Lin, S., & Zhang, Y. (2014). Risk control and rational recreation: A qualitative analysis of synthetic drug use among young urbanites in China. *International Journal of Drug Policy*, 24, 769–775. https://doi.org/10.1016/j.drugpo.2014.06.008
Live Mint. (2016a). Censorship won't solve Punjab's drug problem. *The Mint Live*, June 10. http://www.livemint.com/Opinion/cXeNokCBKYm72odGBKsKYI/Censorship-wont-solve-Punjabs-drug-problem.html
Live Mint. (2016b). Six charts that show the seriousness of Punjab's drug problem. *The Mint Live*, June 10. http://www.livemint.com/Opinion/CbtQvesZxzWezejNXECV8K/Six-charts-that-show-the-seriousness-of-Punjabs-drug-proble.html
Mahi, R. K., Sharma, A., Sharma, K. C., & Sidhu, B. S. (2011). An epidemiological survey of alcohol and drug abuse in a village of district Sangrur, Punjab. *Delhi Psychiatry Journal*, 14(2), 314–322.
Malik, S. (2022). HC deprecates "shoddy probe" in drugs case. *The Tribune*, September 7. https://www.tribuneindia.com/news/punjab/16-yrs-on-hc-raps-police-for-shoddy-probe-429232
McKenna, S. A. (2013). "We are supposed to be asleep?" Vigilance, paranoia, and the alert methaphetamine user. *Anthropology of Consciousness*, 24(2), 172–190. https://doi.org/10.1111/anoc.12012

Mcllwaine, C., & Moser, C. O. N. (2004). Drugs, alcohol and community tolerance: An urban ethnography from Colombia and Guatemala. *Environment and Urbanization*, 16(2), 49–62. https://doi.org/10.1177/095624780401600222
Modi, I., & Modi, S. (1997). *Drug addiction and prevention*. Rawat Publications.
Nadeem, A., Rubeena, B., Agarwal, K. V., & Piyush, K. (2009). Substance abuse in India. *Pravara Medical Review*, 1(4), 4–6.
Nagla, B. K. (1995). *Drug and alcohol abuse: A sociological study of drug and alcohol users in Haryana*. Unpublished Report, Indian Council of Social Science Research.
National Drug Dependence Treatment Centre and All India Institute of Medical Sciences. (2019). *Magnitude of substance use in India*. Ministry of Social Justice and Empowerment, Government of India.
Nyameh, J., Yakubu, I. M., Teru, S., & Titus, A. (2013). Economic implications of drug abuse among the youths. *Journal of Economics and Sustainable Development*, 4(11), 100–103.
Page, J. B. (2022). Anthropology and the study of illicit drug use. In M. Singer, P. I. Erickson, & C. E. Abadía-Barrero (Eds.), *A Companion to medical anthropology* (pp. 275–294). John Wiley & Sons Ltd.
Page, J. B., & Singer, M. (2010). *Comprehending drug use: Ethnographic research at the social margins*. Rutgers University Press.
Parshant, S. (1993). *Drug abuse and society*. Ashish Publishing House.
Parsons, M. A. (2022). Thinking about social determinants of health through the relationality of work and drug use. *Medical Anthropology Quarterly*, 36(2), 272–289. https://doi.org/10.1111/maq.12690
Pathak, P. (2016). Swot analysis of Punjab agriculture. *International Journal of Advanced Research*, 4(4), 871–875. http://dx.doi.org/10.21474/IJAR01/326
Phillip, A. J. (2007). Breaking out of despair. *The Tribune*, April 28. http://www.tribuneindia.com/2007/20070428/saturday/main1.html
Preet, J. (2012). Punjab drug fight loses in Akali-Congress battle. *The Sunday Guardian*, October 13. http://www.sunday-guardian.com/news/punjab-drug-fight-loses-in-akali-congress-battle
Punjabi Tribune. (2022). *Nasheyaan de khatme layi police, taskaran ate siasat dana da gathjor todna zaroori: Sidhu* (To end the drug menace it is necessary to break nexus between police, smugglers and politicians). *Punjabi Tribune*, May 14.
Quraishi, S. Y. (2016). To end drugs, come out of denial first. *The Tribune*, June 29. http://www.tribuneindia.com/news/comment/to-end-drugs-come-out-of-denial-first/258299
Rabinow, P., & Rose, N. (2006). Biopower today. *Biosocities*, 1, 195–217.
Ramachandaran, Rajesh (2023). 'Time to cleanse Punjab', *The Tribune* April 2023.
Ranjan, M. (2019). Red flags from Attari seizure. *The Tribune*, July 7. https://www.tribuneindia.com/news/archive/features/red-flags-from-attari-heroin-seizure-798287
Reith, G. (2004). Consumption and its discontents: Addiction, identity and the problems of freedom. *The British Journal of Sociology*, 55(2), 283–300. https://doi.org/10.1111/j.1468-4446.2004.00019.x
Room, R. (2005). Stigma, social inequality, alcohol and drug use. *Drug and Alcohol Review*, 24(2), 143–155.
Rose, N. (2000). Government and control. *British Journal of Criminology*, 40(2), 321–339. https://doi.org/10.1093/bjc/40.2.321
Royal Commission on Opium. (1894). *First Report on royal commission on opium with minutes of evidence*. Eyre and Spottiswoode.

Sachadev, J. S., Yakhmi, R. S., & Sharma, A. K. (2002). Changing pattern of drug abuse among patients attending de-addiction centre at Faridkot. *Indian Journal of Psychiatry*, 44(4), 353–355.

Sahni, A. (2019). The border war with drugs. *The Tribune*, July 7. https://www.tribuneindia.com/news/archive/features/the-border-war-with-drugs-798241

Sandhu, R. S. (2009). *Drug addiction in Punjab: A sociological study*. Department of Sociology, Guru Nanak Dev University.

Sawhney, S. (2014). *The drug problem in Punjab*. Delhi Policy Group Issue Brief. www.delhipolicygroup.com/uploads/publication_file/1073ssue_Brief_-The_Drug_Problem_in_Punjab_Sawhney.pdf

Sehgal, M. (2014). Den of drugs: How Punjab politicos are linked to Rs. 700-crore drug racket. *India Today*, January 12. https://www.indiatoday.in/india/north/story/punjab-politicians-in-dock-for-alleged-connections-to-drug-lords-176476-2014-01-12.

Sengupta, A. K., Kannan, K. P., & Srivastava, R. K. (2009). *The challenge of employment in India: An informal economy perspective*. Academic Foundation.

Sharma, M. (2021). Hey Buddy . . . Come with me and be drug free. In R. Kumar & N. Gupta (Eds.), *Human rights, youth and drugs* (pp. 83–99). Regal Publications.

Sharma, N. (2017). Centre's heroin seizure figures baffle police, other agencies. *Hindustan Times*, April 22. https://www.hindustantimes.com/india-news/udta-haryana-centre-s-heroin-seizure-figures-baffle-police-other-agencies/story-4KW8ayOW1A5oHMMg8yIuUK.html

Sidduqi, H. Y. (1992). *Drug abuse in Faridabad*. Ministry of Social Welfare, Government of India.

Singer, M. (1994). AIDS and the health crisis of the US urban poor: The perspective of critical medical anthropology. *Social Science and Medicine*, 39(7), 931–948.

Singer, M. (2008). Drugs and development: The global impact of drug use and trafficking on social and economic development. *The International Journal of Drug Policy*, 19(6), 467–478. https://doi.org/10.1016/j.drugpo.2006.12.007

Singer, M. (2012). Anthropology and addiction: An historical review. *Addiction*, 107(10), 1747–1755. https://doi.org/10.1111/j.1360-0443.2012.03879.x

Singh, A. (2010). Strategies adopted by wives of addicts: A sociological study of women in rural Punjab, India. *International Journal of Sociology and Anthropology*, 2(8), 162–170.

Singh, G., & Lal, B. (1979). Drug abuse in Punjab. *British Journal of Addiction*, 74, 411–427. https://doi.org/10.1111/j.1360-0443.1979.tb01370.x

Singh, J. (2022). Wanted drug smuggler Sarabjit Sander killed in Canada. *The Tribune*, February 24. https://www.tribuneindia.com/news/punjab/wanted-drug-smuggler-killed-in-canada-372498

Singh, M. P. (2016). Why Rajasthan is shuttering its opium husk shops. *Indian Express*, March 31. https://indianexpress.com/article/explained/end-of-the-high-why-rajasthan-is-shuttering-its-opium-husk-shops/

Singh, R. (2012). *Drug addiction*. The Kalgidhar Trust.

Singh, S. (2001). Drug: Badal's silence baffling. *The Tribune*, January 16.

Society for Promotion of Youth and Masses, & NDDTC, AIIMS. (2016). *Punjab opioid dependence survey*. Ministry of Social Justice and Empowerment, Government of India and Department of Health, Government of Punjab.

Sydow, D. L., & Sandel, R. H. (1998). Making student retention an institutional priority. *Journal of Research and Practice*, 22(7), 635–643. https://doi.org/10.1080/1066892980220701

The Narcotics Drugs and Psychotropic Substance Act, 1985 (1985), Government of India, New Delhi.
The Tribune. (2001). Drug: Badal's silence baffling. *The Tribune*, January 16.
The Tribune. (2005). A tale of helplessness: Drug addiction in Punjab. *The Tribune*, November 22.
The Tribune. (2008). Region is becoming a drug heaven. *The Tribune*, September 21.
The Tribune. (2013). Akali Dal cannot be blamed for misdeeds of a few, says Badal. *The Tribune*, November 17.
The Tribune. (2014). The flourishing supply chain and its deadly effect. *The Tribune*, June 2. https://www.tribuneindia.com/2014/20140603/main6.htm
The Tribune. (2015). Chemists to maintain record of drugs' sale. *The Tribune*, June 17. https://www.tribuneindia.com/news/archive/features/chemists-to-maintain-record-of-drugs-sale-94639
The Tribune. (2015). Cough syrup bottles seized in Baddi. *The Tribune*, May 7. https://www.tribuneindia.com/news/archive/features/cough-syrup-bottles-seized-in-baddi-77255
The Tribune. (2015). Drug addiction in Punjab no less than terrorism: Kamal Sharma. *The Tribune*, June 27. https://www.tribuneindia.com/news/archive/jalandhar/drug-addiction-in-punjab-no-less-than-terrorism-kamal-sharma-99284
The Tribune. (2015). SC allows poppy husk sale in Rajasthan. *The Tribune*, September 5.
The Tribune. (2015). Security up after synthetic drug haul on Punjab border. *The Tribune*, June 19.
The Tribune. (2016). Alarming rise in drug abuse among youth. *The Tribune*, June 26. https://www.tribuneindia.com/news/archive/features/alarming-rise-in-drug-abuse-among-youth-256960
The Tribune. (2016). Blame game on drugs won't help: Film maker. *The Tribune*, October 12. https://www.tribuneindia.com/news/archive/features/blame-game-on-drugs-wont-help-filmmaker-308323
The Tribune. (2016). Vij blames Punjab for drug supply in border areas. *The Tribune*, May 6. https://www.tribuneindia.com/news/archive/features/story-232568
The Tribune. (2019). Book drug convicts for money laundering, HC tells Haryana. *The Tribune*, April 13. https://m.tribuneindia.com/news/archive/haryana/book-drug-convicts-for-money-laundering-hc-tells-haryana-757544
The Tribune. (2019). Ex-IPS officer Saji Mohan gets 15-yr jail for smuggling drugs. *The Tribune*, August 20. https://www.tribuneindia.com/news/archive/chandigarh/ex-ips-officer-saji-mohan-gets-15-yr-jail-for-smuggling-drugs-819854
The Tribune. (2019). Mohali Court convicts drug lord Jagdish Bhola in three cases. The Tribune, February 14. https://www.tribuneindia.com/news/archive/punjab/mohali-court-convicts-druglord-jagdish-bhola-in-three-cases-728402
The Tribune. (2019). Peddler-jail staff nexus busted, 6 held. *The Tribune*, April 12. https://www.tribuneindia.com/news/archive/punjab/news-detail-756896
The Tribune. (2019). SSP warns black sheep in force, video goes viral. *The Tribune*, June 16. https://www.tribuneindia.com/news/archive/punjab/ssp-warns-black-sheep-in-force-video-goes-viral-788850
The Tribune. (2019). Transit point Amritsar also big drug market. *The Tribune*, July 5. https://www.tribuneindia.com/news/archive/punjab/attari-haul-797244

The Tribune. (2020). Drones used to smuggle arms, drugs from Pak, two arrested. *The Tribune*, December 16. https://www.tribuneindia.com/news/punjab/drones-used-to-smuggle-arms-drugs-from-pak-two-arrested-184958
The Tribune. (2020). Held in smuggling case, BSF constable sacked. *The Tribune*, August 8. https://www.tribuneindia.com/news/punjab/held-in-smuggling-case-bsf-constable-sacked-123698
The Tribune. (2020). Heroin seizure on decline, says BSF. *The Tribune*, January 8. https://www.tribuneindia.com/news/punjab/heroin-seizure-on-decline-says-bsf-22904
The Tribune. (2021). Drugs in 65 cases missing: Police to HC. *The Tribune*, November 20. https://www.tribuneindia.com/news/punjab/drugs-in-65-cases-missing-punjab-police-to-hc-340460
The Tribune. (2021). Majithia booked for drug smuggling, aiding mafia. *The Tribune*, December 22. https://www.tribuneindia.com/news/punjab/majithia-booked-for-drug-smuggling-aiding-mafia-fir-cites-18-stf-report-353121
The Tribune. (2022). 2 Punjab ex-DIGs booked for disposing of drugs sans nod. *The Tribune*, May 4. https://www.tribuneindia.com/news/punjab/2-ex-digs-booked-for-disposing-of-drugs-sans-nod-391497
The Tribune. (2022). 20 Kg ice worth Rs. 208 crore seized; two held, key accused at large. *The Tribune*, June 29. https://www.tribuneindia.com/news/punjab/20-kg-crystal-methamphetamine-worth-208-cr-seized-in-ludhiana-two-held-key-accused-at-large-407774
The Tribune. (2022). 62 kg heroin found hidden in trolley bags at IGI Airport. *The Tribune*, May 12. https://www.tribuneindia.com/news/nation/62-kg-heroin-found-hidden-in-trolley-bags-at-igi-airport-393969
The Tribune. (2022). ADGP-headed task force soon to curb drug menace, says CM. *The Tribune*, June 27.
The Tribune. (2022). Drug racket: Five more PPA cops in police net. *The Tribune*, May 24. https://www.tribuneindia.com/news/punjab/drug-racket-five-more-ppa-cops-in-police-net-397487
The Tribune. (2022). Drugs, sacrilege major challenge for CM. *The Tribune*, March 22. https://www.tribuneindia.com/news/punjab/drugs-sacrilege-major-challenges-for-cm-379564
The Tribune. (2022). DSP arrested under NDPS Act for taking Rs. 10 lakh bribe. *The Tribune*, July 7. https://www.tribuneindia.com/news/punjab/faridkot-dsp-arrested-for-taking-10l-bribe-410116
The Tribune. (2022). Fight against drugs Yadav's top priority. *The Tribune*, July 8. https://www.tribuneindia.com/news/punjab/fight-against-drugs-yadavs-top-priority-410385
The Tribune. (2022). Give status of SIT reports: HC. *The Tribune*, March 30. https://www.tribuneindia.com/news/punjab/give-status-of-sit-reports-punjab-and-haryana-high-court-381882
The Tribune. (2022). Government plans to raise number of de-addiction centres to 500. *The Tribune*, May 8. https://www.tribuneindia.com/news/punjab/punjab-govt-plans-to-raise-number-of-de-addiction-centres-to-500-392782
The Tribune. (2022). Haryana DSP crushed to death by mining mafia. *The Tribune*, July 20. https://www.tribuneindia.com/news/haryana/haryana-dsp-surender-singh-crushed-to-death-by-mining-mafia-413863

The Tribune. (2022). Heroin seizers: Intensify efforts to stamp out cross-border drug trade. *The Tribune*, April 27. https://www.tribuneindia.com/news/editorials/heroin-seizures-389638

The Tribune. (2022). Khattar launches action plan for drug-free state. *The Tribune*, June 27. https://www.tribuneindia.com/news/haryana/khattar-launches-action-plan-for-drug-free-state-407295

The Tribune. (2022). List steps to curb drug trade: HC to centre. *The Tribune*, May 13. https://www.tribuneindia.com/news/punjab/list-steps-to-curb-drug-trade-punjab-and-haryana-high-court-to-centre-394288

The Tribune. (2022). Over 40% inmates found hooked to narcotics in some Punjab jails. *The Tribune*, July 18. https://www.tribuneindia.com/news/punjab/over-40-inmates-found-hooked-on-narcotics-in-some-punjab-jails-413323

The Tribune. (2022). Peddlers fleeing cops kill 2 students in Patiala. *The Tribune*, July 11. https://www.tribuneindia.com/news/punjab/peddlers-fleeing-cops-kill-2-students-411229

The Tribune. (2022). Punjab and Haryana High Court deprecates 'shoddy probe' in drugs case. *The Tribune*, May 25. https://www.tribuneindia.com/news/punjab/punjab-and-haryana-high-court-deprecates-shoddy-probe-in-drugs-case-397776

The Tribune. (2022). Rs 700 crore heroin seized at Attari. *The Tribune*, April 25. https://www.tribuneindia.com/news/punjab/700-cr-afghan-heroin-seized-at-attari-389094

The Tribune. (2022). Rs. 1439-crore heroin seized from Gujrat port. *The Tribune*, April 26. https://www.tribuneindia.com/news/nation/1-439-crore-heroin-seized-from-gujarat-port-389420

The Tribune. (2022). STF seizes 9.4 kg more ice in Ludhiana. *The Tribune*, July 4. https://www.tribuneindia.com/news/punjab/special-task-force-seizes-9-4-kg-more-ice-in-ludhiana-409191

The Tribune. (2022). Tramadol used in large numbers in Punjab and Haryana: HC. *The Tribune*, March 31. https://www.tribuneindia.com/news/punjab/tramadol-used-in-large-numbers-in-punjab-haryana-hc-382240

Thomas, G. (2005). Rival drug gangs turn the streets of Nuevo Laredo into a war zone. *New York Times*, December 14. https://www.nytimes.com/2005/12/04/world/americas/rival-drug-gangs-turn-the-streets-of-nuevo-laredo-into-a-war.html

Times of India. (2017). House panel on Pathankot attack puts Punjab Police SP Salwinder Singh under cloud. *Times of India*, February 14. https://timesofindia.indiatimes.com/india/house-panel-on-pathankot-attack-puts-punjab-police-sp-salwinder-singh-under-cloud/articleshow/57137279.cms

United Nations Office on Drugs and Crime. (2004). *World drug report*. United Nations.

United Nations Office on Drugs and Crime. (2005). *World drug report*. United Nations.

United Nations Office on Drugs and Crime. (2009). *World drug report*. United Nations.

United Nations Office on Drugs and Crime. (2011). *Misuse of prescription drugs: A South Asia perspective*. UNODC, Regional Office for South Asia.

United Nations Office on Drugs and Crime. (2012). *World drug report*. United Nations.

United Nations Office on Drugs and Crime. (2015). *World drug report*. United Nations.

United Nations Office on Drugs and Crime. (2016). *World drug report*. United Nations.
United Nations Office on Drugs and Crime. (2019). *World drug report*. United Nations.
United Nations Office on Drugs and Crime. (2022). *World drug report*. United Nations.
United Nations. (1988). *United Nations convention against illicit traffic in narcotic drugs and psychotropic substances*. United Nations.
Vino, R. (2014). Dynamics of ganja cultivation in Manipur: Case study of a village in Ukhrul district. *Economic and Political Weekly*, 49(33). https://www.epw.in/journal/2014/33/reports-states-web-exclusives/dynamics-ganja-cultivation-manipur.html
Waraich, S. (2018). Punjab's opioid de-addiction rules outdated. *The Tribune*, November 5. https://www.tribuneindia.com/news/archive/comment/punjabs-opioid-deaddiction-rules-outdated-678771
Watts, A. (2020). Women drug peddlers on rise in Muktsar. *The Tribune*, August 8. https://www.tribuneindia.com/news/punjab/women-drug-peddlers-on-rise-in-muktsar-123709
Westermeyer, J. (1976). The pro-heroin effects if anti-opium laws in Asia. *Archives General Psychiatry*, 33, 1135–1139.
Wilson, R., & Kolander, C. (2011). *Drug abuse prevention*. Jones and Bartlett Learning.
Yardley, J. (2012). Indian State finds itself in tight grip of drug addiction. *The New York Times*, April 18. http://www.nytimes.com/2012/04/19/world/asia/drug-addiction-is-a-growing-problem-in-punjab.html?pagewanted=all&_r=0.

# Annexures

## Chapter 1

*Table 1.1A* State-wise number of Focus Group Discussions and number of participants

| *State→* *Composition of FGD↓* | *Punjab* | *Haryana* | *H.P.* | *J&K* | *Rajasthan* | *Total* |
|---|---|---|---|---|---|---|
| Elected Representatives of PRIs | 07 (67) | 03 (24) | 02 (17) | 02 (37) | 02 (16) | 16 (161) |
| Elected representatives of ULBs | 04 (35) | 01 (07) | 02 (19) | – | 02 (28) | 09 (89) |
| Academic institutions (students and teachers) | 04 (50) | 02 (15) | 01 (09) | 01 (12) | 01 (10) | 09 (96) |
| Religious and social organisations | 08 (64) | 02 (19) | 01 (06) | 01 (10) | 02 (10) | 14 (109) |
| Medical experts (Doctors and Para-medical)@ | 07 (59) | 02 (16) | 01 (02) | 02 (11) | 02 (06) | 14 (94) |
| Police Officials+ | 02 (19) | 01 (03) | 02 (22) | – | 01 (07) | 06 (51) |
| Others* | 04 (26) | 01 (06) | 02 (02) | – | 02 (06) | 09 (40) |
| Total | 36 (320) | 12 (90) | 11 (77) | 06 (70) | 12 (83) | 77 (640) |

PRIs – Panchayati Raj Institutions (mainly village panchayats)
ULBs – Urban Local Bodies
* Youth clubs, social welfare groups, *Deras* and knowledgeable individuals
@ Mainly dealing with the drug addicts
+ Senior (district level) officers and Station House Officers (SHOs)
*Note*: Figures in brackets indicate the number of participants in FGDs.

## Chapter 2

*Table 2.1A* Persons arrested under the NDPS Act: 2001 to 2015 (Percent)

| *State/UT* | *2001* | *2005* | *2010* | *2015* |
|---|---|---|---|---|
| Andhra Pradesh | 2.52 | 2.52 | 2.08 | 2.61 |
| Assam | 0.70 | 0.73 | 0.69 | 0.47 |
| Bihar | 2.23 | 1.86 | 2.49 | 1.01 |
| Gujarat | 0.68 | 0.41 | 0.38 | 0.13 |
| Haryana | 5.36 | 4.60 | 3.13 | 3.76 |
| Himachal Pradesh | 1.02 | 0.82 | 2.12 | 1.30 |
| Jammu & Kashmir | 0.57 | 0.56 | 1.64 | 1.51 |
| Karnataka | 1.94 | 1.18 | 1.26 | 0.95 |
| Kerala | 2.30 | 1.56 | 2.59 | 7.76 |
| Madhya Pradesh | 4.86 | 4.31 | 4.39 | 2.57 |
| Maharashtra | 2.38 | 6.07 | 5.69 | 33.54 |
| Odisha | 0.56 | 0.48 | 0.69 | 1.24 |
| Punjab | 9.27 | 15.66 | 18.57 | 20.41 |
| Rajasthan | 3.56 | 4.18 | 4.60 | 2.29 |
| Tamil Nadu | 16.06 | 13.05 | 5.04 | 3.13 |
| Uttar Pradesh | 38.37 | 32.59 | 39.01 | 11.71 |
| West Bengal | 2.74 | 1.79 | 2.95 | 3.25 |
| Total States | 97.41 | 94.11 | 98.91 | 99.03 |
| All India | 100.00 | 100.00 | 100.00 | 100.00 |

*Source*: Computed from Table 2.1.

*Table 2.2A* Gender composition of arrested persons under the NDPS Act (Percent): 2005 to 2015

| *States* | *2005* | | *2010* | | *2014* | | *2015* | |
|---|---|---|---|---|---|---|---|---|
| | *Male* | *Female* | *Male* | *Female* | *Male* | *Female* | *Male* | *Female* |
| Andhra Pradesh | 95.56 | 4.44 | 90.69 | 9.31 | 95.08 | 4.92 | 94.47 | 5.53 |
| Assam | 87.90 | 12.10 | 87.03 | 12.97 | 97.40 | 2.60 | 98.58 | 1.42 |
| Bihar | 98.73 | 1.27 | 99.77 | 0.23 | 99.54 | 0.46 | 99.01 | 0.99 |
| Gujarat | 93.53 | 6.47 | 95.42 | 4.58 | 95.71 | 4.29 | 98.70 | 1.30 |
| Haryana | 95.71 | 4.29 | 95.19 | 4.81 | 96.86 | 3.14 | 96.70 | 3.30 |
| Himachal Pradesh | 96.77 | 3.23 | 96.31 | 3.69 | 97.04 | 2.96 | 96.39 | 3.61 |
| Jammu & Kashmir | 95.77 | 4.23 | 99.47 | 0.53 | 99.32 | 0.68 | 99.22 | 0.78 |
| Karnataka | 92.23 | 7.77 | 93.32 | 6.68 | 97.18 | 2.82 | 96.81 | 3.19 |
| Kerala | 95.28 | 4.72 | 97.65 | 2.35 | 99.14 | 0.86 | 99.72 | 0.28 |
| Madhya Pradesh | 94.79 | 5.21 | 96.31 | 3.69 | 95.78 | 4.22 | 95.69 | 4.31 |
| Maharashtra | 95.63 | 4.37 | 94.61 | 5.39 | 99.59 | 0.41 | 99.60 | 0.40 |
| Orissa | 96.95 | 3.05 | 97.92 | 2.08 | 99.29 | 0.71 | 100.00 | 0.00 |
| Punjab | 91.11 | 8.89 | 93.30 | 6.70 | 95.42 | 4.58 | 94.27 | 5.73 |
| Rajasthan | 97.25 | 2.75 | 98.36 | 1.64 | 99.05 | 0.95 | 98.97 | 1.03 |
| Tamil Nadu | 84.15 | 15.85 | 88.98 | 11.02 | 86.00 | 14.00 | 85.97 | 14.03 |
| Uttar Pradesh | 99.26 | 0.74 | 99.86 | 0.14 | 99.29 | 0.71 | 99.87 | 0.13 |
| West Bengal | 87.81 | 12.19 | 96.17 | 3.83 | 97.05 | 2.95 | 96.85 | 3.15 |
| **Total (States)** | **94.28** | **5.72** | **96.59** | **3.41** | **97.27** | **2.73** | **97.43** | **2.57** |

*Source*: Computed from Table 2.2.

*Table 2.3A* Incidence of drugs reported under the NDPS Act (Percent of national total): 1991 to 2020

| *States* | *1991* | *1995* | *2001* | *2005* | *2010* | *2013* | *2015* | *2020* |
|---|---|---|---|---|---|---|---|---|
| Andhra Pradesh | 0.64 | 2.83 | 2.67 | 1.91 | 1.54 | 1.60 | 1.41 | 1.45 |
| Assam | 0.53 | 0.56 | 0.60 | 0.42 | 0.61 | 0.77 | 0.41 | 1.64 |
| Bihar | 0.53 | 0.95 | 1.08 | 1.26 | 2.14 | 1.39 | 0.94 | 1.61 |
| Gujarat | 1.31 | 1.39 | 0.49 | 0.34 | 0.28 | 0.14 | 0.11 | 0.51 |
| Haryana | 3.89 | 6.08 | 5.42 | 4.85 | 2.94 | 3.26 | 3.27 | 5.12 |
| Himachal Pradesh | 0.41 | 0.42 | 0.94 | 0.82 | 2.02 | 1.53 | 1.22 | 2.57 |
| Jammu & Kashmir | 0.21 | 0.25 | 0.46 | 0.65 | 1.42 | 1.12 | 1.16 | 2.04 |
| Karnataka | 0.48 | 0.94 | 1.27 | 0.99 | 1.02 | 0.84 | 0.69 | 6.78 |
| Kerala | 2.06 | 1.52 | 2.11 | 1.39 | 2.60 | 2.81 | 8.08 | 8.31 |
| Madhya Pradesh | 5.33 | 7.29 | 4.54 | 4.12 | 3.96 | 3.43 | 2.16 | 5.28 |
| Maharashtra | 20.02 | 3.80 | 1.90 | 4.64 | 3.65 | 7.83 | 37.36 | 7.88 |
| Orissa | 0.41 | 0.96 | 0.48 | 0.33 | 0.37 | 1.05 | 1.02 | 1.97 |
| Punjab | 6.22 | 7.34 | 9.15 | 15.17 | 18.62 | 42.27 | 20.00 | 11.55 |
| Rajasthan | 4.48 | 3.21 | 2.89 | 3.31 | 3.94 | 2.72 | 1.74 | 4.59 |
| Tamil Nadu | 22.14 | 10.95 | 17.38 | 14.92 | 4.96 | 4.36 | 3.00 | 9.03 |
| Uttar Pradesh | 21.13 | 44.25 | 41.90 | 36.20 | 44.95 | 18.54 | 12.81 | 18.15 |
| West Bengal | 2.19 | 1.66 | 2.08 | 1.65 | 2.67 | 2.83 | 2.54 | 2.72 |
| Total | 94.24 | 97.73 | 97.27 | 94.62 | 99.08 | 98.36 | 99.06 | 96.31 |
| All India | 100.00 | 100.00 | 100.00 | 100.00 | 100.00 | 100.00 | 100.00 | 100.00 |

*Source*: Computed from Table 2.4.

## Chapter 3

*Table 3.1A* Percentage distribution of operational holding across states

| *Holding size* | *Punjab* | *Haryana* | *H.P.* | *J&K* | *Rajasthan* |
|---|---|---|---|---|---|
| Marginal | 14.13 | 49.29 | 71.43 | 83.79 | 40.12 |
| Small | 18.98 | 19.29 | 17.41 | 11.29 | 21.91 |
| Semi-medium | 33.66 | 17.07 | 8.26 | 4.10 | 18.50 |
| Medium | 27.93 | 11.81 | 2.60 | 0.78 | 14.78 |
| Large | 5.28 | 2.54 | 0.30 | 0.04 | 4.69 |
| Total holdings ('000) | 1,093<br>(0.8) | 1,628<br>(1.1) | 996<br>(0.7) | 1,417<br>(1.0) | 7,655<br>(5.2) |

*Source*: Government of India, All India Report on Agriculture Census, 2015 to 16.

*Note:* Figures in brackets indicate percentage share in total operational holdings of India.

## Chapter 4

*Table 4.1A* International factors responsible for the drug menace: Households' perception

| *State→* *Factors↓* | *Punjab* | *Haryana* | *H.P.* | *J&K* | *Rajasthan* | *Total* |
|---|---|---|---|---|---|---|
| Easy availability* of drugs | 930 (97.08) | 150 (98.68) | 148 (97.37) | 148 (97.37) | 148 (97.37) | 1,524 (97.32) |
| Corruption | 28 (2.92) | 02 (1.32) | 04 (2.63) | 04 (2.63) | 04 (2.63) | 42 (2.68) |
| Total | 958 (100) | 152 (100) | 152 (100) | 152 (100) | 152 (100) | 1,566 (100) |

* Because of the proximity to the international border.
*Note:* 'Household' means drug addicts' households (950) and non-drug addict households (616). Hidden drug addicts' households (190) have not been included as their address was not known.

## Chapter 5

*Table 5.1A* Types of intoxicants and drugs consumed by the addicts: Households' perception

| *States* *Drugs* | *Punjab* | *Haryana* | *H.P.* | *J&K* | *Rajasthan* | *Total* |
|---|---|---|---|---|---|---|
| Traditional | 72 (7.52) | 53 (34.87) | 130 (85.53) | 53 (34.87) | 37 (24.34) | 345 (22.03) |
| Synthetic | 457 (47.70) | 35 (23.03) | 16 (10.53) | 84 (55.26) | 38 (25.00) | 630 (40.23) |
| Pharmaceuticals | 429 (44.78) | 64 (42.10) | 06 (3.95) | 15 (9.87) | 77 (50.66) | 591 (37.74) |
| Total respondents | 958 (100) | 152 (100) | 152 (100) | 152 (100) | 152 (100) | 1,566 (100) |

*Table 5.2A* *Sources of drug supply: Household's perception*

| *States* *Drugs* | *Punjab* | *Haryana* | *H.P.* | *J&K* | *Rajasthan* | *Total* |
|---|---|---|---|---|---|---|
| Drug peddlers | 420 (76.36) | 51 (51.00) | 57 (57.00) | 55 (55.00) | 50 (50.00) | 633 (66.63) |
| Friends | 69 (12.55) | 32 (32.00) | 22 (22.00) | 27 (27.00) | 24 (24.00) | 174 (18.32) |
| Chemists | 47 (8.55) | 14 (14.00) | 14 (14.00) | 12 (12.00) | 16 (16.00) | 103 (10.84) |
| Others | 14 (2.54) | 03 (3.00) | 07 (7.00) | 06 (6.00) | 10 (10.00) | 40 (4.21) |
| Total | 550 (100) | 100 | 100 | 100 | 100 | 950 (100) |

## Chapter 6

*Table 6.1A* Estimates based on the number of friends indulging in drug addiction

| *Range (in Nos)* | *Punjab* | *Haryana* | *Himachal Pradesh* | *J&K* | *Rajasthan* | *Total* |
|---|---|---|---|---|---|---|
| Up to 5 | 825 | 87 | 195 | 225 | 126 | 1,458 |
| 6–10 | 1,376 | 200 | 240 | 256 | 336 | 2,408 |
| 11–15 | 741 | 234 | 130 | 117 | 143 | 1,365 |
| 16–20 | 684 | 360 | 126 | 36 | 180 | 1,386 |
| 21–25 | 483 | 115 | 0 | 0 | 23 | 621 |
| 26–50 | 1,520 | 684 | 190 | 76 | 190 | 2,660 |
| 51–75 | 630 | 63 | 0 | 0 | 189 | 882 |
| 76–100 | 1,320 | 88 | 264 | 0 | 176 | 1,848 |
| 101–200 | 1,204 | 451 | 0 | 0 | 451.5 | 2,107 |
| 200 and above | 6,012 | 0 | 0 | 0 | 250.5 | 6,262 |
| Total responses | 14,795 | 2,282 | 1,145 | 710 | 2,065 | 20,997 |
| Total respondents | 660 | 120 | 120 | 120 | 120 | 1,140 |

*Source*: Computed from the information provided by 1,140 addicts.

## Chapter 7

*Table 7.1A* Reasons for saying 'Yes' about the positive role of PRIs and ULBs

| *State→ Reason↓* | *Punjab* | *Haryana* | *H.P.* | *J&K* | *Rajasthan* | *Total* |
|---|---|---|---|---|---|---|
| Active participation in controlling drugs | 202 (46.98) | 23 (50.0) | 35 (53.03) | 21 (56.77) | 24 (57.14) | 305 (49.11) |
| Resolution against drugs | 150 (34.88) | 17 (36.96) | 11 (16.67) | 09 (24.32) | 04 (9.52) | 191 (30.76) |
| Motivational role, sports, etc. | 65 (15.12) | 06 (13.04) | 17 (25.76) | 05 (13.51) | 03 (7.14) | 96 (15.46) |
| Support by the state administration | 13 (3.02) | 0 (0.00) | 03 (4.55) | 03 (5.41) | 11 (26.19) | 29 (4.67) |
| Total | 430 (100) | 46 (100) | 66 (100) | 37 (100) | 42 (100) | 621 (100) |

*Source*: Table 7.7.

*Table 7.2A* Reasons for saying 'No' about the positive role of PRIs and ULBs

| *State→ Reason↓* | *Punjab* | *Haryana* | *H.P.* | *J&K* | *Rajasthan* | *Total* |
|---|---|---|---|---|---|---|
| Indifferent attitude | 254 (48.11) | 48 (45.28) | 40 (46.51) | 80 (69.57) | 56 (50.91) | 478 (50.58) |
| Vote politics | 139 (26.33) | 21 (19.81) | 30 (34.88) | 13 (11.30) | 08 (7.27) | 211 (22.33) |
| Addiction to intoxicants/ drugs | 65 (12.31) | 03 (2.83) | 07 (8.14) | 07 (6.09) | 08 (7.27) | 90 (9.52) |

| *State→ Reason↓* | *Punjab* | *Haryana* | *H.P.* | *J&K* | *Rajasthan* | *Total* |
|---|---|---|---|---|---|---|
| No agenda to control drugs | 43 (8.14) | 28 (26.42) | 09 (10.47) | 08 (6.96) | 30 (27.27) | 118 (12.49) |
| Engaged in the drug trade | 11 (2.08) | 04 (3.77) | 0 (0.00) | 01 (0.87) | 04 (3.64) | 20 (2.12) |
| Non-cooperation from administration and police | 16 (3.03) | 02 (1.89) | 0 (0.00) | 06 (5.22) | 04 (3.64) | 28 (2.96) |
| Total | 528 (100) | 106 (100) | 86 (100) | 115 (100) | 110 (100) | 945 (100) |

*Source*: Table 7.7.

*Table 7.3A* Households' satisfaction with government efforts

| *State→ Reason↓* | *Punjab* | *Haryana* | *H.P.* | *J&K* | *Rajasthan* | *Total* |
|---|---|---|---|---|---|---|
| Satisfied | 355 (34.97) | 20 (13.16) | 86 (56.58) | 46 (30.26) | 66 (43.42) | 553 (35.31) |
| Not satisfied | 623 (65.03) | 132 (86.84) | 66 (43.42) | 106 (69.74) | 86 (56.58) | 1013 (64.69) |
| Total | 958 (100) | 152 (100) | 152 (100) | 152 (100) | 152 (100) | 1566 (100) |

*Table 7.4A* Reasons for Households' dissatisfaction with government efforts to control the drug menace

| *State→ Reason↓* | *Punjab* | *Haryana* | *H.P.* | *J&K* | *Rajasthan* | *Total* |
|---|---|---|---|---|---|---|
| Indifferent attitude | 274 (43.98) | 79 (59.85) | 33 (50.00) | 40 (37.74) | 56 (65.62) | 482 (47.58) |
| Political patronage | 174 (27.93) | 34 (25.76) | 06 (9.09) | 24 (22.64) | 24 (27.91) | 262 (25.86) |
| Corruption | 175 (28.09) | 19 (14.39) | 27 (40.91) | 42 (39.62) | 06 (6.98) | 269 (26.55) |
| Total | 623 (100) | 132 (100) | 66 (100) | 106 (100) | 86 (100) | 1,013 (100) |

# Index

Note: Page numbers in **bold** indicate a table on the corresponding page.